THE
BRAINWASHING
OF
MY DAD

How the Rise of the Right-Wing Media
Changed a Father and Divided Our Nation—
And How We Can Fight Back

JEN SENKO

sourcebooks

Copyright © 2021 by Jen Senko
Cover and internal design © 2021 by Sourcebooks
Cover design by Sourcebooks
Cover images © Leontura/Getty Images, StuckPixels/Getty Images, xavierarnau/Getty Images

This book is (in part) a memoir. It reflects the author's present recollections of experiences over a period of time. Some names and characteristics have been changed, some events have been compressed, and some dialogue has been re-created.

This publication is designed to provide accurate and authoritative information in regard to the subject matter covered. It is sold with the understanding that the publisher is not engaged in rendering legal, accounting, or other professional service. If legal advice or other expert assistance is required, the services of a competent professional person should be sought.—*From a Declaration of Principles Jointly Adopted by a Committee of the American Bar Association and a Committee of Publishers and Associations*

All brand names and product names used in this book are trademarks, registered trademarks, or trade names of their respective holders. Sourcebooks is not associated with any product or vendor in this book.

Published by Sourcebooks
P.O. Box 4410, Naperville, Illinois 60567-4410
(630) 961-3900
sourcebooks.com

Library of Congress Cataloging-in-Publication Data

Names: Senko, Jen, author.
Title: The brainwashing of my dad : how the rise of the right-wing media changed a father and divided our nation, and how we can fight back / Jen Senko.
Description: Naperville, Illinois : Sourcebooks, [2021] | Includes bibliographical references.
Identifiers: LCCN 2021001194 (print) | LCCN 2021001195 (ebook) |
Subjects: LCSH: Communication in politics--United States. | Mass media--Political aspects--United States. | Right-wing extremists--United States. | Brainwashing--United States.
Classification: LCC JA85.2.U6 S46 2021 (print) | LCC JA85.2.U6 (ebook) | DDC 320.97301/4--dc23
LC record available at https://lccn.loc.gov/2021001194
LC ebook record available at https://lccn.loc.gov/2021001195

Printed and bound in the United States of America.
VP 10 9 8 7 6 5 4 3 2 1

For my dad and my country.

Table of Contents

A Note to the Reader

This book is based on the documentary film *The Brainwashing of My Dad*, which was released in 2016. In its pages, you will see some references to interviews with various experts that were taken either directly from the documentary or from additional footage from the interviews that didn't make it into the film.

Though the main emphasis of this book is on right-wing media, I analyze some events from the last four decades that helped push the country to the right and were made possible largely because of the formidable and calculated influence of right-wing media. I argue that these events were flashing warning signs we failed to address as "conservative" extremists changed the very face of the Republican Party in service of the interests and agendas of a small number of influencers intent on gaining wealth and power at the expense of the vast majority of Americans.

The most powerful tool the extreme Right has used to accomplish their goals over the past forty years has been right-wing media. My experience watching my father, once a liberal Democrat, become more and more entrenched in conservative talk radio and Fox "News" (quotations are mine—the programming on Fox can usually barely be classified as real news) showed me there is nothing more dangerous and destructive than a media monopoly with a political agenda creating an echo chamber. In the case of right-wing media, that echo chamber is deliberately constructed to stoke anger, fear, and hatred in its listeners and viewers. The most frightening thing about the media outlets that push right-wing ideals, however, is how they inspire complete loyalty and devotion in their audiences. After he discovered ultra-conservative talk radio host Rush Limbaugh, my dad became 100 percent devoted to Limbaugh and his school of thought. And once Fox News appeared on his TV, he never wanted to turn it off. Without access to any other news sources, he lost his ability to think critically and question the lies he was being fed.

The events I describe in this book should have served as red flags indicating the changes and division right-wing media was fostering in our society. As of this writing in 2020, objective facts no longer mean much, and most Republicans of today are not the old-school Republicans of yesteryear, with their adherence to fiscal conservatism and conservation. The majority of the Republican Party today is complicit in the dismantling of the checks and balances in our system of government, the resurgence of White supremacy, and the unabashed and coordinated power grabs that have defined the political landscape of the past four years. Their radical ideology does not represent the views of most Americans and has become a chillingly real threat to our democracy.

In *The Brainwashing of My Dad*, I first refer to these extremist Republicans who have adopted a far-right brand of libertarianism as "New Republicans." This new interpretation of Republican values really started to take hold during the years when Newt Gingrich was Speaker of the House as the Republican Party abandoned their interest in bipartisanship and began to be more openly vocal against social safety net programs, child labor laws, immigration, energy regulations, and civil rights. Also cropping up during the Gingrich years were what I will call "New Democrats." These Democrats signed on to corporatism, free market ideology, free trade, deregulation, and other conservative ideals in an attempt not to be left behind with the conservative turn the country was taking. Still, many Democrats sincerely and with good faith sought to find common ground with their New Republican colleagues, unaware or in denial that the New Republicans had changed the rules of engagement.

Later in the book, as the Republican party continues its shift to the right, especially with the creation of Fox News, I change the label from "New Republicans" to "Cult Republicans." Cult Republicans share many of the characteristics of people in a religious cult—they subscribe unquestioningly to all the beliefs held by their media choices and their leaders, oblivious as to whether those leaders have their best interests in mind or not (mostly not).

Under Donald Trump's administration, Cult Republicans dominated the political landscape, encouraged by a president who
constantly lied to the American people, incited violence any time
he felt it politically protected his power, and compromised not
only America's reputation worldwide but our national security.
Right-wing media supported him every step of the way, disguis-
ing his demagoguery as populism and normalizing his pathologi-
cal behavior to the point that each new scandal broke a little more
gently than the last. This is a dangerous road to go down.

In the end, the message I hope readers take away from this
book is that no matter what political party you affiliate with, think
carefully about the media you consume. Engage with a variety of
news sources. Question what you hear, especially if the content
triggers emotions such as anger or fear. Invest in independent
media outlets. It would behoove us all to think deeply and gather
knowledge before making up our minds about the big issues our
country is grappling with. We all need to shift to the side of truth
and demand it from our media. Let's join as one and fight for the
common good and for the soul of our country.

Introduction:
What Happened to Dad?

Once upon a time, there was an average American family living in an average American town. After the family moved to a new state, the father left his car pool and began a long solo commute to work. And gradually, he began to change. He looked the same. He dressed the same. But something was very different.

But this isn't a story about just one man. It's the story of a media phenomenon that changed a father...and divided the nation.

My family's kitchen in the 1960s looked like many other Americans'—scratched linoleum flooring, wooden cabinets with metal handles, a yellow rotary dial phone hanging on the wall by the bread box, its coiled cord stretched and loose from me pulling it taut to try to get some privacy during my long conversations with my girlfriends. The kitchen was always warm and full of the smells of whatever my mother had been cooking.

One afternoon shortly before my seventh birthday, I was sitting at the Formica kitchen table, drawing horses as I often did. It was late in the day. In about an hour, I expected my dad to come home, and I would proudly show him my drawing. As I was deep in concentration, making sure I got the horse's conformation correct and listening to the sound of rain beating against the window, the door connecting the garage to the kitchen swung open earlier than usual. I looked up, surprised, and smiled as Dad stepped into the kitchen, his dark hair plastered to his head, revealing his slightly receding hairline. He had an odd look on his face—almost mischievous—and his detective-like raincoat was oddly puffed out around the top.

"Frank?" My mother turned from the sink, wiping her hands on a frayed towel. "What are you doing home?"

Dad winked at her. "Heh heh." He chuckled slyly. "A little surprise for Jennifer's birthday since she's been begging—"

Before he could finish his sentence, the bulge under his raincoat wiggled, and out popped the head of an adorable puppy, shaking his ears and reaching up to lick my dad's chin with a small, pink tongue.

"What? Oh, Daddy!"

I screamed and leaped out of my chair, dancing around my dad as he extracted the puppy—which I named Streak because of the thin white streak on his chest—from his raincoat and placed him in my arms. I couldn't hold him long because he wiggled so much. I put him down on the floor where he jumped and wiggled some more. He was as excited as I was.

My two brothers and I had been begging for a dog for months. Dad loved animals, but he and my mom weren't sure we were responsible enough to take care of a pet. My mother was clearly surprised by the new puppy and maybe just a little annoyed that Dad hadn't discussed it with her first. But I barely noticed as I sat down on the floor and let Streak lick my face, breathing in his wet dog smell and practically crying with ecstasy as Dad looked down on us, his face creased with the huge smile that he wore so often throughout my childhood. I thought, *I have the best dad ever!*

Decades later, that smile would be little more than a memory as my dad transformed into a person I barely recognized—a person who raged more than he laughed, who viewed the unknown with suspicion, and who inexplicably railed against institutions like PETA that protected the welfare of the animals he used to love so much. So what happened to my dad?

My father, Frank Senko, was born in 1922 in New Castle, Pennsylvania, the first child of my grandfather's second wife. His first wife, with whom he had two children, died in the flu epidemic of 1918. The family was so poor that Dad swore he actually walked barefoot to school. The Roaring Twenties didn't roar so loudly for the Senko family, and my dad often told stories about how he and his siblings would occasionally sneak a carrot out of the nearby farmer's garden and eat it raw or steal potatoes to bake in a bonfire. My grandparents' relationship was troubled, and eventually my grandmother left the family. My grandfather married again and had three more children.

By the time my father was a teenager, Hitler had come to power in Germany. Dad enlisted in the army as soon as he turned eighteen, despite the fact that his job in a factory manufacturing ammunition for the war allowed him a deferment. All his buddies were going overseas, and he wanted to join them. As he put it, "America was fighting the Nazis, and everyone wanted to kick their ass." He served as a medic in WWII, returned home, and went to college on the GI Bill, earning his master's degree and becoming an electronics engineer. A few years later, he and my mother met in New Jersey and married a year or two later. My mom had a son, my brother Greg, from a previous marriage, and I was born on June 23, 1954.

On the surface, Dad was living the American dream, but he quietly struggled with his new identity as an electronics engineer and as a husband, father, and provider. His own upbringing had provided no such role models or experience in the social norms of the middle-class life he now inhabited. His poverty-stricken childhood and unsettled homelife steeped in old-world Eastern European culture left him ill prepared to fit in with the other guys he worked with, who had martinis at lunch and knew which fork to use in fancy restaurants.

However uncomfortable he may have felt among his cowork-ers, at home with us kids, my dad was in his element. He talked to us in funny voices and created a mishmash of words from different languages, including German, Ukrainian, and Polish, that only we could understand. One of his best tricks was to burp the entire sentence "All right, Louie. Drop your gun." Whenever someone would ring the doorbell, he would announce, "He just left." No one knew why he said things like that, but he thought it was hilarious. I guess like a lot of dads, he was a horrible joke teller, but he didn't need jokes—he was funny without trying. He was boisterous and loud and would talk to anybody, the natural life of the party.

Dad was creative when it came to fixing things, mostly because he didn't want to pay to have someone else work on them. His fixes may have looked like jerry-rigged contraptions, but they always functioned well enough. Aesthetics did not concern him. He built an insulated doghouse with a shingled roof for Streak and converted the garage of our house in New Jersey to a TV room, complete with 1970s fake-wood paneling. He built a passageway from the new garage to the basement, which came in handy during my teen years for sneaking boys in and out of the house.

Dad didn't like the wasteful, throw-away mentality of most Americans, remembering the hardship of the Great Depression of his childhood and how his family had to scrimp and save just to get by. In a sense, he was an early environmentalist. He wasted nothing and believed in conserving energy, hollering at us constantly about leaving lights on, not wasting toothpaste in the tube, and—the cardinal sin in his book—wasting food.

On the rare occasions our family ate in restaurants, we'd have to look down the price list on the menu first before we picked something to eat. As my friend's mother, Mrs. Poole, once said, my father "could squeeze a nickel till the buffalo shit." So although it was sometimes hard for us kids not being able to get the latest styles of shoes or clothes growing up, he was able to put all of us through college as a result of all that saving. And for my dad, that meant success in his own life.

The first political conversations I remember overhearing at home were about President John F. Kennedy, whom my parents adored. I remember the 1960s as a time full of hope. With Martin Luther King Jr.'s activism and JFK leading the country, it felt like we were on the verge of solving many of the challenges that had plagued our country. And my dad was totally on board, an upwardly mobile registered Democrat who hoped to contribute to a better future for his children and for America.

But I wouldn't have written this book if my dad had remained the same person he was in the 1960s and 1970s. Over the next twenty years, especially in the late 1980s and 1990s, Frank Senko as I had known him began to disappear. He was replaced by a man I no longer knew, who disparaged the very social programs that had allowed him to create a successful life, who spouted virulently anti-"illegal alien" comments, and who constantly listened to conservative talk radio and watched Fox News on TV.

As I watched my dad change, I realized something else was changing right along with him: the visibility and power of right-wing media. It became clearer and clearer to me that there was a connection, that my dad was internalizing the political opinions people like Rush Limbaugh espoused to the point where he was no longer forming his own opinions at all. He became a parrot of the right-wing media he immersed himself in, repeating conspiracy theories and blatant lies verbatim. And he turned his volcanic anger on anyone who dared to voice a different opinion or fact-check some of his claims.

Disturbed by what I saw happening to my dad, I started researching the right-wing media outlets that began gaining power in the late 1980s and gathered momentum with each carefully calculated lie that fell from the mouths of talk show hosts and news anchors. I soon realized that not only were the radical talk radio and news shows my dad was addicted to changing his beliefs in fundamental ways, but they were specifically intended to do so. The simple truth is that while the rest of us were busy going about our daily lives, right-wing corporate forces were engaged in a vast conspiracy to deliberately build a media machine designed to foster fear, anger, and division that would benefit their economic interests. And my dad, along with millions of other Americans, got bamboozled by it.

CHAPTER 1

The Great Depression, the New Deal, and the Nazi Propaganda That Paved the Way for Extreme Right-Wing Media

When any of us kids wanted to stay home from school because we had the sniffles, my father would boast that he had never once missed a day of school. Even at a young age, Frank Senko valued education...and a warm, quiet, one-room schoolhouse. For him, school represented a safe haven away from his turbulent and poverty-stricken homelife. My dad's family certainly didn't experience the roar of the Roaring Twenties, struggling to get along even during a time of relative prosperity for many Americans.

During the 1920s, the country transformed from a *mixed market* economy to a *free market* economy. A mixed market economy allows for a significant government role. Profit-seeking is not the sole motivation. The motivation is the overall health of the economy. Free marketeers advocate for a strictly reduced government role and believe the market should solely by driven by competition and profits.

The Republican Party dominated the White House during this era, with three consecutive presidents: Warren Harding from 1921 to 1923, Calvin Coolidge from 1923 to 1929, and Herbert Hoover from 1929 to 1933. Though there were improvements in the lives of some American families with the advent of electric lighting and indoor flush toilets, income inequality was the dark underside of the 1920s. The rich were growing richer, and the poor had to struggle along with no safety net.

During this time, the stock market was booming. Opportunistic investors were taking bigger and bigger risks, often buying stocks on credit with very low interest rates. But behind the scenes lay a troubled agricultural sector, low wages for working-class people, bank loans unable to be liquidated, and lots of debt.

The Great Depression

The stock market crashed on October 29, 1929, just months after Herbert Hoover became president. Billions of dollars evaporated from the economy as stock prices spiraled, and by 1932, the stock market would be worth only about 20 percent of what it had been before the crash. Two devastated investors even jumped out windows to their deaths, unable to deal with the lightning-fast downward spiral. Many folks rushed to the banks to withdraw their savings, leading to bank runs and a domino effect of bank collapses, because the commercial banks had used their depositors' savings to invest in irresponsible ventures that had now also bottomed out. Unemployment levels rose to record highs, hitting almost 25 percent in 1932.

The nation was devastated. People were starving. They couldn't pay their rent or mortgages. Breadlines wrapped around entire blocks, and soup kitchens set up by charitable organizations and churches were overflowing with hungry people. This was the world in which my father spent his childhood.

President Hoover believed in virtually no role for the government and wanted to promote capitalism and individualism. He believed that banks and businesses just needed to show confidence to force a quick recovery and that the Depression would get better by virtue of individuals helping their neighbors and people pulling themselves up by their bootstraps. But in fact, matters were only getting worse. The jobless and homeless formed communities of shacks, known as shantytowns and then as "Hoovervilles." Many people felt that the government urgently needed to step in to save the millions of people who were struggling, but Hoover's administration was reluctant to engage in any wide-scale economic programs.

The New Deal

By the time Franklin Delano Roosevelt was elected in 1932, the country was ready for change. Lifting the economy out of the Depression that the free market economic climate had created was a priority for millions of Americans, and FDR had a solution for them: the New Deal, a series of government-managed economic and social programs designed to create economic recovery and a social safety net for its citizens. My mother clearly remembers she and her friends feeling hopeful as he took office.

FDR's first move was to restore confidence in and stabilize the banking system with the Emergency Banking Act, opening the Federal Reserve to supply unlimited amounts of money to banks and creating 100 percent deposit insurance. Although this governmental control over banking was controversial at the time, it went a long way in reinstating the public's trust in banks and slowing the economy's downward spiral.

Within his first one hundred days in office, FDR established the Federal Emergency Relief Administration, which spent $500 million on soup kitchens, blankets, employment initiatives, and nursery schools. Some of the other projects created construction jobs, supported professionals in the arts, educated workers, and gave jobs to nearly five hundred thousand women. Some of the many programs FDR's administration enacted in this time period include the Civilian Conservation Corps, which gave unemployed men jobs working on conservation projects in national parks and other natural areas; the Agricultural Adjustment Administration, which supported farmers; and the Public Works Administration, which spearheaded the construction and maintenance of roadways and bridges across the country. Little by little, FDR's New Deal started America on a new path toward equality and growth.

Many of the laws and institutions we take for granted today, including things like Social Security, can be traced to the New Deal era. FDR's expansive vision of a supportive government that extended opportunities to its citizens allowed for more federal intervention to help banking, agriculture, and public welfare. It provided social safety nets, gave GIs the opportunity to get an education or housing, and much more. The people loved these programs, while the free marketeers called it socialism.

Very significantly for the discussions we'll explore in this book, FDR signed the Communications Act into law in 1934. To avoid a monopoly on media and undue influence by any one company or person, this law regulated radio, telephone, and telegraph communications by limiting ownership and cross-ownership licensing. FDR had the foresight to be concerned about how much influence media could have on people, largely because he could see the alarming creep of right-wing propaganda going on in Germany. He believed consolidated media ownership could be dangerous for democracy. (Boy, did he prove to be right!)

The Communications Act also determined that technology was an interstate good, like railways and highways, and should be monitored and regulated as such. To implement the Communications Act, the Federal Communications Commission (FCC) was created. The FCC's duty was to issue licenses and frequencies to radio operators and to bring order to the burgeoning new industry. They determined ownership by what best served the public interest, requiring diversity in ownership, political discourse, hiring, and programming. Companies broadcasting content considered obscene or profane could be penalized. As such, the FCC had the responsibility of educating the public on the dissemination of news and centralized all the authority pertaining to news and media in the United States.

Not everyone agreed with FDR's regulatory approach, but the success of the New Deal was impossible to deny. Day by day, month by month, the United States clawed its way closer and closer to economic recovery, bolstered by FDR's liberal programs (again, deemed "socialistic" by his critics) and focus on benefits for everyday people. He easily won a second term in office.

In FDR's acceptance speech for his 1936 nomination, he introduced the term *economic royalists* to describe the super rich who wielded enough wealth and power to directly influence American policies. Economic royalists fought against social safety net programs, partly because these social programs were partially funded by levying higher taxes on the rich. This resistance to tax-supported social initiatives would continue for the next several decades and remains a hallmark of today's Republican Party.

FDR went on to serve over three terms as president—the only president to be elected four times—until his death in 1945. His unmatched popularity was due in large part to his refusal to allow the ultrarich to dictate the shape of American government and his belief in and support for the everyday American—and that government should be a force for good.

Propaganda in Nazi Germany

Meanwhile, back when America was just entering the Roaring Twenties, in Germany a young man named Adolf Hitler joined the Nazi political party—a far-right, fanatically anticommunist, racist, and nationalist party with a paramilitary culture. Many Germans were desperate for a strong leader after their defeat in WWI, and postwar Germany was fertile ground for someone like Hitler to rise to power. And rise he did.

Adolf Hitler was born in Austria in 1889. His interest in the Nazi Party was predated by his membership in the German Workers' Party in 1919, in which he became known for speeches he gave in beer halls, catering to dissatisfied soldiers who raged against the outcome of WWI.

Hitler engaged in "unrelenting propaganda through the party newspaper," and its audience grew, and with party meetings and beer hall speeches, so did Hitler's notoriety, arousing passion and anger in the men he appealed to. In these speeches, he portrayed the Germans as innocent victims and "the Jews" as "like a disease...that needed to be resolved." He blamed Jews for the ills of both communism and capitalism and demanded that newspapers should be "propaganda organs that spoke to German emotions" rather than unbiased sources of news and information.

By the time he attracted the interest of Nazi Party leaders who invited him to join their ranks, Hitler had begun to understand the nearly limitless power of propaganda and how he could use it to further the Nazi Party's agenda. A lot of the tactics we see now in the world of right-wing media are directly connected to the methods of the Nazi party, often to a chilling extent.

Hitler believed propaganda must not include the whole truth but only those elements of the truth that are favorable to one's own side of the argument. He wrote that its "task is not to make an objective study of the truth, in so far as it favors the enemy, and then set it before the masses with academic fairness; its task is to serve our own right, always and unflinchingly." He focused on appealing to broad masses of people who are ruled not by reason but by sentiment and emotions. He also wrote that propaganda "must confine itself to a few points and repeat them over and over," creating a powerful echo chamber from which it is difficult for people to break free.

Hitler originally came up with an idea known as "the big lie." As he put it, "the broad masses" are more likely to "fall victim to the big lie than the small lie," because "it would never come into their heads to fabricate colossal untruths, and they would not believe that others could have the impudence to distort the truth so infamously."

Hitler met the writer and activist Joseph Goebbels in 1924 when he, too, joined the Nazi Party. They bonded immediately, and Goebbels became one of Hitler's most trusted associates. Goebbels began exploring how propaganda could help the Nazis further their agenda and gain influence with the German people. Together, Hitler and Goebbels would create a propaganda machine unlike anything the world had ever seen.

Goebbels had two goals: to cement the perceived strength of the Nazi Party in peoples' minds and to build up Hitler as a mythical hero. In 1933, Hitler was elected chancellor and made Goebbels his propaganda minster. In this role, one of the first things Goebbels did was make sure radios were cheap enough that nearly everyone could afford to buy one. Goebbels believed radio was the most effective way to get a message across. In fact, Goebbels presciently said, "What the press has been in the Nineteenth Century, radio will be for the Twentieth Century." Goebbels intuited the benefits of the fact that "the still-new invention brought news, music, dramas, and comedy right into the home. Goebbels saw its potential to transmit Nazi messages right into the daily lives of Germans."

At the core of the content Goebbels curated to broadcast across Germany and the world was anti-Semitism, which was also incorporated into most of the newspapers and movies available to the German people. The content was carefully "designed to mobilize the German population to support all Nazi military and social efforts, including the deportation of Jews and others to concentration camps." Eventually, Goebbels made it "a treasonable offense to listen to overseas broadcasts" to make sure Germans were unable to access different points of view that might make them question the things they were hearing on Nazi radio. Like Hitler, Goebbels believed the bigger the lie, the easier it would be to sell to the public, especially if the lie was repeated often and propagated by what would appear to be official sources. He has been widely quoted as saying, "If you tell a lie big enough and keep repeating it, people will eventually come to believe it."

Goebbels used the basic propaganda principles that Hitler had established:

- ▸ Avoid abstract ideas and appeal instead to the emotions.
- ▸ Constantly repeat just a few ideas using stereotyped phrases.

- ▸ Give only one side of the argument.
- ▸ Continuously criticize your opponents.
- ▸ Pick out one special enemy for vilification.

It's easy to see how many of these tactics are used today by far-right media outlets and how the big lie became a staple communication strategy in Donald Trump's presidential administration, with "alternative facts" and declarations about "fake news" appearing nearly every day.

Hitler's Rise to Power

In the 1920s and 1930s, except for a handful of journalists and FDR to some extent, Americans were not concerned about the propaganda campaigns in Germany, nor the cartoon-like character, Adolf Hitler. They laughed at his wacky antics and shrill voice. Many people, especially Americans, could not imagine him being taken seriously as a political influencer.

Despite his cartoonish demeanor, by the mid-1930s, it was becoming evident that Hitler was unstoppable. His nationalistic philosophy appealed to many people. Leon Botstein, American scholar and president of Bard College said, "Most German Jews didn't question that they would live and die in Germany. They thought Hitler was temporary or that he was so extreme that there would be a reaction against him."

In 1934, Hitler proclaimed himself the führer (leader) of Germany, seizing control of the military.

Responding to Hitler's invasion of Poland five years later,

France and Great Britain declared war on Germany in September 1939, heralding the beginning of WWII.

America in WWII

The United States was just beginning to emerge from the Depression as WWII began, and Americans didn't want to become involved in a war. But after Germany's ally, Japan, bombed Pearl Harbor in December 1941, there was no denying it—America was at war.

My dad enlisted in the army and was trained as a medic. He never had to use a gun in the war, nor found any use for one afterward. He didn't have the stomach for hunting.

America's entrance into WWII spelled trouble for Hitler. Over three million German troops that invaded the Soviet Union had already been pushed back by the Russians. By 1944, the Allies were gaining ground against the Axis powers after several decisive battles and bombing of German air forces. Hitler killed himself in April, and on May 8, 1945, Germany surrendered. The war ended in the summer of 1945 with Japan's surrender after the nuclear bombings of Hiroshima and Nagasaki.

After WWII, it was a new era in America. The GI Bill provided a range of benefits like low-cost mortgages and loans, tuition, and living payments and helped returning soldiers adjust to civilian life. They received unemployment benefits until they could find work. Once again, social programs improved life for millions of Americans by providing a safety net for those who needed it most. However, with the new social programs came the fear of socialism, the growing power of labor unions, and the threat to the conservative ideology which served them, leading to a growing resentment by the economic royalists and free marketeers.

Frank Senko after the War

After returning home, my father happily took advantage of the GI Bill. He went to the Newark College of Engineering and got his master's degree, living at his older sister Olga's house in Nutley, New Jersey, while he buried himself in his studies. He graduated and became a civil service engineer at Fort Monmouth while continuing to take classes at night to better himself and his position in his job.

One night, his buddies convinced him to leave his studies and go down to the local bar and have some beers. There were some pretty gals there dancing!

My father joined the merriment. Then he saw my mom, Eileen, and asked her to dance. They danced the rest of the night together and felt like they had known each other for their entire lives. It turned out Eileen worked at Fort Monmouth in New Jersey too. She had a job as a secretary and was living at home with her mother and father. She was divorced and already had my brother Greg from her previous marriage. My father and mother dated for a couple of years before they married and had me and my younger brother, Walter. Frank Senko had come a long way from the trials of his Depression-era childhood. Thanks to some help from the government, he was now living the American dream.

★ CHAPTER 2 ★

The Right Is Declared Dead

My dad, in addition to wanting us kids to get a good education, also wanted us to "have some culture," something he had no opportunity to experience during his own childhood. So every now and then while we were growing up, we would take day trips into New York City to see a show or go to a museum.

One Saturday morning, Dad made us get up early to get ready to go to the Museum of Natural History. He made his special pancakes, tossing in pieces of whatever fruit in the house that were about to go bad. With lots of butter and syrup, we loved his pancakes anyway, in part because he made them with such joy, whistling away at the stove. After breakfast, we hurried to get dressed as we were running a little behind schedule. Streak looked longingly at us as we hopped in the car and sped off toward the bus station.

My dad drove like a cowboy in our red Ford family station wagon and parked at the Red Bank bus parking lot. The five of us got on the bus and took it straight to Port Authority.

After we got off the bus and walked outside Port Authority, a homeless Black man was standing right by the glass doors amid the hustle and bustle of the city. My younger brother and I were scared because we had never seen a homeless person before. This man didn't have any shoes on! He turned to my father. He asked my dad if he had any spare change for a cup of coffee. My mom stood back, looking like she wanted to walk away as quickly as she could. My father surprised us all when he called the man sir, had a little conversation with him, and handed him some change. *Well, my Catholic self thought, that's what Jesus would do.* My dad treated the man like an equal. That moment made such an impression on me, I never forgot it.

In many ways, despite our Catholic roots, my family was quite socially liberal. My brothers and I were taught racism was bad. Our parents encouraged us to treat all people equally and to especially have sympathy for Black people on account of the horrors they went through at the hands of White people and the prejudice they still had to endure. I remember this attitude being pretty much accepted as just "the right thing to do" while we were growing up. But of course, there were (and are) plenty of people who didn't see racism quite the same way. Standing outside the bus terminal, watching my dad treat that homeless man with such dignity, it would have shocked me to know that my dad would eventually become one of them.

★ ★ ★

Both my parents loved President Kennedy and were very happy when he was elected in 1961. With Martin Luther King Jr. leading the civil rights movement, President Kennedy in office, and the incredible advances in science, we all felt really hopeful about the future of America. If landing on the moon was possible, people thought solving poverty and racism would also be possible. Then, on November 22, 1963, President Kennedy was assassinated.

Nearly everyone from my generation remembers where they were when they heard about the assassination. I was in Mr. Harris's fifth grade class. After Mr. Harris was mysteriously called out of the classroom for a few minutes, he came back in, his face ashen, and told us President Kennedy had been shot.

Our dinner at home was quiet that night. Even my little brother sensed the dark mood that enveloped us. My dad, for a change, did not have much appetite and hung his head over his food. I wasn't sure, but I thought his eyes looked wet.

We had the news on. The small black-and-white TV sat on a little rickety stand by the kitchen table. Earlier in the day, my mother had watched live as Walter Cronkite, usually so reserved and calm, tearfully removed his glasses, looked up at a clock, and announced, "President Kennedy died at one p.m. central standard time, two o'clock eastern standard time, some thirty-eight minutes ago." In an interview fifty years later, Cronkite said, "Those whose jobs often involve great emotional stress develop an amazing stoic power to defer emotion, a power that momentarily eluded me."

My parents were as perplexed and distraught as we kids were. How could something like this happen? Conspiracy theories began to fly around. My parents openly wondered how one lone man could do something as monumental as assassinate a sitting president.

While writing this book, I asked my mother about that day. My mom said, "The thing I will never forget is when Kennedy was shot. How Ida Gikow [our neighbor] came over and was so distraught and cried to me, 'Eileen, do you know what this means?' But she never told me, and I often wonder what she meant."

At the time, conspiracy theories were rare, but many Americans believed Kennedy's murder was more than the work of just one man—a theory that persists to this day. In the modern day, however, conspiracy theories and their offspring—"alternative facts" and "fake news"—have become commonplace, largely thanks to media outlets that proliferate them.

In the '40s and '50s, the U.S. economy boomed and the middle class grew. But that didn't stop the resentment of the economic royalists and free marketeers. In 1954, when *Brown v. Board of Education* found segregation to be unconstitutional, Southern economist James McGill Buchanan argued that paying taxes for poor kids, and especially Black kids, to go to school was exploitative of the wealthy! In fact, he didn't think the wealthy should pay any taxes for things like public education, social security, libraries, roads, etc. So, he started organizing. Charles Koch joined him and helped fundraise and organize. Today, Buchanan has been called the architect of the radical right. Not long after Buchanan started organizing, in 1958, a fervently anticommunist group with these shared beliefs, called the John Birch Society, was created. It had an impact. A Republican presidential candidate in 1964 adopted its platform. That was Barry S. Goldwater.

"Goldwater! Goldwater!"

As a kid, I never sensed political arguments getting heated between the grown-ups, not even during Thanksgiving. They always seemed to be having fun, enjoying each other's company, laughing it up or debating spiritedly, even if they belonged to different political parties. I remember only ever hearing one blustery outburst, and that was from my best friend. It was on the playground, and she wanted me to chant "Goldwater! Goldwater!" along with her. I declined to do it because my parents were for Lyndon B. Johnson, and I liked Mr. Johnson too. I adopted my parents' politics and had a strong sense of right and wrong. Also, Mr. Johnson was connected with President Kennedy and was for the same stuff that the wonderful Mr. Martin Luther King was for.

That chant was the only reason I knew my friend's parents were Republican. The differences between the Democratic and Republican parties weren't as stark back then, as it seemed like everyone pretty much wanted the same thing—a paycheck good enough that their wives could stay home to take care of the kids if they wanted, possibly a second car and maybe a pool in their backyard, and Social Security and a pension when they retired.

And back then, that was not only possible, it was the norm for the middle class.

★ ★ ★

To understand the trajectory of how our country moved to the right, I had to go back in time. As a kid, I vaguely remember some of these events. The 1960s were very relevant and resonated with me because it felt like they reflected my family's values and much of what I related to.

In 1963, the country was still trending liberal, and there were more Democrats than Republicans. Many of my friends' parents still remembered how FDR had saved them from the Depression, and Kennedy's magical allure didn't end after his death. Lyndon B. Johnson's presidency continued in that vein.

But after Johnson signed the Civil Rights Act of 1964, many White southerners, opposed to racial equality and integration, started looking for ways to push back. Former Arizona senator Barry Goldwater strategically came out against the civil rights movement during his presidential campaign, garnering sympathy with those voters.

In general, the trajectory of the United States was still progressing toward social liberalism, but not for Goldwater supporters. Goldwater, in coming out against the Civil Rights Act, used a new strategy, at that time called Operation Dixie (later called the Southern Strategy), developed by and for Republicans to win White voters in the South by appealing to their racism and fear of change. In an interview I conducted with political activist Noam

Chomsky, he described the calculated strategy of the Republican Party to gain voters in the South: "The South had been voting Democratic. The Republicans realized they could change the party labels in the South by appealing to the racism and the strong opposition to the civil rights legislation and making that their stand." And that's exactly what Goldwater hoped to do.

My parents were both FDR and JFK Democrats and thought Goldwater and other ultraconservative people like him were really far out of the mainstream. They were still fiercely grateful to FDR for helping pull the country out of the Depression and for providing social safety nets and giving GIs opportunities that they would not otherwise have had. They thought it was crazy that anyone would want to take away the benefits that had made such a difference to so many Americans, and one extremist conservative group that especially made them scratch their heads was the John Birch Society.

One day around the time Goldwater was running for president, I remember running home from playing with my friend, JoAnne. I didn't want to be late, as I knew my dad would be home because it was supper time. When I got to the front door, I noticed a pamphlet stuck between the screen door and the front door. It looked important, so I brought it into the kitchen where my parents were sipping their manhattans and chatting while dinner was cooking. I shoved it at them. They looked at it and laughed. My dad said, "This is from that nutty Birch Society." My mom looked at me and said, "Throw it out. Those people are kooks."

Robert W. Welch Jr. founded the John Birch Society in 1958.

The John Birch Society was named after avid anticommunist Baptist minister and Air Force captain John Birch, who was killed by Chinese Communist soldiers a few days after WWII ended. "Birchers" believed in extremely limited government. They also fervently believed that communists were waiting to take over the United States at any minute. Claire Conner, a woman who grew up indoctrinated in the ideology of the John Birch Society and later authored the book *Wrapped in the Flag: What I Learned Growing Up in America's Radical Right, How I Escaped, and Why My Story Matters Today*, had compared the ideas of the Republican Tea Party group to the John Birch Society's philosophy when I met her in 2014. The Republican Party of today is nearly identical to the "nutty" John Birch Society.

But despite Goldwater's supporters and fringe groups like the Birchers when I was growing up, extreme conservative ideals did not get enough traction to impact society in any major way. After Johnson hammered Goldwater in the 1964 presidential election, the Right was declared "all but politically dead." Nobody wanted to be a conservative in the mid-1960s; conservatism was so out. After Goldwater's defeat, the Right started planning to hit back hard any way they could to retake control of the national conversation. And over time and with patience and stealth, they did.

★ **CHAPTER 3** ★

News in the Age of Walter Cronkite and Nixon on the Rise

In the 1960s, most folks got their news through the same few outlets. Cable and the internet didn't exist, so the newspaper, radio, and broadcast television were how we got updates about what was going on in the world. The *CBS Evening News* with Walter Cronkite and the other newscasts on ABC and NBC mostly consisted of the major national and international news stories, presented "in-depth" in two or three minutes, along with an occasional sprinkling of opinion. It was accepted that the point of the news was to be objective and report the facts, not to make a profit or cater to a specific audience. Cronkite, who was the anchorman for CBS from 1962 to 1981, was known as "the most trusted man in America" thanks to his reserved and calm approach to delivering the news of the day. I remember Walter Cronkite. He seemed like your really smart, really kind, scholarly uncle.

In addition to watching the nightly news, my parents subscribed to the *Newark Star-Ledger* and *LIFE* magazine. On
Sundays we would all sit in the living room after church and
read. My younger brother and I read the funnies and occasionally looked at *Time* magazine. My parents always begged me to
read just one article in the newspaper. I did as they asked, but I
never understood what I was reading. It was like a foreign language to me. I saw no real reason to be interested in politics or
current events, since nothing seemed like it could really change
that much. As I got older, of course, I would become much more
invested in the events of the world around me and would eventually begin to research exactly where our news comes from and
why it is presented to us the way it is.

After Goldwater lost the election to Johnson, the extreme
Right realized they were quickly losing influence over American
society. The energy in the United States was leaning more
and more liberal, and the conservative agenda was seen as
backward-looking and out of touch. Influential people within
the Republican Party realized they needed to do something
drastic to convince voters that the conservative point of view
was the only correct one. They began to establish organizations
to market the notion of "liberal bias" to the public. Liberal bias
is a theory constructed by these ultraconservatives, or New
Republicans, who accused mainstream media of promoting
liberal ideas over conservative ones, and it has persisted into
the twenty-first century. In 1969, Reed Irvine, an economist
who was invested in promoting a conservative agenda, helped

form a watchdog group called Accuracy in Media (AIM), one of the first groups to take a targeted approach toward discrediting the media and pushing for more airtime for conservative ideals.

AIM supported the war in Vietnam and felt the eventual public loss of support for the war was due to liberal bias within the media. More recently, they have been involved in publicizing conspiracy theories and denying climate change. David Brock, political consultant, commentator, and founder of media watchdog group Media Matters for America, described AIM's goals to me as follows: "Basically, the idea of this group was to counter their feeling that the media was opposed to Nixon's policies in Vietnam. That's how it began, but you could see how the campaign to discredit the media in the eyes of the conservatives would lay the groundwork for a vast alternative media that would come later... It opened up space for conservatives to get a foothold in the media."

In addition to labeling the media as liberally biased to sow doubt about the impartiality of reporting, those on the right knew they'd also have to control the media and change the way news was presented. If the media was objective, it would have to be honest about the New Republicans' actual policies, and they would no longer have an appeal to 90 percent of the country, so they started to clamor for "fairness" and "balance" rather than objectivity.

Brock described how objectivity was key to journalistic standards in the 1960s:

There was a universal agreement, I think, that the goal
of journalism was objectivity and to discern the truth of
conflicting claims. The conservatives moved the argument from objectivity to one of "balance." Under the
rubric of balance, the conservatives do better because
the way the media now treats balance is there's 99 percent of scientific consensus on global warming. One percent of scientists funded by the coal industry say that is
not true. But they're presented in a balanced way, giving
credit to both sides. And so, the conservatives were able
to infiltrate the op-ed pages of the country on the same
notion that you have the liberal columnist and the conservative columnist.

This focus on balance happened slowly at first, but over
time, it became the new standard in reporting. With constant
accusations of being liberally biased, mainstream media eventually fell all over themselves trying to prove they were balanced,
often at the expense of being accurate. Average people like my
parents weren't consciously aware of this organized attack on
mainstream media because they were used to trusting their
newspapers and television news. It never occurred to them that
anyone would spin the media one way or another to promote a
hidden agenda.

Ultimately, the New Republicans' goal was to sell the majority of the country on policies that benefited billionaires and mul-
tinational mega corporations. Groups like AIM slowly began

to have an effect on the media that would take decades to fully form, but the leaders of this movement were willing to wait, and as we will see, their patience would pay off.

During this time period, I was in junior high, and I was fascinated and excited by what I saw on the television news special programs my parents would sometimes watch. I saw hippies protesting the Vietnam War and demanding equal rights for Blacks and women. These rebels also wanted the constraints and old-fashioned mores of society lifted. They wanted to be able to "do their own thing," whatever that may be, as long as it didn't hurt anybody else—a philosophy my dad had often preached.

All of it stirred my own inner rebel and resonated with me since I had been badly bullied in school and often felt like an outsider. I was also inspired by my big brother, Greg. One day, he suddenly stopped combing his hair back and up in a pompadour like a greaser and was the first one in his high school to comb his hair forward over his forehead like the Beatles! He fit right into the counterculture, and I wanted to follow in his footsteps.

By the time I entered high school at the end of the '60s, it seemed that most people were leaning toward progressive social changes. These ideas permeated everything from styles of dress, household, and commercial design to TV shows like *Rowan & Martin's Laugh-In*. Everyone knew the terms *women's lib*, *hippie*, and *Black power*, and it seemed like the hippies might actually change the world.

My parents were a bit uncomfortable with my attraction to the hippie movement because of its association with drugs. Along with the social revolution, pot, quaaludes, MDA, LSD, and speed became part of the culture. Like other hippie teens of that time, I experimented a little bit with all of it, which probably didn't help my grades, frustrating my education-minded father. Though they were concerned about drug use, my parents still believed in the protests and the social movements. I think they saw these movements as an extension of what the Kennedys and MLK had stood for: the common good and equality for all. The casualness and informality of the time actually felt natural for us as a family.

Both my parents leaned liberal, my dad even more so than my mom. He even sewed patches on my blue jean bell-bottoms, proud and happy that I was "extending the life of my clothes" and not asking for new ones.

Eventually, a little bit of a backlash against hippie culture began. And thus came an opportunity for a man who would do great things for the extreme conservatives looking for a breakthrough in their ability to take back control of the national conversation: Richard Milhous Nixon.

Richard Nixon was born in 1913 in California. His father ran a gas station and a grocery store and had struggled to earn a living. This gave Nixon a strong sense of ambition. He became a zealous McCarthyite and rabidly anticommunist. In 1952, after a turn in the senate, he was General Dwight D. Eisenhower's running mate. After a lackluster presidential bid in the 1960 election, where he lost to John F. Kennedy, Nixon ran again as the Republican nominee in 1968 against Vice President Hubert Humphrey.

George Lakoff, the director of the Center for the Neural Mind & Society and a cognitive linguist, philosopher, and best-selling author, said, "When Nixon was running for president, he had a problem. And that problem is that in 1964, Goldwater lost. In 1964, 'conservative' was a dirty word. Everybody wanted to be a liberal. So Nixon comes along in '67 and says we have to get working people to vote for Nixon. How do we do this when all these people in the unions are Democrats? Well, what Nixon's folks discovered was that between '64 and '67, three major things changed in the country."

The first of those three things was the antiwar movement. A lot of working men had been in the military and saw college kids who resisted the war as commie ingrates who hated America. The second was the women's movement. Many men felt threatened by "radical" feminism and "bra burners." The third was the civil rights movement. Many working men in the South were racist or were scared African Americans were going to take their jobs. So Nixon capitalized on the multifaceted fears of White men to build a following, and it worked.

Unlike Goldwater, Nixon was able to use the Southern Strategy quite effectively during his presidential campaigns. Many conservative-leaning voters in the South left the Democratic Party because of its civil rights agenda, as did Northern voters who were uncomfortable with the changes brought about by the civil rights movement. Nixon's campaigns also actually pushed the Republican Party itself further to the right by fusing ideas about the role of government in the economy, women's place in society, racial grievance, law and order, and White evangelical Christianity.

Racism and the antiwar backlash by veterans were not the only tools used for division at the end of the 1960s. Nixon also promoted what he called "traditional family values," implying that women should stay at home, raise children, and dress like ladies. This was a great way to capture the vote of the working men who felt threatened by women who wanted to work, be measured for something other than their looks, and be seen as equal to men, what some called "radical feminism." Instead of encouraging and helping men expand their visions of themselves and allowing women to participate meaningfully in the workforce and society, Nixon and his followers stirred up and exploited anger, frustration, fear, and indignation in susceptible voters. These were some of the same types that Rush Limbaugh would later exploit. But Nixon couldn't do this all on his own, of course; he needed some serious help to smooth out his image and convince voters to adopt his agenda. Nixon was not the most charismatic man, and by his own admission, he was "shy," not a "buddy-buddy boy," unable to "let his hair down." Luckily for him, in 1968, he met Roger Ailes.

The (Evil) Genius of Roger Ailes

Roger Ailes, just twenty-seven years old when he and Nixon met for the first time, had grown up in a factory town in Warren, Ohio. Ailes, who had hemophilia, was medically fragile and spent many hours during his childhood watching TV. As a college student, majoring in radio and television at Ohio University was a natural fit. He was ambitious and climbed the ladder quickly at a locally produced television talk-variety show. By the time Nixon appeared as a guest on the popular *Mike Douglas Show*, it was nationally syndicated, and Ailes had won two Emmy Awards for its production.

Ailes convinced Nixon that he desperately needed to better understand the television medium to reach voters. Nixon was at first taken aback by the brash young TV producer, but Ailes won Nixon over and convinced him to hire him as his personal television consultant in his presidential campaign against Vice President Hubert Humphrey.

Like everyone else who had watched it on television, Ailes had seen how Nixon had bombed in his debate against John F. Kennedy in 1960. For people listening to the debate on the radio, it wasn't clear who won, but to people watching it on TV, the loser was painfully obvious. Nixon appeared sweaty, shifty-eyed, and clearly nervous. Kennedy, with his relaxed, cool demeanor, good looks, and smart answers, dominated in the new visual format of televised debates. Ailes had his work cut out for him to make sure Nixon wouldn't have a performance like that again, but he really wanted to help Nixon. It was said he was personally infatuated with him. I have my own theory, which is that Ailes believed he knew television better than anyone, and Nixon was the perfect person he could exercise his talents on. Ailes was young and ambitious and brash. What a challenge Nixon, who was intelligent but had no television appeal whatsoever, would be.

My mother remembers watching the 1960 debate and thinking "what a fake" Nixon was. "He seemed stumbling compared to Kennedy, who was relaxed and smiling. Generally, I disliked Nixon intensely. Thought he was a crook, deceitful, unsure of himself...despicable." She said, "I really don't remember Dad watching the news with me. Isn't that strange? It seems we were not that much into politics then. At least Dad wasn't." Not yet anyway.

Even after that disastrous debate, Nixon did not understand how big of a role television played in his failure to attract voters during his first presidential campaign. He thought TV was a gimmick, and he blamed the media for his loss. Roger Ailes eventually convinced him that he badly needed coaching on how to come across on television, and the two began working together in February 1968.

In an interview with me, Gabriel Sherman, an NBC News/MSNBC contributor and author of *The Loudest Voice in the Room: How the Brilliant, Bombastic Roger Ailes Built Fox News—and Divided a Country*, said, "Roger Ailes understood that TV is about one thing. It's about emotion and that you need to communicate with the audience and hook into them on an emotional level." When I asked Sherman about Ailes and Nixon, he said, "Roger Ailes coached Richard Nixon on how to communicate his ideas to the average American who is watching TV every night at the dinner table. He told Nixon, 'America is dumb. So give them something simple, boil it down, and they'll get it.'" Ailes told Nixon he needed snappy one-liners (the art of the soundbite!), to appear as if he had a sense of humor, and to be aware of camera angles.

To start, Ailes had Nixon do what appeared to be live town halls, taking risks by answering questions on live TV. But the audience members were plants, all carefully selected to look just diverse enough to appeal to a broad viewership. The audience members asked predetermined softball questions and were directed to applaud Nixon's answers. No reporters or journalists were allowed to attend. The staged town halls were the perfect opportunity for Nixon to perform in a safe space and make him look like he was a hit with the American people.

Ailes left nothing to chance, even telling him he needed to buy long socks because nobody wanted to see a flash of his leg "over a droopy sock." Ailes became so involved with crafting Nixon's new image that once Nixon became president, Ailes even orchestrated the lighting of the White House Christmas tree, which up to that time had been a much more casual and spontaneous event.

The rebranding of Richard Nixon was possibly the single biggest factor for his presidency, in which he appealed to a group of people that became known as the "silent majority"—blue-collar workers, WWII veterans, and others who had no interest in joining the antiwar, civil rights, or women's rights movements. They considered themselves average Americans—those who were okay with where things stood and were resistant to change. Putting Nixon in office changed everything for the Republican Party.

After Nixon was elected, the Republican Party continued to strategize on how to wrestle more working-class voters away from the Democratic Party, specifically through race and class issues. Capitalizing on White working-class voters' fear of the unknown, Nixon positioned himself as an enforcer of law and order, a president who would defend White voters against the perceived threats of urban, non-White influences in their lives. As a result, the cultural divide between rural and urban Americans grew wider.

Nixon especially capitalized on this growing cultural hostility by creating a new definition of the "elite" as the people and groups advocating for progressive social movements. If you happen to be a liberal and have been called elite and have been puzzled as to why you were called this, this is where it started. By rebranding who the elite in America were, Nixon successfully turned working-class people's criticism away from the super-rich country club types who financially backed the Republican Party and toward the Democratic Party and its liberal ideals. His administration called this the *blue-collar strategy* and portrayed the silent majority as victims of these so-called elites hell-bent on destroying traditional American values. Ultimately, this rhetoric convinced many working-class voters that the Republican Party, despite its true allegiance to rich donors and business owners, was fighting for the everyday man and his traditional family values. George Lakoff said about Nixon's strategy, "He created conservative populism. 'We're gonna bring them together and have them vote on the basis of their morality *against* possibly their self-interest!' Not vote on their economic issues but vote on their 'moral' issues."

Journalist and historian Rick Perlstein echoed Lakoff's thoughts, framing Nixon's strategy as an issue of cultural populism versus conservative populism: "The brilliance of Nixon was to base a politics that was based on deference to money and plutocracy and frame it in terms of a kind of cultural populism. The idea that the real snobs are not the people who hire and fire, but the people who kind of decide cultural trends."

The idea was, simply, to divide the American people. And, of course, it worked.

Two Secret Memos that Changed Everything

By 1970, Nixon's honeymoon with the press was starting to wear thin, and the continuation of the Vietnam War was gnawing at his approval rates. Neither Ailes nor Nixon liked the coverage in the news about him, and they needed to find a way to fix it. A secret memo from this time period, discovered in the annals of the Nixon Library by John Cook from Gawker, was titled "A Plan for Putting the GOP on TV News." It outlined a clear strategy for using the media to promote the agenda of the GOP (short for Grand Old Party, a nickname for the Republican Party). It's unclear whether the memo was written by Ailes, but his hand-written notes appear all over it.

The memo set out a detailed plan for getting television stations to promote GOP-friendly news. It outlined a way to avoid "the censorship, the priorities and the prejudices of network news selectors and disseminators" and deliver "pro-administration" stories to viewers. The plan laid out specifically how the administration could use biased media to create GOP viewers and thus GOP voters. It stated that "people are lazy" and that they want their "thinking done for them." It went on to say that "29% rely on TV only" for their news coverage and that "44% say TV is more believable than any other media." The administration could easily feed a lazy audience pro-White House propaganda and get them to feel positively about Nixon no matter what was really going on with Vietnam and other hot-button issues through tactics such as creating prerecorded media segments to send out to TV stations across the country, providing them with free content to run to their audiences. It was a win-win situation: independent TV stations could save money, and the Republican Party would expand their reach. For unknown reasons, the strategy outlined in this memo never quite got off the ground at the time, but the thought processes regarding what was basically government-funded propaganda were all in place.

A PLAN FOR PUTTING THE GOP ON TV NEWS

For 200 years the newspaper front page dominated public thinking. In the last 20 years that picture has changed. Today television news is watched more often

than people read newspapers.
than people listen to radio.
than people read or gather any other form of communication.

The reason: People are lazy. With television you just sit--watch--listen. The thinking is done for you. *29% rely only on TV*

As a result more than half the people now say they rely on television for their news. Eight out of 10 say they tune in radio or TV news at least once daily. *59% rely primarily on TV*

Network television news is only half the story. People are also concerned about their localities. As a result, TV news is one-half network, one-half local. *44% say TV is more believable than any other medium.*

To make network TV news from Washington you must have a story with national priority. Otherwise, you don't get on network and, therefore, you are not seen in any locality.

To date, local stations have not been able to carry Washington news unless it made the network because, literally, they haven't been able to get it there from here.

A page out of the Roger Ailes memo "A Plan for Putting the GOP on TV News," with Ailes's handwritten notes on it. Via Gawker.

Despite the success they had created together, Ailes and Nixon's relationship frayed over time. Nixon lost trust in Ailes, feeling he was going rogue. Ailes was eventually fired from the Nixon White House in 1974 after being caught leaking info to author Joe McGinnis, who wrote the damaging book *The Selling of the President 1968*, which covered Nixon's "repackaging" during his initial presidential campaign.

Ailes took a job at the Television News Network (TVN), a network funded and owned by the Coors family, famous for their popular beer brand. The Coors family wanted a conservative network to counter what they viewed as the "liberal" TV networks, such as NBC, CBS, and ABC.

Reese Schonfeld, who worked with Ailes in the early days of TVN and later cofounded CNN, said this about Ailes' and the Coors brothers' goals for TVN:

> Their goal was to be like a tugboat to the *Queen Mary*. They would just be going along and pushing the boat a little further to the Right and a little further to Right, and their goal was ultimately to put the great ship of ours over Right as far as they could. Ailes didn't know anything about news, and he doesn't know news now, but he sure does know television. He's as good at television as anyone in the country, and he is a great propagandist.

Right-wing media would push the country to the right. Credit: Maryam Hajouni.

Ailes was the perfect hire for TVN: he knew propaganda and had studied the dramatic camera angles and the use of chiaroscuro and music that the Hitler propagandist filmmaker Leni Riefenstahl used in the masterful Nazi propaganda film commissioned by Hitler, *Triumph of the Will*. Ailes had even used some of these techniques for Nixon's television appearances. Wouldn't you know it, the motto for TVN was "Fair and Balanced."

Just a year after the "Plan for Putting the GOP on TV News" memo, there was another, even more startling memo—the mother lode of secret memos in fact, drafted in August 1971—and this communication, later known as the Powell memo, would forever change the American political landscape.

Lewis Powell, a corporate lawyer from Virginia whom Nixon would soon appoint to the Supreme Court, was secretly commissioned by the education director of the U.S. Chamber of Commerce, Eugene B. Sydnor Jr., to write a manifesto. It was titled "Confidential Memorandum: Attack on American Free Enterprise System." The Powell memo fearfully and woefully described the economic climate of the early 1970s this way: "No thoughtful person can question that the American economic system is under broad attack. The government, the media, the universities, of course...and that Ralph Nader is destroying the free enterprise economy."

Wait. What? Ralph Nader? I remembered Nader's name well from my childhood, but I certainly didn't remember him as one of the bad guys. My parents revered him as a hero, and it seemed everybody did!

Nader, a lawyer from Connecticut, first came into the public spotlight in 1965 with the publication of *Unsafe at Any Speed*, a book critical of the safety of American automobiles. Following the book's publication, Nader quickly became a household name as he pursued governmental reform related to safe and ethical business practices and consumer protection.

The Powell memo reflects how the corporate establishment felt their feet were being held to the fire by Nader and the many Americans who agreed with him about governmental regulation and that as a result, the free market economy was in jeopardy and socialism was taking over. (There's that scary word, socialism, again.)

The memo was a call to arms for the business community and corporations. In it, Powell laid out very detailed plans for selling a free market economy to the masses. The memo was basically designed as an anti–New Deal blueprint for conservative business interests to retake America, despite the activism of people like Nader.

George Lakoff explained the actions Lewis Powell was laying out to combat these social movements as if in Powell's own words:

> We have to get wealthy conservatives to put their money together to appoint professors at major universities to teach our principles. We have to set up and support organizations in major universities to do this. He [Powell] said we couldn't trust universities. We have to set up our own research establishments, which became the think tanks. We have to make sure that they get published. So we have to start journals. We have to start publishing houses to start publishing their books. And we have to buy media so their ideas could get out. Not only that, but [Powell would say,] "We need spokespeople. So we're going to need training institutes to train ordinary citizens who we believe are on our side to learn to think and talk that way so they can be in the media. So we're gonna have to train them and keep in touch with them so that we can get booking agencies and book them on radio and TV."

The Powell memo concluded as follows: "It hardly need be said that the views expressed above are tentative and suggestive. The first step should be a thorough study. But this would be an exercise in futility unless the Board of Directors of the Chamber accepts the fundamental premise of this paper, namely, that business and the enterprise system are in deep trouble, and the hour is late."

Thus was born the most effective all-encompassing plan for the "vast right-wing conspiracy" that would ultimately lead to the Republican Party's control over America. This memo was an unequivocal rejection of not only the progressive movements of the 1960s but also the growing power of the middle class. It was an elaborate and strategic plan to save corporations and big business from the perceived onslaught of socialism and anticorporatism that came as a result of the progressive social and economic movements across the country.

Powell's main triumph in the memo was to outline a detailed method for cultivating positive attitudes toward the free market in everyday Americans. He sought to mold society to value business and small government and privatization over anything else. The scope of Powell's ideas was hugely ambitious, but with billionaires and the business community supporting the plan with patience, lots of funding, and cooperation, it would work.

How exactly would it work? The Powell memo called on the business community and corporate libertarian billionaires to fund think tanks and lobbying organizations and to get pro–free market professors teaching at colleges. The plan also included influencing the judicial system to lean more conservative and more pro–big business. It advocated for constant surveillance of textbooks and media. Media outreach, of course, was also emphasized.

Strength lies in organization, in careful long-range planning and implementation, in consistency of action over an indefinite period of years, in the scale of financing available only through joint effort, and in the political power available only through united action and national organizations.

From the Lewis Powell memo "Confidential Memorandum: Attack on the American Free Enterprise System." Via the Powell Papers at Washington & Lee University School of Law Scholarly Commons.

Jeff Cohen, cofounder of the online activist group RootsAction.org, media critic, author, lecturer, and former liberal Fox News pundit, explained, "You had a series of institutions formed and funded. These were right-wing think tanks, putting forward stuff that basically wasn't academically sound or intellectually sound but had good propaganda value."

The think tanks hired scientists, researchers, and academics to conduct studies whose results would inevitably come up with findings to support the benefits of a free market, a small, ineffectual government, deregulation, and a no-taxes ideology. In an article that appeared in the *New York Times* in 2016, Eric Lipton and Brooke Williams wrote, "Think tanks, which position themselves as 'universities without students,' have power in government policy debates because they are seen as researchers independent of moneyed interests. But in the chase for funds, think tanks are pushing agendas important to corporate donors, at times blurring the line between researchers and lobbyists. And they are doing so while reaping the benefits of their tax-exempt status, sometimes without disclosing their connections to corporate interests."

The vast majority of Americans were clueless about this strategic push to influence their thinking, despite the fact that the *Washington Post*'s Jack Anderson reported on the leaked contents of the Powell memo in 1972. A regular person like my dad just somehow began seeing things a bit differently as time went on and the messaging from the New Republicans grew stronger and more prolific. Dad gradually started devaluing college education and began seeing governmental assistance to those in need as government interference or allowing lazy people to take advantage of the system. Once friendly to and eager to talk to foreigners, he began to eye them with suspicion, thinking they might be illegal immigrants.

To be honest, my own thinking had changed. I remember having a conversation in the 1980s with my very politically informed boyfriend, Randy, about how our government spends so much money on poor people and people on welfare. He patiently informed me that it was only about 3 percent of our budget then, and for comparison, he showed me how much we spent on the military (an astronomical amount!). I was shocked. I was under the impression that there was so much more spent on welfare than what was actually spent, and the question of how I got that impression in the first place got me thinking.

The effects of the Powell memo started to seep into our culture almost immediately; the 1970s were called "the me decade" as people were focused on their individual rather than the common good. It got worse. Movies like 1987's *Wall Street* portrayed how the culture valued a "greed is good" philosophy. Ideologically, the country had moved a very long way from President Kennedy's 1961 inaugural address when he famously said, "Ask not what your country can do for you but what you can do for your country."

This major shift in many Americans' minds not coincidentally was beginning to coincide with the Right's way of thinking, as conservative think tanks cast doubt upon the value and effectiveness of public education, undermined publicly funded research, and continued to push a conservative agenda secretly backed by billionaires.

Regarding the Powell memo, Cohen concluded, "So they set up this infrastructure, and then ultimately, it led to the right-wing media itself, where they were setting up their own channels of communication, and that was the big boom in right-wing talk radio, nationally and across the country in every locale. And ultimately, the Fox News channel."

The Powell memo has been incredibly influential—probably even beyond Powell's wildest dreams. It impacted the realms of politics, judicial law, media, education, and beyond, establishing the ultraconservative thought foundations that continued to gain popularity over the next several decades. Yet today, it is not talked about or recognized for its gargantuan influence.

★ ★ ★

The day after I graduated high school, my parents moved to Maryland for my dad's work for the government. He was working on a new technology called "electronic mail." I had no idea what that meant, but it sounded important.

The 1972 election was the first one in which I could vote, but I still wasn't paying much attention to politics. I just knew all my friends hated Nixon. I voted for Shirley Chisholm, the first African American woman to run for president. I thought that was so badass. I had to support her.

The voting age had changed from twenty-one to eighteen in 1970 because, as the saying went, if you were old enough to fight, you were old enough to vote. And the younger voting age changed the dynamic of the election slightly, although not enough to avoid Nixon's reelection and what we can look back on now as the kickoff of the organization of the far-right movement as we know it today.

CHAPTER 4

From Nixon to Reagan and the Rise of the New Republicans

By the 1972 presidential election, neither of my parents were talking about politics much anymore. After JFK, Bobby Kennedy, and Martin Luther King Jr. were killed, my parents didn't seem as excited about where the country was going, and my dad in particular seemed almost detached from politics. They were settling into their new house and busy dealing with my younger brother, Walter, now a junior in high school, who was having trouble adjusting to the move.

I didn't move to Maryland with them immediately. Having worked part-time in the last couple of years of high school, I used my savings to rent a cheap room by the beach for the summer. One day at the end of the summer, in our tattered bell-bottom jeans and T-shirts, my friend and I hitchhiked to my parents' new home in Oxon Hill, Maryland. I liked the digs.

And the backyard butted up against a farm with horses on it! My dad told me firmly that if I chose to live there, I would have to either get a job or enroll in the community college. I chose community college and enrolled in some night classes, becoming a part-time student.

Looking back on it now, I realize that my brother Walter was really struggling and that his behavior was due to an emerging mental illness that he would struggle with for the rest of his life. But my dad blamed my brother's issues on listening to bands like the Beatles and smoking pot because it coincided with the time he began to change. It was an easy blame (and much less painful than the truth.) My mother, being at home all day, got to see more of my little brother. Concerned that Walter's issues went beyond pot smoking and garden-variety rebellion, she convinced my father to get him counseling, but Walter only went for a few sessions, refused to go to more, and the idea of him getting counseling was dropped. It was around this time that my dad began to view hippies and their associated liberal beliefs with suspicion. Despite this, though, I am pretty sure he voted for McGovern, if only because he was still a registered Democrat at that point.

The Problem with McGovern

George McGovern's popularity had made many long-time Democrats nervous, as he embodied many of the liberal ideologies that emerged in the late 1960s and early 1970s. Some people "were worried about his antiwar views, while others thought that he went against traditional Democratic principles. For many, unfairly or not, McGovern came to symbolize a candidacy of radical children, rioters, marijuana smokers, draft dodgers, and hippies." The candidacies of Howard Dean and Bernie Sanders reminded me of McGovern's.

Nixon, of course, had learned how to leverage his image more effectively to appeal to voters, and the Republicans were getting good at using marketing-like tactics via the media to promote their agenda. In his reelection campaign, Nixon used the divisiveness of race and war, corporate money, red-baiting, impugning the patriotism of Democrats, and dirty tricks like wiretapping to win over voters. With many Democrats already on the fence about whether McGovern was the right choice for the country, Nixon won the election in a massive landslide, garnering almost eighteen million more popular votes than McGovern—the widest margin of any U.S. presidential election. Nixon's reelection opened the door to a new generation of Republicans who would grow ever more conservative over the next couple of decades as their influence in media expanded.

Watergate and the End of Nixon

After the election, Nixon's internal memos show that he felt his strategy of painting Democrats as a party of racial quotas and urban welfare was successful. He believed he had won by mobilizing a nonpartisan majority against liberalism, rather than just propping up the core Republican Party.

But of course, Nixon's second term in office didn't last long, ending in the infamous Watergate scandal. Nixon resigned in

1974, and his vice president, Gerald Ford, took over. He seemed like a nice man to me—an accidental president also prone to physical accidents even though he was an accomplished athlete in his youth.

By the time Nixon left office, he had done significant damage, well beyond Watergate and the stain on the presidency. The true legacy of his administration was the division he successfully sowed to gain power, and to the detriment of our country, Nixon's sins went unpunished. Ford pardoned him, giving the impression that the powerful can get away with crimes.

The Influence of Televangelism

Sometime before I went off to college to finish my degree after completing community college at home, I remember coming across televangelism for the first time, catching a program from the famous TV pastor Oral Roberts. It seemed like a new phenomenon to me, but broadcast evangelism (the zealous spreading of the Christian gospel publicly through the use of media) had been around for a long time, starting with religious radio shows in the 1930s. I remember not quite knowing what I thought and felt about this new phenomenon, but something about it left me a bit queasy.

Billy Graham was one of the first major radio and TV preachers, rising to prominence in the 1950s and gaining power and followers over the next four decades. Reporter Laurie Goodstein described Graham's influence in a *New York Times* article on his death at the age of ninety-nine: "Mr. Graham took the role of evangelist to a new level, lifting it from the sawdust floors of canvas tents in small-town America to the podiums of packed stadiums in the world's major cities. He wrote some 30 books and was among the first to use new communication technologies for religious purposes."

In 1960, according to author Anne Nelson, "the Federal Communications Commission opened up a new world of opportunity for fundamentalist preachers, giving commercial broadcasters the right to sell airtime they had previously given to traditional churches as a public service. The new ruling allowed fundamentalists the chance to compete in the marketplace and develop telemarketing as a profit center."

Perhaps in part due to the success and pioneering of Billy Graham, evangelism, helped along by the television-broadcast version of the medium, televangelism, continued to grow in influence in the 1960s and 1970s; in 1979, conservative activist Paul Weyrich helped found the Moral Majority, a political action group comprised of conservative fundamentalist Christians, led by prominent Southern Baptist televangelist Jerry Falwell. The Moral Majority preached that the nation's morality was in decay. They were for the traditional family (which meant against gay people), values, prayer in schools, the "right to work" anti-union agenda, and what they called fairness and justice (lowering taxes for the wealthy). They were against political correctness and abortion, and they believed the culture we were living in was "an ever-widening sewer."

This was when the resurgence of conservative evangelism, a

movement called the New Christian Right, arose. The movement largely relied on the ideologies of nineteenth-century evangelicalism, which were typically "characterized by racism, a hostility to Native Americans, an imperialist mentality, superpatriotism, a promilitarist stance, and a deep suspicion of 'foreign' ideologies such as Catholicism and socialism."

The televangelist broadcasters in particular were very influential, especially since, as they weren't considered news and religious services were broadcast as a public service, the FCC did not hold them to the public standard rules.

A preacher named John MacArthur once wrote the following about televangelists:

Someone needs to say this plainly: The faith healers and health-and-wealth preachers who dominate religious television are shameless frauds. Their message is not the true Gospel of Jesus Christ. There is nothing spiritual or miraculous about their on-stage chicanery. It is all a devious ruse designed to take advantage of desperate people. They are not godly ministers but greedy impostors who corrupt the Word of God for money's sake. They are not real pastors who shepherd the flock of God, but hirelings whose only design is to fleece the sheep. Their love of money is glaringly obvious in what they say as well as how they live. They claim to possess great spiritual power, but in reality, they are rank materialists and enemies of everything holy.

What is particularly striking to many today are the offenses that evangelicals once found to be deal breakers, such as adultery, but now tolerate in their elected official or candidate. Televangelists are media masters, well trained in the art of selling a specific message and indoctrinating followers. It's no surprise the Republican Party's own media strategies have mirrored televangelism in many ways over the past few decades.

The Religious Right later went on to stealthily insert their agenda in an even more nefarious way. After Reagan was elected, in 1981, a group of evangelicals, fundamentalists, oil barons, oligarchs, gun lobbyists and other Republican operatives gathered to form a group called the Council for National Policy. They coordinated an attack on civil liberties, the social safety net, and waged their own information war on broadcasting. They worked with the Koch brothers using state-of-the-art apps and shared highly detailed and personal voter data in order to manipulate voters and church-goers and to outmaneuver Democrats. I would wager that this shadowy organization that Anne Nelson uncovered and talked about in her book, *Shadow Network*, was possibly as influential as the Lewis Powell memo.

Shortly after I came across televangelism, I transferred to Pratt Institute to finish my degree. In a departure from my previous failing grades, I graduated on the dean's list. My dad was exceedingly proud of my educational success and impressed with the life I was building for myself as an adult.

Although my dad had backed away from politics in recent years, he had become slightly more conservative in some ways.

It came as a welcome surprise to me that Dad liked and admired the new friends I made at college, who came from all over the country and included people of color and several gay guys. Dad drove to Brooklyn to help five of us move into a brownstone we were renting together and was impressed when my friend Alex, one of my gay buddies, wearing a crisp pink shirt, changed a tire on my dad's car in ten minutes flat. I was very proud of my dad for being so open, willing, and able to kibitz, as he called it, with anybody—even people who were completely unlike him. That day at the brownstone was one that would live on in my memory, eventually becoming a somewhat painful reminder of the man my father had once been.

During and after my college years, Gerald Ford's short presidency was fairly uneventful, and the Democratic Party was able to take back the White House when Jimmy Carter ran as an outsider against the incumbent. He was a liberal thinker who pardoned all the draft evaders of the Vietnam War and established a national energy policy, even going so far as to put solar panels up on the White House. It seemed like the country was recovering from the damage Nixon had done. I remember feeling both men were decent, but I preferred Jimmy Carter. In addition to seeming like a truly good person, he seemed really smart.

Due to some of the beginning effects of the Powell memo, however, President Carter acted in accordance with the new trending views on deregulation. He signed into law the Motor

Carrier Act, which deregulated the trucking industry and ended up having a negative impact on truckers' earnings.

When Carter ran for a second term in 1980, Ronald Reagan ran against him on the Republican ticket. Also running in that election, on the Libertarian ticket for vice president, was the little-known billionaire David Koch.

Who was this David Koch running on the Libertarian ticket? David Koch's father, Fred Koch of Koch Industries, a huge manufacturing company, was one of the founding members of the radical John Birch Society in the 1950s. Koch's platform was founded on his advocacy for abolishing government programs and institutions such as Social Security, the FBI, the CIA, and public schools. Although he ran for president as a Libertarian, David Koch and his brother Charles would eventually become highly influential within the Republican Party in its most extreme right-wing form.

Libertarianism and the New Republicans

In the early 1980s, most Americans were not familiar with libertarianism, a relatively new political framework conceived in the early 1970s. Merriam-Webster defines a libertarian as "an advocate of the doctrine of free will, and a person who upholds the principles of individual liberty, especially of thought and action." Some Libertarians so value individual freedom that they tend to prefer laws that honor the right of the individual more than those that serve the good of society. The *Stanford Encyclopedia of Philosophy* further elaborates on how that

translates in the real world: "Libertarians endorse strong rights
to individual liberty and private property; defend civil liberties
like equal rights for homosexuals; endorse drug decriminaliza-
tion, open borders, and oppose most military interventions."
In contrast to its *social* liberalism, libertarianism embraces
highly conservative economic policies such as an unregulated
market, extreme deregulation of business, protected rights to
private property, and no taxes. Another brand of libertarianism
is the so-called left libertarian. They tend to be more egalitarian
in their approach; for instance, they might believe that there
should be a limit to how much natural resources (land, water,
minerals, etc.) one can own.

The following text was David Koch's platform and manifesto.
I was shocked when I first came across it a couple years ago. I
don't know if I was more shocked by what it said, or that anyone
running for office would actually put it on paper. It clearly lays
out what the goals of these corporate libertarian billionaires actually were.

- We urge the repeal of federal campaign finance laws,
  and the immediate abolition of the despotic Federal
  Election Commission.
- We favor the abolition of Medicare and Medicaid
  programs.
- We oppose any compulsory insurance or tax-supported
  plan to provide health services, including those which
  finance abortion services.

- We also favor the deregulation of the medical insurance industry.
- We favor the repeal of the fraudulent, virtually bankrupt, and increasingly oppressive Social Security system. Pending that repeal, participation in Social Security should be made voluntary.
- We propose the abolition of the governmental Postal Service. The present system, in addition to being inefficient, encourages governmental surveillance of private correspondence. Pending abolition, we call for an end to the monopoly system and for allowing free competition in all aspects of postal service.
- We oppose all personal and corporate income taxation, including capital gains taxes.
- We support the eventual repeal of all taxation.
- As an interim measure, all criminal and civil sanctions against tax evasion should be terminated immediately.
- We support repeal of all laws which impede the ability of any person to find employment, such as minimum wage laws.
- We advocate the complete separation of education and State. Government schools lead to the indoctrination of children and interfere with the free choice of individuals. Government ownership, operation, regulation, and subsidy of schools and colleges should be ended.
- We condemn compulsory education laws...and we call for the immediate repeal of such laws.

- We support the repeal of all taxes on the income or property of private schools, whether profit or non-profit.
- We support the abolition of the Environmental Protection Agency.
- We support abolition of the Department of Energy.
- We call for the dissolution of all government agencies concerned with transportation, including the Department of Transportation.
- We demand the return of America's railroad system to private ownership. We call for the privatization of the public roads and national highway system.
- We specifically oppose laws requiring an individual to buy or use so-called "self-protection" equipment such as safety belts, air bags, or crash helmets.
- We advocate the abolition of the Federal Aviation Administration.
- We advocate the abolition of the Food and Drug Administration.
- We support an end to all subsidies for child-bearing built into our present laws, including all welfare plans and the provision of tax-supported services for children.
- We oppose all government welfare, relief projects, and "aid to the poor" programs. All these government programs are privacy-invading, paternalistic, demeaning, and inefficient. The proper source of help for such persons is the voluntary efforts of private groups and individuals.

- ► We call for the privatization of the inland waterways, and of the distribution system that brings water to industry, agriculture and households.
- ► We call for the repeal of the Occupational Safety and Health Act.
- ► We call for the abolition of the Consumer Product Safety Commission.
- ► We support the repeal of all state usury laws

David Koch's extreme libertarian anarchist vision was definitely not how most Americans thought our government should work. But over the years, more Americans, like my father, came to be swayed to ascribe to some of these ideas, and many of them took hold within the New Republican party.

At this point, with Ronald Reagan's election on the horizon, the United States was about to enter a golden age of conservatism unlike any seen before, and the effects of it would resonate for decades.

In an interview I did in 2011 with my dad, who had always prized education, he parroted much of the Koch manifesto. I doubt he ever actually read it—it's more likely he heard the basic outline from talk radio or TV—but he quoted parts of it word for word. This was the first interview I had with him on camera. It was a beautiful summer day. We were on the back porch, and I was just starting the movie and began cautiously attempting to film him with an unobtrusive little camera so he would speak candidly. With a carefully crafted tone of nonjudgmental curiosity, I asked him why he was a Republican. He started out speaking calmly, but as he answered me, he got more and more agitated. He at one point declared with passion, "We should get rid of the Department of Education and the Department of Energy!"

This conversation encapsulated the dangers of right-wing media as I saw them manifested in my dad. He spouted views that directly contradicted his personal values and philosophy, he was incredibly emotional and angry, and he was obviously using language that had been provided to him by an external source, which he then internalized and repeated back. The last thing he said as he jutted his chin out and nodded his head was, "I used to be a Democrat, but now I'm a Republican! Before I became a Republican I was fat, dumb, and happy." I had to agree—at least about the happy part. He was clearly unhappy now. And I was unhappy that he was so bitter and full of anger.

CHAPTER 5

"Let's Make America Great Again"

At the time of Reagan's election, my dad still wasn't paying much attention to politics. He was generally more interested in his bowling nights and what my mom was making for dinner. Though my parents still watched the news every night together after dinner and read the Sunday paper every week to keep up with current events, I can't recall them having any discussions about politics. What I did observe during this time was a sweetness between my parents. My dad would be really happy when he got home from work. He'd whoosh in the side door to the kitchen, where my mother would be cooking dinner. He'd grab her, bend her backward like they did in the old black-and-white movies, and plant a kiss on her. Then he'd ask "What's for dinner, Babe?" and make himself, my mother, and my grandmother each a manhattan. Sometimes he'd make my grandmother a second one. He'd kid around with her, and she would affectionately admonish him for being so "noisy."

Sharing Ayn Rand with Dad

I moved home a year after I left college because I was having a hard time trying to figure out how to navigate this new life. In the 1960s when I was little, I had envisioned my life would be entirely different than what was now expected of me, and even what I expected from myself. At the time, my good friend Mike Mentzer was building his career as a professional body builder, even once competing against Arnold Schwarzenegger.

Mike helped me out a lot, talking on the phone with me nearly every day during this rough period. Like me, Mike had been raised Catholic. When he turned away from Catholicism, he discovered the author and philosopher Ayn Rand, and he told me to check out her books and her philosophy. I did, and her teachings about how selfishness was a virtue were a stark contrast to the beliefs entrenched in me by my Catholicism. Mike convinced me that a large part of my angst was due to low self-esteem, and I thought he was right. Reading Ayn Rand and seeing how her philosophy actually made having good self-esteem a virtue, I dove in. I read everything she wrote, even passing *Atlas Shrugged* along to my dad. I eventually moved on from Ayn Rand's philosophy, but I have sometimes painfully wondered if reading her work contributed to the changes I saw in my dad a few years later.

Let's Make America Great Again...without the Government!

Ronald Reagan was key in jerking the country to the right even more than Nixon did. Reagan, a former popular Hollywood actor and union leader who became governor of California in 1966, won the 1980 presidential election. Comfortable under the spotlight, Reagan was dubbed the Great Communicator. His optimism and enthusiasm made it easy to convince voters that the free market would steer the country in the best direction. Reagan introduced into the mainstream the idea that smaller government was always better because government itself was largely ineffective. Indeed, Reagan once pronounced, "The economic ills we have suffered have come upon us over several decades. In this present crisis, government is not the solution to our problem. Government *is* the problem."

Personal responsibility and deregulation were touted throughout the course of his presidency in a philosophy that became known as Reaganomics, or trickle-down economics. Historian and author Rick Perlstein explained trickle-down economics as follows:

> One of the brilliant innovations was a new theory of how taxation works or how the economy worked. It used to be that conservatives or the Republicans were all about balanced budgets. They were all about making the people eat their spinach. They came up with this new theory called "supply-side economics." Supply side

basically means you give money to businesses, and that way they'll basically produce more plenty that will trickle down to ordinary people.

Reagan claimed that undue tax burdens, social spending, and excessive government regulation hampered growth. It was a great theory for the already rich, but multiple studies have shown that trickle-down economics doesn't work, and it would end up hurting the very working-class voters who trusted Ronald Reagan with their economic future. With Reagan's sunny personality and positive spin, many people, including Democrats, bought it. I still wasn't very political, but I didn't buy Reagan's sunny act. I thought there was something dark about him and his administration. It scared me a little. But other Democrats did buy into it.

Perlstein explained what made some Democrats vote for Reagan: "There are two things that made the Democrats want to vote for Ronald Reagan. Reagan developed this political vocabulary that made traditional conservative economic ideas sound really positive and really good to ordinary people. And what Ronald Reagan was promising these voters was to return to a simpler time."

Reagan made it seem to many like he would take America back to some really great place it had been in the past while never explicitly saying what that place was, using the slogan "Let's Make America Great Again." (That should ring a bell!)

Claire Conner explained that a stealth movement born in the roots of the John Birch Society and adopted by the Heritage

Foundation (the first conservative think tank created not long after the Powell memo) was literally intended to move the country backward, but rather than to a quaint, pastoral former America, the extreme Right actually wanted to revert the country to a darker place before FDR and the New Deal. It was shocking—a jolt—to hear Claire say the following:

> They [the Birch Society and wealthy corporate libertarians] saw 1900 in America like the apex of when we were great as a nation. 1900—before the income tax, before the Federal Reserve, before any progressive legislation was considered or passed. Before child labor laws, before women had any rights, before women even had the right to vote. Robert Welch, who was the founder of the John Birch Society, talked a lot about 1900 as these glorious times in the American History. And he said, "There were pockets of poverty." If you know anything about 1900, you are now laughing. "Pockets of poverty, however," he said, "but it was a healthy kind of poverty. Poverty free from government interference, where every man understood that relief from dire want is entirely his own responsibility. Thus, the blessings of liberty outweighed the poverty."

In his bid to make poverty great again, Reagan also began the foundation for fulfilling another goal to build a super-rich class who could influence government with their money. One of the first things he did to help the uberwealthy class was fire the professional air traffic controllers who were on strike. This move had the ripple effect of diminishing the power of unions and their ability to bargain for higher wages. Reagan also cut income taxes for the wealthy from 70 percent down to a meager 28 percent, though as has been pointed out, "the 70 percent rate didn't kick in until $212,000, which in today's dollars is over $600,000." Because he was working closely with the Heritage Foundation, who always pushed for lower taxes for the wealthy, Reagan asked the anti-tax activist Grover Norquist to start the advocacy group Americans for Tax Reform. To belong to the group, any elected official or candidate for office had to pledge never to vote to raise taxes for any reason.

Reagan also helped create the super-rich class through widespread deregulation. Political commentator and liberal radio host Thom Hartmann explained how this worked:

We have now a very politically active super wealthy class, whereas from basically World War II until the late '70s, that class was just quietly and slowly involved in businesses and building their wealth. The average CEO made over thirty times what the average employee did, because the top marginal tax rate was 90 percent. [As of this writing, the average CEO makes around 287 times more than his or her average employees.] And back then, you couldn't shift income into other forms of compensation like stock options and things like that. All those rules changed under Reagan and made it possible for people to be very wealthy very quickly if they were in a position of ownership or leadership in a large corporation. What they have done is they shifted so much power to those who have great money or those corporations who have great money. I mean, it's so powerful. How do you resist it?

Reagan made government smaller and the rich richer and more powerful, and he also helped to make corporate monopolies bigger. His Justice Department relaxed antitrust enforcement, which helped create a "previously unimaginable rise of monopoly power." And all along, he was selling himself through the media as an approachable, looking-out-for-the-little-guy kind of president.

Back then, there were still just three networks dominating TV broadcasting. Their editorial positions were pretty indistinguishable, and extremists didn't get airtime. It was the same with the mainstream newspapers, with only the *Wall Street Journal* being somewhat more conservative than its competitors.

But then came Roone Arledge, the president of ABC News in the late '70s and early '80s. He was not political but "figured the country was turning conservative and that a conservative slant would be in fashion." Arledge, a brilliant and sophisticated sports broadcaster with a good sense for entertainment, wanted to make the television news as entertaining as possible—whatever would draw a crowd. Under his direction, the news reporting coming from ABC became much more emotion-driven and biased. Viewers responded to the content, which often focused on performative patriotism and heavy use of curated photography to communicate a specific message, and soon the other news outlets began to follow suit. The major newspapers picked up cues from these changes as well, and the style of reporting changed in a way that often focused on Reagan's perceived strengths as a president and less on how "the oil industry, the automobile makers, defense contractors, banks, the nuclear-power industry" supported him. Nor did they mention the ballooning deficit looming in his second term.

This change was in part because the media was also "reacting to the battering" they were taking from right-wing critics. They did not want to be charged with accusations of liberal bias, which had become louder and more frequent. AIM, the conservative think tanks, and the right-wing machinery were beginning to exert their influence.

Reagan's Top Three Gifts to the Right-Wing Media Machine That Caused FDR to Roll Over in His Grave

RUPERT MURDOCH

The most significant but little-known contribution Reagan made to the development of right-wing media was done unceremoniously. In 1985, Reagan made Australian publishing magnate Rupert Murdoch a naturalized citizen of the United States—a decision that would prove to be much more influential than almost anyone could have imagined.

Keith Rupert Murdoch, who went by his middle name, grew up in Australia, accustomed to wealth and privilege. His father died when Murdoch was just twenty-one years old. He took over as managing director of News Limited, which his father had owned, and inherited a family trust of newspaper shares. Murdoch eventually started buying up newspapers all over Australia, shaping himself into a media mogul.

By his midforties, Murdoch realized he could influence national politics through his readership. He was responsible for getting his choice of people in power in Australia and then, when they were no longer useful to him, getting them out of power, all by painting them as bad for the country in the media he owned. He even successfully led an effort to repeal the country's fairly new carbon tax, which had been popular at first.

Murdoch took over newspapers throughout Australia and then New Zealand, and he eventually expanded his reach into the United Kingdom. He purchased a British newspaper, the now defunct *News of the World*, in 1969. The publication did not follow journalistic norms or codes of conduct; instead, it specialized in sordid stories.

Murdoch had great influence over the British government too. But that wasn't enough for him. In 1973, he purchased two newspapers in San Antonio, Texas, and he also briefly owned the *Village Voice*. He moved to the United States in 1974 and purchased the *New York Post* in 1976, then quietly added to his

American media empire over the next couple of decades through the acquisitions of Twentieth Century Fox and HarperCollins. Reagan made him a U.S. citizen in 1985. And then, in October 1996, Murdoch finally realized the culmination of his dreams when he got Roger Ailes to help him create Fox News. Sometime in 2007, he notably acquired the *Wall Street Journal*. (FDR rolls a little.)

THE FEDERAL COMMUNICATIONS COMMISSION

In 1987, Reagan weakened the power of the FCC. The FCC, as mentioned earlier, was originally created by FDR to regulate the media industry and limit ownership of media outlets in America. It had the responsibility of educating the public and disseminating the news. Reagan's first step was to drastically cut the funding for the FCC. Then he "staffed the FCC with prominent media businessmen who were intent on slashing government regulations...the equivalent of letting the fox guard the chicken coop." They aggressively deregulated the broadcast industry, claiming they wanted the marketplace to determine who controls TV and radio and deliberately overlooking the ways in which deregulation would put more power into the hands of huge companies.

Reagan's FCC thought of the television as "a toaster with pictures"—just another household appliance rather than a core instrument of our democracy. They also lifted its children's policy guidelines, which limited the number of commercials for certain ages and stated that children's shows and their hosts shouldn't sell products and should provide educational and informational programming, and, in 1984, ruled that stations could air as many commercials as they pleased. The FCC was unwilling to restrain the broadcast industry with regulation overseeing any morality or accuracy in programming. The *marketplace* would determine programming for children! Thanks for the endless commercials, Mr. Reagan!

(FDR rolls a little more.)

THE END OF THE FAIRNESS DOCTRINE

The third and arguably the single most influential thing Reagan did that gave America a huge shove to the right was block Congress from signing the Fairness Doctrine into law in 1987.

The Fairness Doctrine, which had been introduced in 1949, was explained to me in an interview with Steve Rendall, cofounder of and former senior analyst for the media watchdog group Fairness and Accuracy in Reporting (FAIR):

> Broadcasters were required to one, cover matters of public controversy, and two, cover them by including different voices—with a variety of voices, not just from the same point of view. It said if you are watching or listening to your local television or radio station, and there are points of view that are not being included in the discussion, and you wish for them to be in there, go complain to your station. If they don't give you satisfaction, then send a complaint to the FCC. It didn't guarantee equal time. What it did was it reminded broadcasters that they

had a public trust, and they should include some views that might go against their own or might not be popular or favorable to them.

The goal of the Fairness Doctrine was to ensure that broadcast license holders covered controversial issues of importance in an honest, equitable, and balanced way. At the time, the doctrine had large support, as Americans were alarmed by how much influence radio and TV propaganda had had on the people of Nazi Germany. These laws were put into place in an effort to protect the public from that kind of manipulation.

The 1987 veto of the Fairness Doctrine created chaos almost instantaneously within our media, especially radio. With the expectation of honest and accurate reporting discarded, the talk radio industry exploded. And just one year later, extreme conservative shock jock Rush Limbaugh went national.

(FDR does a full turn and then another for good measure.)

Though Dad was dancing Mom around the kitchen in Maryland and my parents were happy, I finally realized I felt most like myself in New York and that since I was finally successfully armed with a decent résumé, it was more likely I could get a job there in my field of graphics. I moved back to New York when Reagan was still in office. At the time, I still didn't think who was in office made a big difference. But then one day, I took a long walk. When I walked across Houston Street, I was immediately struck by the sight of so many more homeless people. I had not seen anything like it in my three previous years in New York. The sidewalks were literally strewn with men and women muttering to themselves. They seemed more disturbed than the usual homeless people. Walking around the Lower East Side, it was like seeing herds of zombies from *The Walking Dead*. They looked like they needed to be cared for in a psychiatric hospital, and they probably *had* been. In a conversation with my mother, I found out that President Reagan had changed a law governing the mentally ill and that the mentally ill were now "free" from the hospital facilities they had been in.

Reagan had repealed most of Carter's Mental Health Systems Act of 1980, which gave grants to community mental health centers. There was to be no more federal funding of services for the mentally ill. The libertarian idea was to let the individual states and families take care of their mentally ill. If they couldn't, well then, so be it. I saw the direct result of the ensuing deinstitutionalization on the streets of New York City, and it sure didn't look like any version of "making America great again" that I could believe in.

This is the moment when I had a bit of a political awakening. It finally hit me—who you have in office *does* make a difference! Up until then, I wasn't that interested in politics, and I didn't really think it mattered.

Now I *knew* it did.

★ CHAPTER 6 ★

How Talk Radio Hijacked My Dad

In 1984, Reagan was reelected in a landslide victory against liberal Democrat Walter Mondale. That year was also when everything began to change for my dad and our family.

In 1984, Dad retired from his job with the federal government at age sixty-two. Both my parents missed being near the shore, so they moved back to New Jersey and settled in Toms River, a town where there was a large retired population. Still energetic, my father got a part-time engineering job three or four days a week, necessitating a long solo commute by car. He didn't want to waste time on music while driving. He wanted to be stimulated mentally, and he discovered talk radio to keep himself company. At that time, Bob Grant was the dominant talk radio personality. Often called the father of conservative radio, Grant was an openly racist, sexist, far-right shock jock. On his WABC radio show, he referred to Blacks and Hispanics as "savages." He believed them to be inferior, and he even once called Martin Luther King Jr. a "slimeball." With his combative and testy style, he was considered a pioneer of the combat talk radio format. Soon, Grant became my dad's commuting buddy.

I didn't know Bob Grant from Joe Namath, but I did know I didn't care for his style of yelling at callers or hanging up on them if they disagreed with him. My mother was not a fan of Grant's either, and she delighted in telling me the story of how she ran into him one day. She was at the Ocean County mall eatery, sitting at a table having lunch, when she saw Grant walk in. She recognized him, and when he passed her table, she asked him, "You're Bob Grant, aren't you?"

He said, "Yes, I am."

She said, "Oh, my husband likes you, but I don't."

He had been walking away and turned to look back at my mother and gave a little laugh. She said she just sat there at the table and did not smile back.

Gradually, it seemed my dad started becoming more agitated after listening to Bob Grant. Eventually, he became consistently more irritable, excitable, and easy to anger. Little did we know a metamorphosis was beginning.

The History of Talk Radio

Along with massive deregulation in the communications industry, there were several other factors that led to talk radio's explosion of popularity in the 1980s. The first was that music had moved from the AM dial to the high-fidelity sound of FM and thus left a void on the AM dial. Broadcasters realized that filling the blank airspace with mainstream news wouldn't make much money. However, *entertainment* made money, and talk radio was entertainment at its finest, even when it masqueraded as news coverage. Human conversation didn't benefit from high-fidelity sound the way music did, so talk radio filled the void on the AM radio waves perfectly.

The second contributor to talk radio's rise was the new accessibility of satellite technology, allowing anyone to broadcast a show nationally. And the third was the fact that when 1–800 numbers became available, you could have callers call in from all over the country. These factors combined to make a pretty powerful storm!

The format of talk radio was, of course, not new. The format first debuted in the 1920s, continuing with Father Charles Coughlin's controversial and anti-Semitic radio broadcasts in the 1930s. Coughlin has often been referred to as the father of hate radio, and he paved the way for all that was to come in this medium.

Many of the most famous conservative talk radio personalities modeled themselves after the 1950s sensation Joe Pyne. His show, *It's Your Nickel*, consisted of Pyne debating his opinions with people calling in. Calls often culminated with him insulting the caller, to the delight of his audience.

The format of talk radio evolved from there, but many of the most popular shows and hosts, including Bob Grant, Rush Limbaugh, Sean Hannity, and Glenn Beck, have stuck with the confrontational tone and high-emotion interactions that these early hosts introduced.

There haven't been many successful liberal talk radio hosts. Ed Schultz, Randi Rhodes, and Alan Colmes tried to make inroads but "simply failed to draw a large audience." You may wonder why conservative talk radio programs have been so phenomenally popular while equivalent liberal shows have foundered. Aside from big money to support it, the secret seems to lie in the inflammatory approach favored by these so-called conservative hosts. Abram Brown of *Forbes* says of liberal talk radio shows, "It's not the same as a Limbaugh or a Hannity. It's more general, not really railing against the system. No one is yelling. 'We need to get rid of the Republicans! They're the worst thing to happen to this country!' But you'll hear conservative radio hosts say that about liberals on their programs."

Brown makes another good point that speaks to that: "Tell your audience that the mainstream media is corrupt and biased, then there's all the more reason to turn to your conservative talk radio to get the truth." Anger is a hot commodity. Finding an enemy is even hotter. Or as Ailes might say, "It's the emotion, stupid!" (He did not say this.)

A little known but very chilling example of how powerfully influential radio can be is the 1994 Rwanda genocide where an estimated eight hundred thousand citizens were brutally murdered by their fellow citizens (the Hutus). This happened after an intense radio campaign that started in 1993 dehumanized and demonized one group (the Tutsis). Militia groups were formed, and police and soldiers joined them in the killing. Samantha Power, who later served as the U.S. ambassador to the United Nations, said, "Killers often carried a machete in one hand and a transistor radio in the other."

Dad Discovers Rush Limbaugh

After about a year or so of working part-time and his long commute, my dad officially retired. He still occasionally listened to Bob Grant, mostly when he happened to be in his car during the day. But at some point, probably around 1989, my dad discovered another talk radio guy. It was none other than the potentate of right-wing talk radio, Rush Limbaugh, who exploded onto the scene in 1988.

My dad began enjoying what I called his "Limbaugh lunches," where he sat in the kitchen and ate a *very* leisurely lunch while listening to Limbaugh on the radio. Before long, he was listening to Limbaugh for three hours every day, and these lunches were the highlight of his life. My father dominated the kitchen during the middle of the day. My mother wasn't allowed to speak to him when he listened to Limbaugh, so she chose to eat alone in the living room where she watched the news at noon. Since the kitchen opened up to the living room, she often couldn't hear her news because my dad had Limbaugh on so loud. My dad eventually put up heavy sliding wooden doors between the living room and the kitchen. When the doors were closed, my mother had her TV turned up loud enough that she was able to drown out Rush Limbaugh's voice.

My mother couldn't stand Limbaugh. She declared emphatically to me once, "He is not nice!" She claimed that she was raised with certain Christian values and that he did not reflect those values. To her, he was a mean-spirited bully and full of hate. She did not find Limbaugh entertaining or even remotely interesting.

But my dad sure did. Limbaugh's rhetoric tapped the sweet spot of his insecurities, as it did for so many other older White men at the time. Limbaugh had struck gold by speaking directly to American men who felt lost and alienated in a rapidly changing society. He capitalized on their confusion and nervousness about their changing roles and their fears about being left behind in a society that seemed increasingly socially liberal and technologically advanced every year. Rush Limbaugh and the other rising right-wing radio personalities cleverly preyed on their aggrieved feelings.

Limbaugh directly benefited from Reagan's rejection of the Fairness Doctrine. With widespread deregulation, radio stations could blast whatever kind of commentary they wanted without having to present opposing views. As a result, Limbaugh was able to spread his opinions and misinformation without ever having to correct the record or give anyone a chance at rebuttal.

Many older White men like my dad found a hero in Rush Limbaugh. He made them feel understood and validated, so they trusted him completely. He abused that trust by single-handedly manipulating multitudes of older White men to vote against their own economic interests simply by appealing to their deepest fears and insecurities. He seemed like he bravely was bucking the system when he really was supporting it.

Steve Rendall, cofounder of FAIR, sheds more light on Limbaugh's power: "The allure of the Limbaughs and the Grants is that they tap into a kind of resentment, a kind of insecurity on the part of mostly White men, in large part, middle-aged and aging White men, a kind of injured pride that...the world is passing them by. It's typical of demagoguery to say that your problems really aren't problems caused by you and they're caused by these other people that aren't like us."

The Rise of Rush Limbaugh

Rush Limbaugh started working in radio as a teenager and DJed through his twenties. He got a big break in 1984, when he replaced Morton Downey Jr. (pioneer of trash TV in the late '80s) on KFBK-AM in Sacramento, California. He was very successful and was then hired to start a show at WABC-AM in New York City in July 1988.

Limbaugh was charismatic and authoritative, and a devoted following quickly grew. He had a way of making his listeners feel special, like he was only talking to *them*. And he knew how to get a rise out of people. In 1988, he surprisingly agreed to go on a public-access cable TV show called *Miggs B on TV* and said, "People who see you on TV are there for one reason only, and that's to make you mad, and the formula for making you—the viewer, the listener—mad hasn't changed a bit, yet people keep falling for it." In the same interview, he gave his formula for getting listeners: "If you embellish the opinion with confidence and cockiness, then you're getting into generating hatred." Then with a cocky tilt of his head and a smile, he said, "A lot of people say, 'Do you really believe the stuff you say?' Well, that's for you to figure out." Hmm. Unfortunately, they rarely do.

The Rush Limbaugh Show soon became "the most listened to talk radio program in the U.S." Limbaugh's success provided plenty of opportunities for copycat shows to cater to the same audience as well. According to far-right radio personalities like Limbaugh and those who emulated him, America's problems could easily be blamed on liberals, feminists, minorities, and the poor. Limbaugh provided plenty of affirmation for his audience that they were the long-suffering "true" Americans, and the reason their lives weren't going quite as well as they had hoped was not because of billionaires hoarding wealth and resources but, say, because a Black family moved in down the block and property values in the neighborhood tanked.

Limbaugh hammered away at what later became a household term: *the liberal media.* He claimed any media that didn't espouse his extreme views was liberal media, inherently biased and unreliable. He took the vocabulary a step further, entrenching his listeners in a special language that sowed division. All liberals were "libtards" who were ruining the country and his listeners' lives. Cultural changes made some of these older White men feel inadequate or unsure of what their role in society was going to be. Limbaugh exploited that and so turned those feelings of inadequacy to anger that they were supposed to change to keep up with the times. Limbaugh exploited their feelings of vulnerability.

The deceptive thing about Rush Limbaugh is that though he pretended to be for the middle-class average White guy, he was always defending the big corporations like the tobacco companies. It was a great way to sell the free market ideology and deregulation to those unsuspecting folks who wouldn't benefit from it.

Jeff Cohen of RootsAction.org further explained this to me:

In terms of people like your dad, the important thing about a Bob Grant or a Rush Limbaugh is the owners of the media and the owners of radio stations love these guys because they'll never offend anyone in power or any advertiser or any corporation, and they will offer, largely to White, middle-class, working-class males...an explanation of why their lives are screwed up.

So what they'll do is they'll point to every group in society that's "ruining society," except those that actually have the power to ruin society, which is corporate power. So the key is...people that flocked to Rush Limbaugh and flocked to Bob Grant, especially during the '80s and '90s, were people who were economically being screwed, and they were looking around for an explanation that would sort of reinforce their prejudices.

The trouble with Limbaugh is that he was misleading (and enraging) millions of Americans. Cohen continued:

He wasn't just wrong factually. He would take, like, reality upside-down. He became what we call a champion of the overdog. Any powerful group that was being criticized, by scientists or medical people, was the victim. So the tobacco industry was a victim, and that's where he came up with his "conclusion" that, you know, no one's ever proved that nicotine is addictive or is linked to these horrible diseases. He'd say it; he said it more than once. You don't like seat belts? It's Ralph Nader—he made up this stuff.

You know, again, there's no science involved, and cigarettes' secondhand smoke, making you go outside of the restaurant to smoke, it's not true. Here's the real facts, and then he comes up with his false facts.

Cohen and Rendall, the cofounders of FAIR, wrote a book called *The Way Things Aren't: Rush Limbaugh's Reign of Error: Over 100 Outrageously False and Foolish Statements from America's Most Powerful Radio and TV Host*, which lists many of Limbaugh's blatant and sometimes ridiculous lies. They then debunk each lie with research and fact-checking, clearly demonstrating how Limbaugh blatantly said things he knew to be untrue simply because they would appeal to his listenership. The title was a spoof on Limbaugh's *New York Times* bestselling book called *The Way Things Ought to Be*.

Limbaugh had no trouble—and apparently did not feel guilty about—making stuff up. He was able to happily craft a lucrative career while also spreading lies. He falsely claimed that there are more Native Americans alive today than when Columbus arrived; that ice caps melting won't make the sea levels rise; that there's no conclusive proof that nicotine is addictive or that cigarettes cause emphysema, lung cancer or heart disease; and that President Obama shut down NASA space flights and turned the agency "into a Muslim outreach department." His biggest lie of all was when he would say "I'm not making this stuff up, folks!" He was indeed making stuff up. Yet my father bought all of it and swore on the bible of Rush.

Rendall also astutely pointed out why talk radio is so seductive: "Most people don't think about this, but talk radio is something, unlike a lot of other media, that's almost always done alone. People almost always listen to it alone. And they're listening to this one other person, and there's sort of a personal thing there and a connection." That made a lot of sense to me when I thought about my father (and other fathers) on those long drives to work, listening to the rantings of Bob Grant or Rush Limbaugh. Limbaugh easily transformed an army of millions of previously nonpolitical listeners into voters and activists.

It has been well documented that people's social circles tend to shrink as they get older, and the relative social isolation of older White men could very well be another reason people like my dad fell so hard for Limbaugh—he made them feel less alone, even as he stoked their anger and dissatisfaction with the world. Not to mention my dad no longer worked with a group of people, mostly men. He was basically alone, with just my mother and my occasional visit. My older brother was in North Carolina and my younger brother was in California at the time.

My dad's Limbaugh lunches were bad enough, but it turned out that talk radio was merely a gateway for the far-right ideologies to reach my father. In the years that followed, he fell down a rabbit hole that completely took over his life and hammered home the realities of how the media we consume impacts the way we think and how we see the world.

★ CHAPTER 7 ★

The Vast Right-Wing Conspiracy Takes Off

I was so hoping there would be a small chance my dad would be open to Bill Clinton as a presidential candidate, but long before the election, my father's mind had already been poisoned against Clinton by his media choices. The New Republican snail mail readers had already been primed with anti-Democrat hype, and so, too, Rush Limbaugh's listeners, on how "slick" Clinton was, how he supposedly avoided the draft, his rumored and admitted affairs with women, his non-inhaling pot smoking. Clinton was painted as weak, a free love, '60s "brat" whose wife, Hillary, was a god-awful feminist!

After twelve years of Republicans in the White House, I was excited and hopeful for change with Bill Clinton's election. My mother was excited too. My dad—not so much. From what he already "knew" about Clinton, our country was going to go to hell in a handbasket. He believed Bill Clinton was a slick liar, a drug runner, an unpatriotic draft dodger. He was disgusted when Clinton said he would allow gay people into the military, even though Clinton ended up compromising with his "don't ask, don't tell" policy. Dad feared for our country because "Slick Willie" would ruin it somehow. He saw Clinton as a liberal, and as far as he was concerned, if you were a liberal, you hated your country and naively and stupidly cared about poor people and criminals.

It was no longer as in to be liberal as it had been in 1964 when Johnson beat Goldwater and the pundits announced the Right was dead. In fact, the pendulum had fully swung in the opposite direction from the '60s time of peace, love, and anti-materialism. So when Clinton was elected, I figured he was going to have to act more conservative than he probably really was to have a fighting chance at the presidency. Though I knew Clinton had to appeal to the conservatism gaining popularity in America, I naively expected that he would reverse the direction that the country was headed in.

The Republican establishment despised Bill Clinton solely because he was a Democrat, and a popular one at that. It threw a wrench into their plans for one-party rule. What if the majority liked him and voted him in again? That would be a setback for their plan and what was achieved so far with twelve years of Republicans. I think, too, the Right felt threatened by his charisma. Clinton was a real threat to the conservative agenda, and they feared he was appealing even to Republican voters. So as soon as he was elected, the Far Right started to conspire about how to get him removed from office.

Jeff Cohen described the treatment of Bill Clinton by these New Republicans, spurred on by Rush Limbaugh: "There is this backlash against Clinton spearheaded by Rush Limbaugh. Limbaugh almost becomes the leader of the opposition and [pushes] his crazy and paranoid conspiracy theories. Several times he said on the air that Vince Foster, the White House aide for Clinton, had actually been murdered and his body was found at Hillary Clinton's apartment." (Not true. He was found dead in a park.) Cohen said, "No other president in the previous decades had been hammered as relentlessly as Clinton."

David Brock reasserts Cohen's point. A staunch conservative at the time, Brock had written the Troopergate story, which appeared in the conservative magazine *American Spectator*. It stated that several Arkansas state troopers claimed they arranged sexual favors for then-Governor Bill Clinton. They charged that Clinton abused his power by having them scout for women, secure hotel rooms for Clinton and the women, and then cover for him to hide these escapades from his wife. Paula Jones was mentioned as one of the women. She later brought a sexual harassment suit against Clinton. Though the lawsuit was dismissed, Jones appealed it. Clinton settled for $850,000 while still denying the charge. But it all started a chain of events that led to the Monica Lewinsky scandal and Clinton's impeachment.

Brock, along with Ann Coulter, had been recruited by a

financier for former Speaker of the House Newt Gingrich's GOPAC (Grand Old Political Action Committee), a training organization for Republican candidates at state and local levels, to dig up whatever they could find on President Clinton. In an interview in 2002 with the *Washington Post* about his book *Blinded by the Right: The Conscience of an Ex-Conservative*, Brock said, "The conspiracy came to center on the Paula Jones sexual harassment suit; her key legal adviser admitted to me in a private conversation that he did not believe Jones but wanted to use her allegations as a way of setting a perjury trap for Clinton... Hillary Clinton was right that there was a well-organized, heavily financed right-wing conspiracy that was determined to drive Clinton from office."

In an interview with me, Brock explained further:

In early 1998, Hillary Clinton went out on the *Today* show and talked about a vast right-wing conspiracy. I think that the political and media elites basically scoffed at that notion. I was actually watching it when she said that. And I knew what she was saying was true. I mean, to me, conspiracy is a wrongful scheme. And I was involved with it, very much knew firsthand, with people who I was working with in places like the *Spectator* magazine. Back in 1993, shortly after Clinton was elected, it was trying to figure how to get him thrown out of office.

So there was a very well-financed strategic operation

that was put in place essentially right after the election. It was unprecedented in a sense that we expect political campaigns to be hard fought but then when they are over, they're usually over.

So something called the Arkansas Project was established by the *American Spectator*, which was essentially a dirt-digging operation on Clinton's past. And a lot of the scandals that came out from the Arkansas Project, ranging from Whitewater to Filegate to Travelgate and to the Troopergate story, I was involved in. There were also allegations of the murder of Vince Foster and drug running to the airport.

There were all sorts of scandals that were drummed up in the early and mid-1990s. And the goal was to throw sand in the gears of Clinton's ability to govern, to slow him down, and to drown him under investigation. And ultimately, change the outcome of the democratic election.

And Rush Limbaugh, named by Reagan as the number one voice for conservatism at that time and drawing twenty million listeners a week, helped spread any and all rumors and conspiracy theories about Bill Clinton.

Along with attacking Bill Clinton relentlessly, there was another more general effort against Democrats put forth by Newt Gingrich. Gingrich basically changed the rules for how the parties would work together. He turned politics into war and declared that the Democratic Party should be treated like the enemy. And henceforth, they were. Gingrich even admitted so himself in a speech to the Heritage Foundation, saying, "This war has to be fought with a scale and a duration and a savagery that is only true of civil wars." In fact, in a petty move, he encouraged the Republican freshmen to move to Washington without their wives and families so that they couldn't mingle, be friendly, and develop relationships with other members of Congress across the aisle. Incivility became the new standard operating procedure.

The Headquarters of the Vast Right-Wing Conspiracy

In 1993, the year Clinton entered office, political activist Grover Norquist expanded his Americans for Tax Reform advocacy group to include weekly strategy meetings initially held on Wednesday mornings in DC. Any group that wanted support for their issue had to sign the "no tax pledge" and had to be against abortion rights and for gun rights. Then they could join and bring their issue up at a meeting.

Tom Medvetz, George Lakoff's student at the time and now associate professor of sociology at the University of California and author of *Think Tanks in America*, spent almost a year going to these meetings. According to Medvetz,

> The Wednesday meetings were held every week in downtown Washington, DC. It was a chance for representatives with different elements of the conservative

movement to come together and talk about their com-
monalities and differences.

There were people there from groups that represented a full gamut of political issues on the right from
the fur trade commission to evangelicals. The real genius
of the meeting is that you can get these dozens of people
who might not otherwise agree in the same room every
seven days talking and sort of ironing out their differences. As long as you're on board with pro-life, pro-gun,
and the anti-tax agenda, you are with us.

Opposition to the Clinton health care reform proposals prompted the meetings initially. And so because
they were successful in defeating that proposed legislation, the meeting just sort of gained this momentum, and
it kept expanding.

Medvetz added,

If the conservative movement taught us anything, it is
that there's really a valuable role to be played for people
whose job it is to articulate a common philosophy, a
common brand, if you like. If the Left wanted to learn
from that, it would be that the people who are involved
in different issues that we would label progressive see
themselves not only as just environmentalists or repro-
ductive rights activists, et cetera, but see themselves as a
part of something larger. They can't do that unless there

are people there who are essential to the movement who can articulate how they are all on the same team—to use the Norquist phrase.

Medvetz concluded, "So when Hillary Clinton referred to the 'vast right-wing conspiracy,' I believe she had in mind the full gamut of conservative organizations, from legal foundations to media organizations to think tanks to advocacy groups, and including the Wednesday meetings as its linchpin. After that, people would call the Norquist meetings the headquarters of the vast right-wing conspiracy."

What Norquist accomplished with these Wednesday meetings was nothing short of brilliant. He created a huge network where factions with seemingly nothing in common could come together to pledge to help each other. The Americans for Tax Reform meetings in effect built an army of New Republicans who were ready to vote in lockstep as long as they were in agreement on taxes, abortion, and guns. Norquist understood that there was strength in numbers. Norquist later revealed his goal was to get the government small enough to be able to "drown it in a bathtub."

Another brilliant aspect of Americans for Tax Reform was the consistency in their messaging. The organization wrote up talking points for right-wing media and pundits every day. Lakoff explained, "They have people writing up talking points, which then get sent out to all the people who are going to be booked on radio and TV. And by five o'clock at night, everybody is going to be saying the same thing."

Democrats were playing please-like-me while the New Republicans ran them over, crying foul or complaining about liberal media. The New Republicans were playing a brilliant game of offense. The Democrats didn't know what hit them. They were either too busy apologizing or, like the New Democrats with their more conservative ideology, hopping on board.

The mainstream media did not fare any better. Psychologist Julie Hotard put it well in a column she wrote for Medium, comparing the mainstream media to someone in an abusive relationship:

They try to empathize with the abuser—to understand him and see events from his point of view. They try to change their own behavior, to get the abuser to change. Maybe they try to be nicer. Maybe they try to be more aggressive. The abused spouse often tries to take all the responsibility for the abuser's behavior.

This doesn't work because the abuser isn't acting abusive because of their partner's actions. The abuser is abusing because of their own issues—for example, the belief and feeling that they are entitled to act controlling and abusive toward others.

The Republican Party kept playing into the Far Right's agenda, the media was complicit in furthering their messaging, the Democratic Party seemed unable to fight back, and no one broke the cycle.

Dad's Hatred for Bill Clinton

Meanwhile, my dad was being swept along in the rushing tide against Clinton. I would have to say he was even *obsessed* with Bill Clinton.

One of the times I visited my parents and stayed overnight, I got up in the morning and saw my father bent over in his easy chair, reading. It was unusual to see him reading in the morning. He rarely read books at all anymore. I noticed he was holding a book about Bill Clinton. I believe it had "Slick Willie" in the title. Dad's face was screwed up in concentration, and he didn't even notice me.

I wanted to say, "Isn't it enough that you get mailers from the Republicans and listen to Rush Limbaugh rant about Clinton on his show three hours a day? Now you have to read a book about him? Are you *trying* to give yourself a heart attack?" But I was too scared to do that. I didn't want to hear him rage. I felt helpless and worried.

Dad hated Bill Clinton with a mad passion, and he also jumped on the anti-Hillary bandwagon. He thought the Clinton health care plans were "socialistic" and would "centralize power in Washington." And Rush Limbaugh was breathlessly telling his listeners fantastic lies about both Clintons. My dad also believed Bill and Hillary were murderers. Take your pick of conspiracy theories!

As both Jeff Cohen and David Brock mentioned, one of Limbaugh's go-to lies was that the Clintons had killed Vince Foster, a White House deputy counsel during President Clinton's first year in office. Foster was deeply frustrated by politics inside Washington and had been taking the antidepressant trazodone. His unexpected death was ruled a suicide, but that didn't stop the New Republicans from accusing Bill and Hillary of murdering him. Limbaugh used nothing more than his authoritative tone to convince millions of people he was in the know about what the Clintons were *really* up to in the White House.

Rush Limbaugh's flock believed him because he was the determiner of their facts. This was the beginning of the end of facts mattering, or the start of "alternative facts," a term Kellyanne Conway, who served as Donald Trump's campaign manager in the 2016 election, would coin years later.

Having been fully convinced by Limbaugh that the Clintons were crooks and murderers, my dad could not speak about President Clinton rationally. He'd get red in the face and refer to him as Slick Willie to the family even though he knew *we* liked President Clinton. This was a bone of contention between him and my mother. My mother liked Clinton and his vice president, Al Gore, and didn't appreciate my father bashing them in front of her. She just wanted him to respect her opinion. After many explosive arguments, she tried to just avoid talking politics with him. But this was difficult because my dad ate and slept his new politics, all day every day.

Meanwhile, the changes I saw in my dad became deeply unsettling to me. Not because he didn't agree with me but because he seemed to be getting sucked into something that was literally changing his personality. The constant rage he exhibited was exhausting, and I couldn't imagine it being healthy for him. It felt like I was watching my father disappear into a cult.

Occasionally, the thought struck me, *Was he brainwashed?* I think my mom may have even said that to him once or twice. When I looked up the definition of brainwashing, it seemed to fit what I saw happening to my dad: "a forcible indoctrination to induce someone to give up basic political, social, or religious beliefs and attitudes and to accept contrasting regimented ideas."

I knew deep down that the new fanatical Right was trying to diminish Clinton simply because he was a Democrat—and a popular one at that. Clinton, being a people pleaser and ever the politician, tried to work with them, but this new Republican Party didn't want a healthy democracy. They wanted one-party rule to be able to enact their corporate libertarian agenda, and they were determined to get it by any means necessary, mercilessly destroying any Democrat or moderate Republican who stood in their way.

The Bipartisan Telecommunications Act

In my mind, one of the largest contributions to the growth of the far-right media apparatus happened in February 1996, when Bill Clinton signed the Telecommunications Act, a revision of FDR's original Communications Act. FDR's legislation had regulated and restricted ownership of telephone, telegraph, and radio communications. Later, it applied to television and the internet as well. The number of media companies a single entity could own was restricted to avoid monopolies and to prevent any one company or person from having inordinate influence. But the Telecommunications Act changed all that.

Jeff Cohen described the effect of this new legislation as follows:

One of the biggest steps forward to handing our whole media system to a handful of corporations was completely bipartisan. It was the 1996 Telecommunications "Reform" Act, and I put reform in quotes intentionally. Consumer rights advocates were calling it the Time-Warner Enrichment Act, but President Bill Clinton and the Democrats were getting huge soft money donations from the big media and telecommunications companies. So was the Republican Speaker of the House, Newt Gingrich, and together behind closed doors, they developed this Telecommunications Act, which gave away the media to these few big companies. These few fat companies got even fatter. The mainstream media didn't scrutinize it because they were getting rich at the top, and when you have that kind of bipartisan corruption, corrupting our media system, it explains why we ended up with the media system we have.

The Telecommunications Act allowed for cross-ownership of any communications business. It set the conservative media dogs free to start monopolizing the U.S. media landscape and enabled a few giant corporations to buy up smaller media outlets. This is why we have only five or six corporations controlling almost all the media today. In contrast, in 1983, there were fifty companies that had meaningful control over various media outlets.

Largely as a result of this act, by 2015 Rupert Murdoch became the executive chairman of the world's second-largest media conglomerate, News Corporation. It was the largest media conglomerate the United States had ever seen, and it would allow Murdoch to unleash his influence on the American public in a way that never would have been possible before the deregulation of the media industry.

Fox News Is Hatched and "the News" Is Never the Same

Less than eight months after the Telecommunications Act was passed, Murdoch launched Fox News.

Murdoch, who had "long wanted in on the TV news business," had previously tried to buy CNN, but it was "snapped up by Time Warner." Sometime in the fall of 1995, Roger Ailes heard that Murdoch was going to try to rival CNN with his own network and let Murdoch know that he would be interested in getting on board. With Murdoch's experience in running successful and influential media companies and Ailes's talent for creating compelling TV programming, they were the perfectly matched diabolical team.

Ailes recycled the slogan he had crafted for TVN decades before as Fox News's tagline—"Fair and Balanced." This language implied that other media outlets were too liberal and signaled to viewers that Fox would not have any liberal biases. In fact, the language "fair and balanced" could subtly indicate to some conservatives that this new network might even have a conservative bias and thus be the dream network for them.

Murdoch, who financed the early years of Fox, and Ailes were passionate about getting the network off the ground for different reasons. Ailes wanted to be able to push the country to the right by providing news that would facilitate that and that was presented the way he wanted it to be interpreted. I believe he thought it could also serve to help a future president conservatives wanted to protect (like Nixon). Back in 1972, when he was at TVN, he told the *Washington Post*, "I know certain techniques, such as a press release that looks like a newscast. So you use it because you want your man to win." But Ailes felt more importantly that it was crucial to put out news that was always favorable to the GOP.

In one of our interviews, Rick Perlstein said, "He [Ailes] says things like, 'If we can convince the audience that we are fair and balanced, we could actually move the audience to the right by introducing some right-wing themes surreptitiously.'"

Gabriel Sherman gave further insight:

Roger Ailes feels that he is speaking for the people who used to be in charge in America and are now sharing power with all of these other groups. And he talks about Fox News as part of this mission to protect this division of America.

Roger Ailes came of age at the time when these divisions existed, but they were not reflected in our media culture, and through the force of his personality and genius in using the television to advance a political message, he was able to use the media to bring these divisions to the surface and cement them. So now we do not have a media culture that is separate and independent of our politics.

Oh, without question, Fox News divided the country, because now you could not talk about media without talking politics.

Ailes understood how to generate fear, but he was also a master of creating the feeling of safety—as long as the viewer stuck with Fox News. Fox set itself up as the group that exclusively represented the outraged victim. Once a victim, the viewer would get the desired effect: fear turned to self-righteous anger and hatred against anything liberal or Democratic.

Ailes believed displaying emotion is key in hooking your audience. The display of emotion hooks the viewer and convinces them to think, "They *must* be telling the truth. They're practically having a heart attack telling us about this!" One of the goals, as Ailes said, was "riling up the crazies" by making them angry and paranoid. He created a patriarchal, patriotic, John Wayne kind of world.

For Murdoch, Fox was another opportunity to make money by selling his low-brow brand of media and to influence the

American government just as he had done in Australia and, to some extent, the UK. On the political side, I've wondered if he might have been motivated to spread his hodgepodge brand of libertarianism. His political leanings are hard to pigeonhole. He would support leftist politicians as well if they were likely to let him buy more media and give him control over the content: low-brow with the emphasis on sensationalism. However, it's important to note he thinks and has said that "authoritarian countries can work."

The late Edward S. Herman, economist, media scholar, and social critic, said of Fox News,

Fox News is a real and fairly important development, because what it does is bring out explicit right-wing views, right into the heart of the media, and making no, hardly any pretense at objectivity. It sometimes makes statements suggesting that it's being fair, but it's blatantly biased, and it has Republican politicians on. It hardly minces words that it has a political agenda. It's also important in that it's had an effect on the rest of the media. It was already pretty nice to the right wing, but it [the rest of the media] has to go even further to be nice to the right wing.

David Brock added,

The most dangerous thing about Fox News is not the fact that it exists and speaks to its audience of a few million people. It's the effect that Fox can have on the rest of the media. Time and again, you will see a false and wrong story that is aired and starts moving through the Fox News channel on any given day and it bleeding over and spilling over into mainstream institutions of journalism. Media critics coined this term the Fox effect to mean media is an ecosystem and all media affects all other media. So the existence of Fox News and having that wrong approach to journalism out there has a toxic effect on the rest of journalism. They air the stories, and they start to bang the drums that the mainstream media is censoring and won't report to try to pressure and guilt the mainstream media into following their lead.

Right-Wing Media Tactics

With Fox News established and conservative talk radio more popular than ever before, the Far Right had a media infrastructure in place. It had the potential to become incredibly powerful and convince millions of Americans that the New Republican ideals were the only way forward for our country, and all that was left for the far-right extremists to do was hone their tactics.

Many conservative media outlets employ psychological operations (psyops) and propaganda-type tactics to a chillingly effective degree. These tactics are extremely important to recognize—if we can be aware of them, we will be less likely to fall prey to their influence.

A 2008 Emory University study found that watching Fox News directly causes a rightward shift in a viewer's attitude. In an article on the study, journalist Dylan Matthew wrote, "The effects of CNN and MSNBC on centrist voters are mostly negligible…. But Fox News increases Republican voting odds for centrists, for Democratic viewers…and Republicans already inclined to vote that way…. Watching three minutes more of Fox News per week in 2008 would have made the typical Democratic or centrist voter 1 percentage point likelier to vote Republican." The study's authors reported that "Fox is substantially better at influencing Democrats than MSNBC is at influencing Republicans." They estimated that in 2000, "58 percent of Fox viewers who were initially Democrats changed to supporting the Republican by the end of the election cycle."

So what exactly makes the right-wing media machine so powerful? It has to do with their well-studied and highly effective tactics. Let's take a look at some of them.

LIE AND SKEW

As Joseph Goebbels said, the bigger the lie, the better, and if you keep repeating it, it becomes believable. One reason the lying tactic is so effective is because people are conditioned to believe authority figures when they say something. No one wants to believe they are being lied to.

Repetition is key for this strategy to function. Writer Emily Dreyfuss describes it as:

a glitch in the human psyche that equates repetition with truth. Marketers and politicians are masters of manipulating this particular cognitive bias... The effect works because when people attempt to assess truth they rely on two things: whether the information jibes with their understanding, and whether it feels familiar... Researchers have found that familiarity can trump rationality—so much so that hearing over and over again that a certain fact is wrong can have a paradoxical effect. It's so familiar that it starts to feel right... Your busy brain is often more comfortable running on feeling.

Related to lying is skewing. Dr. Jonathan Schroeder, professor of communication at Rochester Institute of Technology in New York, describes skewing this way:

What these news shows often do is, they will cite a statistic, or they'll cite a finding. But they won't really tell you where it's from. They won't tell you much about the study. They won't tell you who's compiling that statistic. They just cite it out of thin air. Who put this statistic out? Is this scientifically proven? Was it peer reviewed? Who paid for it?

This kind of language, in science, mathematics, graphs, charts, and tools like that, often gives an air that this is scientifically proven or this is revealed by data. Again, we don't usually have the time to really think about what does that chart show? How is this chart created in such way that leads us to think about one particular outcome or one particular conclusion?

The Far Right, of course, has set up plenty of organizations and think tanks whose purpose is to manufacture and disseminate information that looks convincing but is easily skewed to promote their agenda. After all, most average people won't question an "official" study to determine who ran it or funded it. They just take the information as conclusive and move on, forgetting that there are plenty of ways for humans to skew data to suit a particular argument.

CREATE CONFUSION AND DOUBT

Another favorite tactic of the Far Right is to create confusion and sow doubt, leaving people exhausted and less likely to question the messages they are being fed. David Brock calls it "the noise machine."

Eric Boehlert, who was a senior writer at the media watchdog group Media Matters at the time of my interview with him, explained how the noise machine works, saying, "The noise machine is really designed to create confusion, create misinformation, create fear. It's the deliberate dissemination of misinformation in order to confuse the viewers and news consumers and get them all riled up. The Republican noise machine is when the Republican Party works in concert with Fox News, with Rush Limbaugh, with AM talk radio. It's really just designed to distract or to attack and smear people."

Noam Chomsky has talked about how right-wing media gives credence to climate change deniers just to create doubt about the science. "One of the worst things, other than demonizing Democrats, has been the massive attempt to create climate change denial—that is a *huge* problem because it could destroy the planet," he said.

It's easy to look back to history for examples of how organizations have deliberately created messages meant to confuse their audience. A memo from the R. J. Reynolds Tobacco Company in 1969 revealed how they dealt with the scientific data indicating that smoking had an adverse effect on people's health: "Doubt is our product since it is the best means of competing with the 'body of fact' that exists in the mind of the general public." It successfully created confusion for decades about the adverse impact of tobacco use.

Journalist Heather Hogan wrote, "Instead of presenting outright lies as facts, confusion is implemented by presenting deliberately vague generalities so the audience can fill in the blank with the messages they've already received about people who have already been othered. It's talking around an idea with willful ambiguousness for the purpose of obscuring facts."

Creating confusion and doubt in someone's former beliefs leaves them vulnerable to whatever information is given to them next. What right-wing media has done so successfully is to create doubt about an issue, then give their audience an alternative answer that only they can provide. The messaging then becomes: *All other media is not to be trusted. You can only trust us. Come to us for the answers, and you will belong.*

Related to creating confusion and doubt is gaslighting, a manipulation technique whereby someone makes you question your own memory or sanity by disavowing previous statements or accusing you of making something up when you know you haven't. Right-wing media pundits are masters at gaslighting and use this technique to rebalance power if they ever find themselves on the losing side of a debate.

BLAME AND DIVIDE

The blame-and-divide tactic works by getting people so mad at one another that they don't notice who is really causing their problems and won't join together to oust the truly guilty parties. This makes them capable of feeling nothing toward the group that's blamed and able to dehumanize them.

The purpose of blame and division is to create an enemy, which is why so much of right-wing media frames the world in terms of "us" versus "them." In this way, in-groups and out-groups are created, and "once two groups identify themselves as rivals, they are forced to compete in order for the members to maintain their self-esteem." In the case of right-wing media, the in-group is identified as the viewing audience and the out-group, of course, is the "Dems" or "libs" intent on the disempowerment and destruction of the in-group. The listener, watcher, or reader feels special and privileged to belong to the in-group: *These people are like me. They are my teammates, my tribe.* Meanwhile, they feel inherently threatened by anyone belonging to the out-group.

Blame and division are similar to psyops tactics employed

by military forces. A U.S. Army captain who asked to remain anonymous reached out to me to tell me why the U.S. military is extremely reluctant to use psyops techniques. The military might use psyops in a situation where they turn one civilian group against another to make it easier to go into a country once it's divided. The danger is that when they divide a civilian population, it "can cause irreparable damage long after the campaign has ended." According to the captain, "It is easy to manipulate biases and prejudices, but once you go down that road, it is almost impossible to return...and the consequences can be deadly."

The captain shared his thoughts with me about the right-wing media machine: "It's just so clear to me that this is what Fox News, Rush Limbaugh, and their ilk are doing, and the damage they are causing to this country is immense."

BRAND AND LABEL

Branding works by creating an image that will stick in a consumer's mind. Whether the image created is accurate or not doesn't matter. Democrats, liberals, and progressives have been branded as radical socialists, America-hating destroyers of cities and states, election-stealing, Christian-bashing elitists who want to kill Christmas and are anti-police and pro-crime! The Far Right sees all liberals as these caricatures. Meanwhile, the Republican Party has done a good job of branding themselves as the only political party that truly loves America; they've even managed to make the American flag proprietary to their party in some cases. Have you ever noticed that Republicans are almost always the ones driving around town with flags streaming from the backs of their pickup trucks and that Twitter profiles featuring the American flag emoji in their bios often belong to Trump supporters?

The Far Right's ability to use branding to their advantage is clearly on display in how they have convinced millions of people that mainstream media is inherently liberal. The opposite is true, actually—all major news outlets tilt slightly conservative, simply because they need to appeal to the broadest audience possible. But this media branding has been so effective that I've even heard some Democrats use the term *liberal media*. This is a perfect example of branding something successfully through repetition, even when the label is false.

When I asked Dr. Jonathan Schroeder how political parties might label each other or negatively brand a policy they don't want to see supported, he said, "Well, part of it is just getting a hold of the narrative or controlling the story. So if you think of an advertising campaign the Republicans did when Obamacare was first being introduced, they would show a bunch of coffins in the background and associated the idea of Obamacare with death squads. And so, without even making any verbal argument, they were making a powerful visual argument."

Another simple, less sophisticated form of branding is name-calling. Rush Limbaugh was famous for name-calling, constantly using vocabulary like "the Democrat Party," "feminazis," "libtards," and "snowflakes" that simultaneously entertained his audience and made them feel superior for not being categorized under those labels.

INCITE EMOTION, ESPECIALLY FEAR AND ANGER

As we have discussed, newscasters in the past reported the news unemotionally to show you that they, in their role as objective purveyor, were just reporting what was happening that was newsworthy, without editorializing or adding their own opinions to the facts.

Since Rush Limbaugh's style of talk radio became popular, however, Fox has taken his blustery, emotion-driven model and transferred it over to TV news, where it is arguably even more effective. Roger Ailes understood that displaying emotion on the screen and creating emotion in the audience are what keeps people invested and interested. And when it comes to viewership, fear and anger are by far the most powerful emotions, so that is what almost all Fox News programing tries to incite in its audience.

According to Dr. Cynthia Boaz, a professor of political science at Sonoma State University, "The idea is to terrify and terrorize the audience during every waking moment. When people are afraid, they don't think rationally. And when they can't think rationally, they'll believe anything."

If a news anchor acts angry, it makes them seem really sincere—especially if they act like they can barely contain themselves. The viewer (often unconsciously) thinks, *Hey, this impartial, professional news anchor is not supposed to let their anger show. They must really believe what they're saying if they can't control their emotions on-air!* Humans are very suggestible, and the viewer often starts to mirror the anchor's emotions, getting riled up in their living room thousands of miles away from the location of the Fox News broadcast. Before too long, the network has gained another sympathetic viewer riveted to the TV screen, watching the news broadcast and thinking, *Yeah! They're mad as hell, just like I am!*

Fear comes into play when dissenting views are aired, such as when a "liberal" guest comes on the show to debate with the conservative anchor or host. The audience then feels indignant. Because of the effective branding we discussed earlier, they already feel like they've been lied to by politicians and liberal or "fake" media. Perhaps the guest is making some good points, causing the viewer some discomfort and fear that their own views might be wrong. Then, when the conservative anchor gets into verbal combat with a so-called liberal (often a milquetoast liberal) on the show and shoots down that liberal's argument, the viewer gets a huge hit of dopamine. The perceived triumph of the in-group over the out-group reassures them and dispels the fear that was initially generated by the issue. The viewer feels engaged, they feel righteous, and they feel that they belong to a community that has triumphed over a common enemy. That swirl of emotion is exciting, and they want to push that lever again and again for the reward.

Fox News and other conservative media outlets have masterfully set themselves up as the group that exclusively represents the outraged victim, and the cycle perpetuates itself: fear turned to self-righteous anger and hatred toward liberals or Democrats and then the feeling of safety by being part of an in-group that speaks for them.

BULLY

You could argue that widespread use of the bullying tactic in media started with Bob Grant's radio show, but later radio personalities like Rush Limbaugh and Mark Levin refined the approach, often hanging up on or humiliating and interrupting callers they disagree with.

Bullying is effective on two levels. First, it shuts the guest up if they are making a point that the bully doesn't want the audience to hear. Second, the fake outrage makes the bully look justified as they try to shame their frustrated guest into silence. The bully often intentionally switches the power dynamic in the conversation, acting like the victim when the guest tries to speak up.

Bullying is not only rampant in the realm of far-right TV or radio personalities; it is also the general practice of those on the right who are in office.

Bullying is in fact standard operating practice for the New Republicans. When the story of Monica Lewinsky's affair with President Bill Clinton broke, it became not only fodder for the tabloids but fuel for right-wing media as they viciously attacked Lewinsky, only twenty-four years old at the time, from every angle. Today, Lewinsky runs an anti-bullying campaign.

All the Clintons were bullied by the Right during Bill Clinton's presidential campaign and both terms, as right-wing media homed in on personal details they could exploit for the entertainment of its audience. Rush Limbaugh took particular pleasure in negative comments about their daughter Chelsea Clinton's appearance and intimations that Hillary Clinton was a lesbian and simultaneously subordinate to her husband but somehow too ambitious for her own good.

Just as with the tactic of inciting anger and fear, when used by the media, bullying allows the viewing audience to cycle through a highly exciting and satisfying circuit of emotions. Watching a perceived enemy get taken down, even through false statements and unproven hypotheses, triggers an emotional response that can be downright addictive.

ACCUSE THEM FIRST

This tactic was a favorite of Joseph Goebbels, who famously said, "The cleverest trick used in propaganda against Germany during the war was to accuse Germany of what our enemies themselves were doing." We see this tactic being constantly used in anti-Democratic right-wing media today, and Donald Trump was a particular fan of it, often accusing his rivals of doing the very thing he had just done himself.

Whatever New Republicans are guilty of that they don't want to be called out for, they will accuse Democrats or liberals of first. It's an extremely clever and devious tactic because it's nearly impossible to argue against. Imagine a Democrat recognizes they were just accused of something they didn't do but the party that accused them *did* do, then turns around and says, "But that's what *you* do!" Or "That's what the Republican Party is guilty of!" They would sound childish and ridiculous, no matter how correct they might be. The party that first levels the accusation will always be able to make it stick more firmly.

A cousin of the "accuse them first" tactic is deflection. Take the Republicans' accusation of Democrats committing voter fraud. There is more of a chance to be struck by lightning than for a person to impersonate someone else at the polls, reports the Brennan Center of Justice. But this claim of voter fraud is used to enact laws to limit voting and to cull voting rolls. Then, a perfect example of accusing them first would be Lindsey Graham lying on Fox to Sean Hannity by saying, "Republicans win because of our ideas and we lose elections because [Democrats] cheat."

INUNDATE

I receive stories all the time from people who claim their parents have Fox News on in their homes 24/7, often even playing on TVs in every room. The constant presence of news media is exhausting and creates an echo chamber that is difficult to separate from once you get sucked in.

Fox News has programming available literally all the time. Rush Limbaugh is on five days a week. There's Michael Savage, Alex Jones, *The Mark Levin Show*, the Drudge Report, Newsmax, One America News Network, Breitbart, the *American Spectator*, the Daily Caller, and the Tea Party Express, to name just a few more media outlets, and then there's the avalanche of anti-Democractic, right-wing subscription emails and snail mail. If you wanted to (and some people do), you could surround yourself with right-wing media content every waking hour of the day without too much effort.

Rush Limbaugh debuted on Armed Forces Radio in 1993.

Despite the fact that "only 3.9 percent of 50,000 listeners indicated a preference" for his show, his presence on the airwaves available to our military soon expanded in a nakedly political move. Carol Wallin from the anti-Rush Limbaugh organization StopRush said, "Republican representative Robert Dornan gathered up seventy of his closest representative friends and got them to sign a letter to the defense secretary at the time. He thought that it was really important for Rush Limbaugh to be played on the Armed Forces Network. That this was absolutely a necessity."

In 2018, the FDA (Food and Drug Administration) was ordered by President Trump to make Fox News the only station permissible to have on in their facilities, and they complied.

Most disturbing of all, another military man I interviewed, Aaron, told me that when he tried to change the channel from Fox in any military facility, he was stopped from doing so.

Pew Research found that 47 percent of conservatives tightly cluster their choice of news around Fox News rather than seeking out a diverse array of sources. With Fox's programming so readily available, it's easy to see how they have become a kind of echo chamber unto themselves.

Perhaps the most disturbing thing is that roughly 91 percent of political talk radio stations can be considered conservative. The Center for American Progress says this "is due to structural imbalances—not popular demand. The complete breakdown of the public trustee concept of broadcast, the elimination of clear public interest requirements, and the relaxation of ownership rules have tipped the scales against localism and allowed the few to indoctrinate the many."

The Left is far less strategic and programmatic about making sure their message is everywhere all the time. Money often comes from many small donors rather than coordinated major donations from a few billionaires, which makes the use of the funds often less targeted and impactful and coordinated messages more difficult to spread.

USE NONVERBAL MANIPULATION

Fox News can claim a lot of firsts in the media world. It was the first blatantly right-leaning TV news show. It was also the first to use very bright colors, cartoon-like graphic images, and alarming text crawlers across the bottom of the screen. In his book *State of Confusion*, Dr. Bryant Welch says, "The sound and visual effects of Fox News are almost carnival-like, with multiple crawlers and a seemingly constant state of news crises created by 'Fox News Alerts.'" This visual stimulation is intentional and effective in that it captivates the audience and makes them less likely to get bored and go looking for something else to watch.

Fox News is also famous for its parade of look-alike blond beauties with long legs, short skirts, and bare shoulders. After Roger Ailes was fired for sexual harassment, Murdoch lifted the ban on wearing pants for their female anchors. Still, the sex appeal to their core base of older men is clear.

When asked about Fox's reliance on stimulating visual content, Gabriel Sherman said, "It's a visual medium, that he [Ailes] wrote in one memo, that you need to communicate with your audience on a gut, sort of emotional, level. It's not about the facts and figures." The mastery of visual effects at Fox News underscores his point.

Frank Luntz, an expert in language manipulation, said, "It's not just language, it's also visuals." Luntz trains some of these television personalities to emote with passion and to use gestures (like visibly counting on their fingers) that will help their audience remember what they say and help communicate an emotion.

LEVERAGE (AND REWRITE) HISTORY

Right-wing TV, radio personalities, and online publications will often reshape or revise history to validate the ideology they are propagating. One good example is the Republican Party's obsession with Ronald Reagan's administration and trickle-down economic policy as a high point for America, despite the fact that trickle-down economics has been proven to widen economic disparity, not to diminish it.

The Texas Board of Education is notorious for rewriting history in their educational textbooks, which is troubling because "the state is one of the largest buyers of textbooks." The elected board members were locked in a battle between those who disregard "Darwin's theory of evolution" and those who believe in Darwinism. They also chose to stress the view that capitalism is king. All the Republicans on the board even voted to rename it the "free-enterprise system" since capitalism had a bad connotation.

Other efforts to rewrite history by the Right were described by journalist Steven Thomma:

> In articles and speeches, on radio and TV, conservatives are working to redefine major turning points and influential figures in American history, often to slam liberals, promote Republicans and reinforce their positions in today's politics.
>
> The Jamestown settlers? Socialists. Founding Father Alexander Hamilton? Ill-informed professors made up all that bunk about him advocating a strong central government.
>
> Theodore Roosevelt? Another socialist. Franklin D. Roosevelt? Not only did he not end the Great Depression, he also created it.
>
> Joe McCarthy? Liberals lied about him. He was a hero.

USE WHATABOUTISM

Whataboutism is a beloved practice New Republicans use as a distraction technique. When something they or their party did wrong is pointed out, instead of addressing the charge, they point out supposed hypocrisy: "Well, what about when such and such Democrat did the same thing?"

They deflect. They distract. It changes the subject and turns the blame around. But it does not refute the initial accusation. I see news analysts fall for this tactic all the time! Rather than having a meaningful discussion about one issue, it becomes a standoff or a "gotcha" moment. News anchors could simply say, "Let's talk about one issue at a time, and right now we're talking about this issue."

CONTROL THE LANGUAGE AND FRAMING

In the world of political battle, carefully crafted words are used as ammunition. Words and labels are chosen to influence an opinion about an issue.

Newt Gingrich recognized that "language matters." Newt's political action committee, GOPAC, published a pamphlet in 1990 called *Language: A Key Mechanism of Control*. The pamphlet provided Republicans with negative words to use to describe Democrats, such as *corrupt, liberal, sick*, and *traitors*. The idea was that if Republicans consistently repeated these words to describe Democrats, they would eventually stick and become a kind of insider shorthand for the whole party. As we can see today, it was an effective tactic. He also provided a list of uplifting words to use to help the New Republicans define their campaign and vision, such as *courage, dream, duty, liberty, freedom, hard work,* and *reform*.

We cannot discuss how political language is used without talking about Frank Luntz, the master wordsmith for the Right. He is a marketer and a public opinion guru (i.e., pollster) and consultant who was first hired by Newt Gingrich to come up with the messaging, slogans, and language to help the Republican Party sell what would normally be considered unpopular policies or, in reverse, to make what would be popular policies held by Democrats seem bad.

As George Lakoff emphasized, "Language is not neutral. In politics, it's anything but neutral. And this became professionalized in 1994 when Newt Gingrich hired Frank Luntz." In hiring Luntz, Gingrich brought the use of language to the forefront of the New Republican Party. He understood that by controlling the language, he could control the narrative.

Luntz has worked with many prominent Republicans, including President George W. Bush. One example of Luntz's influence was with the naming of Bush's anti-environmental initiative as the Clear Skies Initiative. This deceptively titled initiative was framed to appear as if it would decrease air pollution, but it actually resulted in more air pollution. Another example was the timber-industry-friendly Healthy Forests Initiative, which supported logging activity. Then came the Patriot Act, which curtailed Americans' individual freedoms after the 9/11 terrorist attacks, and the controversial No Child Left Behind Act, which mandated standardized testing and held low-performing schools' feet to the fire rather than provide new funding to improve public education.

One of the most successful language manipulations Luntz crafted for the Republican Party was the so-called death tax, his reframing of the estate tax. It was a brilliant revision to get middle- or lower-income people on board for a policy that would only benefit the uberwealthy. When people heard "death tax," the cry rose up: "We can't tax people after they die!" But in reality, this law is only relevant to very wealthy families and collects a tax on inheritance money when the sum totals over $11.8 million.

Luntz said about his testing of his "death tax" language in a focus group, "I have fought over the validity of the death tax since I started working in this space. And I went out and tested it, and my God. It changed the dynamic of how people look at policy!"

Like any good marketer, Frank Luntz keenly understands that what you call something affects its message and the emotions we experience when we hear about it. He said in an interview on *Frontline*, "80 percent of our life is emotion, and only 20 percent is intellect. I am much more interested in how you feel than how you think."

Luntz's counterpart in the liberal space is George Lakoff, the director of the Center for the Neural Mind & Society. Lakoff has written many books about how language affects our feelings and opinions, in particular about political issues. Lakoff talks a lot about framing, or the way language can be deliberately packaged to create a desired effect and make an issue seem either very important or not important at all. He believes that whichever side first frames an issue has the advantage and that their frame will be more accepted than any additional frames laid on top of it. In an article titled "The Power of Positive Persistence," Lakoff wrote, "Framing is about reclaiming our power to decide what's important. Framing is about making sure we set the terms of the debate, using our language and our ideas. Conservatives have beaten progressives at this for decades. It's time for a change."

In general, Luntz has had a lot more influence over our

political language than Lakoff has. For whatever reason, the Democratic Party has not invested the same time and resources in carefully crafted language as the Republican Party has, and it shows in the vocabulary of each of those groups.

In an article titled "Who's Behind the Attack on Liberal Professors?" Dave Johnson, a fellow at the Commonweal Institute, writes about the "mighty Wurlitzer," a term coined by the CIA that refers to the power of propaganda, underscoring the Far Right's ability to promote their message regardless of its veracity:

The right-wing movement's messages are orchestrated and amplified to sound like a mass "movement" consisting of many "voices." Using "messaging"— communication techniques from the fields of marketing, public relations, and corporate image-management— the movement appeals to people's deeper feelings and values. Messages are repeated until they become "conventional wisdom." Examples include lines like "Social Security is going broke" and "public schools are failing." Both statements are questionable, yet both have been firmly embedded in the "public mind" by purposeful repetition through multiple channels. This orchestration has been referred to as a "Mighty Wurlitzer," a CIA term that refers to propaganda that is repeated over and over again in numerous places until the public believes what it's hearing must be true.

One example of the differences in language usage between the two major American political parties is the term *Democrat Party*. Around 1996, a new name for the Democratic Party, the *Democrat* Party, started to gain traction in Republican circles. It seems like a small difference, but the terminology has had a big effect. Roy Copperud, another language expert, has said that the Republicans did not like the positive connotation that *Democratic Party* had, positing that Republicans disliked the implication that Democrats "are somehow the anointed custodians of the concept of democracy," so they shifted the term.

Cognitive psychologist Paul Thibodeaux at Oberlin College pointed out that *Democrat* conveniently rhymes with *autocrat, plutocrat,* and *bureaucrat*. The term's use has become so widespread that I have occasionally heard other Democrats unwittingly use it, unaware of the fact that they have integrated into their vocabulary what is essentially a Republican epithet specifically intended to denigrate Democrats.

Dad Is Introduced to Fox News

For years, my dad would get up at 5:00 a.m. and go meet his friend Don at the Y. They would go for a swim and then go to McDonald's to have breakfast and gush over Rush Limbaugh and his most recent rant. Don was a Limbaugh lover too, but Don was more "in the know" than my dad and also watched Fox News. My father so far for *some* blessed reason did not seem aware of Fox News, until Don introduced him to it sometime in the early 2000s.

My mom had actually been friends with Don first. They had met in the swimming pool at the Y. She introduced Don to my dad, and he and my dad bonded over Limbaugh.

At their McDonald's breakfasts, Don and my father talked about Rush Limbaugh together like a couple of schoolgirls with a mad crush. One would gush, "Did you hear what Rush said yesterday?" "Wow!" They were not alone. Millions of other older White men were crushing all over Rush Limbaugh. Many called themselves Dittoheads. When calling in to his show, callers would often start their comments with "Dittos, Rush" or "Constitutionalist Dittos, Rush" or "Mega Dittos, Rush."

Alas, it was a dark day for the Senko family when Don told my dad that he should check out this network called Fox News. My dad started watching Fox in the morning at breakfast and at lunch in addition to listening to Limbaugh. I was more than disturbed by his new habit. I had seen how the right-wing tsunami of fake news had *already* changed him and, subsequently, the bond of our family. I wasn't sure how much more we could take.

CHAPTER 8

Is Dad Brainwashed?

Then Don gave Dad another horrible idea.

Don told my father he could listen to *more* extremist conservative talk shows by bringing a small radio to bed and wearing earbuds. Even though Dad was wearing the earbuds at night, my mother could still hear the mumbling drone of a ranting voice from his radio as she lay next to him in bed. It kept her awake, so my dad solved that issue "for my mom" by moving into the spare bedroom. For years, he fell asleep listening to volatile words and conspiracy theories, letting them even penetrate his dreams.

At this point, with my dad obsessed with Fox News, talk radio, and extremist conservative email subscriptions he had recently discovered, it was like completely losing him to a cult. He was obsessed. This was his new identity. During his Limbaugh lunches, he also had Fox on the television in the kitchen. When

Rush went to advertisements, he unmuted Fox to see what they were talking about. When Rush came back, he muted Fox again. There was no downtime. Dad expressed more anger toward the world, especially toward people who were different from him. It seemed the only people he liked or related to anymore were White, straight Republicans.

Visiting my parents became a huge source of stress for me. *Would Dad again try to convince me how wrong I was to be a Democrat? Would an argument spring up between him and my mother or between him and I? Would he lose his temper?* I knew he would bring politics up; would I be able to steer him to a different conversation topic? It was distressing to see him so angry and obsessed but also to have to anticipate arguments, dodge conversations, and try to be patient against his denigration of my own beliefs.

I began worrying about Dad's health. He stopped wearing a seat belt because Limbaugh said Ralph Nader made up the idea that they saved lives. When he picked me up at the bus station, he would have a cocktail in the coffee cup holder of his little Toyota. I would tell him, "Dad, you shouldn't drink and drive," and he'd get angry at me. "Why *not* drink and drive? Who says you can't? The damn government can't tell me what to do!"

My mother had brought up more than once that she thought Dad was brainwashed. Could it be? My only familiarity with brainwashing was from a 1962 movie, *The Manchurian Candidate*, and from cult leaders like David Koresh of Waco, Texas, or Jim Jones of the Jonestown massacre, who convinced more than nine hundred members of his cult to commit mass suicide. To me, brainwashing meant that someone had gotten hold of your mind and, using sophisticated and clever psychological trickery or even torture, managed to drum into you thoughts that weren't yours. But I wasn't even sure if brainwashing was a real thing, much less that it could have happened to my dad simply from listening to too much talk radio.

The Emails

By the end of 1996, nearly 10 percent of Americans were on the internet. My dad, having an engineer's mind (and having worked on electronic mail for the government in the 1980s) and being somewhat computer savvy, started using email around 1998.

Shortly thereafter, my dad found some other older people who were on the same political path he was on. Once he started sharing his email address, he became a perfect target for every right-wing group's propaganda. From the Heritage Foundation to English-first groups to the National Rifle Association to Judicial Watch, he probably subscribed to a dozen of them. I think his favorite might have been NumbersUSA, a fervent anti-immigration group. And he gave money to *all* of them.

For years, my father forwarded these emails to family, friends, and acquaintances. He even forwarded them to *my* friends and their family members. The sometimes subtle and sometimes not messages were always targeted against Democrats, liberals, or some Democratic institution or policy.

Some of these emails were deceptively crafted to sound folksy.

They were made to appear to have originated from a friend of a friend. These messages were "plainspoken," and on the surface, they sometimes masqueraded as nonpolitical and nonpartisan, like someone just telling a story of their own experience. This tactic gave the emails some credibility and cover as to the source. But in reality, the emails most often originated from some unidentified political outlet or think tank, and they were written with the intention of getting people to believe that what they were reading was from an ordinary person just like themselves.

I sometimes received these emails from unwitting friends, family members, or coworkers—not necessarily Republicans, which indicated to me that there was some large-scale dissemination of them going on. It seemed people were on autopilot, just forwarding them along without checking into where they had come from or who was profiting from them.

One email I remember in particular was about the McDonald's "hot coffee" lawsuit, in which a woman sued McDonald's because a coffee she purchased was so hot it scalded her when she spilled it, eventually requiring her to get nine skin graft operations. She never fully recovered from the injury. The email raged about how ridiculous the amount awarded to the woman who got burned was. It complained about "frivolous lawsuits" that were clogging up our courts and claimed that it was because of these tort lawyers and these types of lawsuits that hamburgers, milkshakes, and everything else were so expensive. In reality, the woman got only $2.86 million from the suit—a drop in the bucket for a corporation like McDonald's (and barely enough to cover a live-in nurse for the rest of her life) and hardly the reason for any kind of pricing decision. The purpose of this particular email was clearly to discredit class action lawsuits and stifle consumer rights and civil justice.

The one that shocked me the most was about "the war on Christmas" that the godless liberals were supposedly waging by saying "happy holidays." I loved Christmas, and so did most liberals I knew. The claim that the Democrats were trying to kill Christmas was preposterously false. But it helped enforce the other narrative that Christians were being victimized by liberals and Democrats.

My mom, who hated getting these emails, started to learn how to research and fact-check them and would send my father rebuttals debunking these stories.

My dad wasn't the only person who fell for the emails, of course. I was surprised to see that so many people believed them. Even though they were mostly Democrats, the secretaries I worked with in a law office at the time would shake their heads, cluck their tongues, and also forward such emails around the office. The insidious nature of the messages was what gave them such power. These ideas, which were repeated in various ways in different emails, seeming to come from different people and looked like new common truths and realizations that *everybody* was getting on board with, not the product of some right-wing think tank. I would have thought it was genius if I didn't find it so terrifying.

My father continued to badger us for years with these email

attacks against Democrats and liberals, often sending three or four a day when he wasn't listening to Rush Limbaugh or reading far-right snail mail. Everyone in my family begged him to stop sending them, but he was on a mission. He believed he had to warn everyone about how evil and unpatriotic Democrats were. We would only save the country and ourselves if we listened to Rush Limbaugh and became Republicans and hated Democrats like he did. What hurt the most was that his emails were never, ever personal.

My brother Greg was the first one to block my dad's emails. Eventually, my brother Walter and I followed after our pleas for him to stop went unanswered. My mother also threatened to block my dad but never did because she was compelled to debunk the outrageous claims and lies.

How Dad's Brainwashing Affected Our Family

I got the shock of my life one day when my mother emailed me and said that she couldn't take living with my father anymore. She wanted to find an apartment and live on her own. Could I help her?

She was in her late seventies or early eighties at the time, and she was miserable, always having to tiptoe around subjects for fear she'd stir up Dad's wrath, which always lurked barely below the surface. I tried to support her, to talk to Dad, to solve the problem—help her however I could. Eventually, she decided to stay. Leaving him would have been too disruptive and unrealistic at her age.

When I lost my job after the Great Recession, I came to visit my parents for a few days. I was distraught about not having a job and frantic about not being able to find reasonable interim health insurance. My COBRA had run out. I had the urge to talk to the *old* Dad, who had always been ready to help me. I did. I told him how hard it was for me to get health insurance as an unemployed individual. I was frustrated and frightened and near tears. I was on unemployment, and the only insurance policies I could possibly afford didn't pay for lab work and had ridiculously high deductibles. He listened to my story, shook his head with pity, and said he thought that was terrible. He felt bad for me, and in that moment, he said he wished there was some type of government health care I could afford. I was heartened he cared to see beyond the politics, but I wasn't even sure he realized what he was saying was contrary to the New Republicans' beliefs.

Of course, eventually, once the Affordable Care Act was signed into motion, I got emails from him about its evils and non-existent "death panels". After that point, there was no more talk about cheap government-funded health care.

One of the sadder moments for me was when Dad had Limbaugh on the radio in the kitchen. Limbaugh was railing against gay people and how they were supposedly depraved and going to be the undoing of America—his standard fare. But it made my blood boil. I turned to Dad and said, "So are you against gay people now? What about my gay friends you liked so much?" I reminded him of the day he helped me move into the brownstone in New York and how he had joked and kidded around with my gay roommates and how my friend Alex changed his tire in his pink shirt.

I don't remember everything Dad said during this conversation, but there was an angry outburst and some arguing. I tried to remind him of one of his old principles: to each his own. Being gay didn't hurt him or anyone else. He sputtered and cast around for a good answer, something that would align him again with Limbaugh and the whole right-wing philosophy he had bought into. After not being able to come up with any sensible argument for his change of opinion on gay people, he finally bellowed, "I just don't want it in my face!"

I couldn't believe it. My dad's acceptance of my friends had been such a wonderful moment, something that had stuck with me for years and that I had always looked back on fondly. In just a few minutes, he had disavowed everything I thought he stood for. And unfortunately, things would continue to get far worse before they got better.

My mom often begged my father to stop sending her hateful emails about Democrats.

From: Eileen Senko
Subject: Re: Fw: FW: Speaking
Date: February 5, 2012 6:22:53 PM EST
To:
Cc:

Here, have this back. I am not even going to read it. Stop sending me this kind of crap!!!! You are truly brainwashed.

On Sun, 5 Feb 2012 17:39:35 –0500 writes:

I came to dread when he would pick me up from the bus station. If it were that time of day, he would be blasting Rush Limbaugh to a deafening degree.

One time when he was driving me back to their house, I noticed all these SUVs on the road. This was the 1990s, so they were a new and popular phenomenon. In addition to that, they were mega gas-guzzlers at the time. My father had always been so concerned with mileage for any car he owned that he kept a little notebook in the glove compartment, and anyone who drove that car was required to keep precise track of the mileage, the amount of gas left, the amount of gas we put in, and what it cost. You did not want to forget to do this. This is how he kept track of the miles per gallon the car got. He'd thoroughly research the mileage for any car he bought in order to make sure he got a vehicle with the best mileage per gallon.

I did get him to turn down Rush. But I didn't know what would be safe to talk about, so when I conversationally muttered something about "these gas-guzzling SUVs," I thought he would praise me for being aware of their gas usage vs. mileage. Instead, I was startled by his reaction. He was furious. He gave me one of his "the government can't tell me what to do" lines: "We should all be free to buy SUVs if we want, and as a matter of fact, the next car I get may be one!" I couldn't believe this was my father talking, the one who gave my older brother the job of tearing napkins in half every Saturday to save money. After all, who needs to use a whole napkin? I couldn't imagine how much it cost to fill one of these mammoth SUVs's tanks.

So many things that previously wouldn't have bothered him now made his blood boil. Take the Hooters incident. Another time when he picked me up (I had begged my mother to start picking me up, but most of the time it was convenient for him and not her), we passed a Hooters restaurant. Out of the blue, my father began ranting about these horrible feminists objecting to Hooters's practice of scantily-clad waitresses. It wasn't crystal clear what he was so furious about. I surmised he didn't want to be told new "rules." At the time, Rush Limbaugh was calling women "feminazis" because they were demanding social change, equal treatment, and to not have their value judged by how they looked (and not be seen solely as sex objects). This was inconvenient, not fun, and threatening to male privilege. In Rush's eyes, women were trying to spoil all their fun and trying to have the same power as men. This pissed Rush off, so it pissed my dad off.

I had to say *something*. I was sickened this was coming from my dad. I *gently* told him that I thought the feminists might have a point (about objectification) and asked him why that bothered him. He got so flustered and angry he threatened to pull over and have me hitchhike back to their house! I was stunned. His reaction was very hurtful to me. Though I was close to my mom, I don't think I told her about this, because it would have upset her that he was going to make me hitchhike the rest of the way home and that would have caused a huge argument. I didn't want that to be what my short visit was about.

The one thing I thought would never happen was that he also started knocking college. He was being told that liberal professors wickedly turned all kids into liberals. My dad had flipped 180 degrees. Who *was* this man who lived with my mom? He had encouraged all three of us kids to pursue and value education. From the time we were little, he made us read for an hour before bedtime each night, and the value of reading and education were pounded into us.

The painful stories I could give are endless. My older brother, at a later time when I was making the film, told me he felt like our family was coming apart.

Rush Limbaugh had turned my dad into a full-on rebel against anything that could have been interpreted as elitist or Democratic or liberal. This "liberal elitist" button that the Right pressed fed into the discomfort my father had felt in social situations as a young professional when I was growing up. Even though he'd achieved middle-class status, that vulnerable, uncomfortable poor boy who walked to school in his bare feet and the 1950s man whose status was challenged by the martini lunches with the sophisticated guys at work was still in there. Now, finally, he had found somewhere to belong. He was a prime target for demagoguery, and nothing we could do or say would change his mind about the path he was going down.

Should I Make a Movie?

I had always been interested in filmmaking and pursued it in my spare time, even producing a number of short films and directing award-winning documentaries, *Road Map Warrior Women* and *The Vanishing City*. I thought films were an incredible medium for exploring life's issues, and then I saw a documentary that changed my life.

The Hunting of the President is a 2004 documentary directed by Nickolas Perry and Harry Thomason and narrated by Morgan Freeman that illustrates how New Republicans attempted to sabotage President Clinton. I had known the relentless and mostly warrantless attacks against Clinton were part of something bigger and more nefarious on the part of the Republican Party, and now I had confirmation of it. There was so much in the film that resonated with what I had seen and heard in my own life and in the media, but what really blew me away were the interviews with David Brock. He was a whistleblower, but better than that, he was a convert. He had been a conservative operative and investigative reporter and author who then switched sides and was shining a light on Republican media tactics and the New Republican agenda. After his conversion, he wrote books about the Right, including *Blinded by the Right: The Conscience of an Ex-Conservative* and *The Republican Noise Machine: Right-Wing Media and How It Corrupts Democracy.*

After getting to know Brock's work, I started reading more related books. My friends would get annoyed because instead of going out at night, I'd be home sitting in bed, reading. It seemed to me that no one in mainstream media shared my alarm as to how dangerous Rush Limbaugh, Fox News, or right-wing media was. I feared that if this new far right-wing media was not openly challenged, it would not only continue to divide my family and strain some of my friendships but that it could also threaten the very fabric of the country. One day, I vowed, when I had enough time and more experience, I would make a documentary about it.

The 2000 Presidential Election

By the end of the Clinton presidency, I was much more invested in politics than I had ever been before. I studied as much as I could about right-wing media and their push to the bring the country to the right, all with the desire to hopefully be able to sound the alarm with the documentary I hoped to make.

The 2000 presidential election was ripe for trouble from the start. George W. Bush, the governor of Texas and an oilman, ran against Vice President Al Gore, a staunch environmentalist who touted renewable energy. During the campaign, Gore distanced himself from President Clinton because of the sex scandals associated with him, but Clinton, with his likability, the robust economy, and his surplus, was still very popular.

From the beginning, Gore was painted as arrogant and elitist in media outlets like Fox, and his image suffered from an interview shown on mainstream media in which Gore said, "I took the initiative in creating the internet." The media latched onto that sentence, twisting it to make it seem Gore said he *created* the internet, and painted him as a liar. It stuck so well that twenty years later, people still joke about how Gore "invented the internet." Meanwhile, right-wing media pushed the image of Bush as a likable, friendly guy you'd want to grab a beer with, a drastic contrast to Gore's supposed uptight, intellectual demeanor.

During the debates, there was no doubt Gore was the more intelligent, experienced candidate. To me, it was like watching a college professor debating a grammar school student who had a cookie hangover and no sleep the night before. But Al Gore was criticized for sighing in frustration with Bush's lies and lack of knowledge.

Going into the election, Bush and Gore were deadlocked in the polls. NBC first called the election for Gore at 7:50 p.m. EST. Others followed suit (Associated Press, ABC, CBS, CNN, Fox, and NBC). Then at 9:55, CNN said Florida was actually too close to call. Then other networks took their predictions back. Later, they gave the election to Bush, then retracted it again. Gore had called Bush to concede and then later retracted it when he learned how close the election was. The most obvious problem in Florida was that many paper ballots, counted by machine, were sometimes hard to decipher and could only be determined by being recounted by hand.

Gore sued to hand count them—the Florida Supreme Court said the hand count could continue—then Bush sued to stop the recount. And so began the dramatic controversy of the 2000 presidential election and the perfect storm of dubious influence with Jeb Bush, George W. Bush's brother as governor in Florida, the partisan Republican secretary of state, Katherine Harris, rejecting ballots as spoiled if they had hanging or dimpled chads (not completely punched through), voter disenfranchisement by being purged or through problems with confusing ballots and a new electronic voting system that sometimes lost votes.

In Volusia County, one computer even showed Al Gore getting minus nineteen thousand votes.

Gabe Sherman explained how Gore was negatively depicted on Fox: "What happens in 2000, another year when Fox News exploded in the ratings: the Bush/Gore recount. How did Ailes cover that story? He covered it as not that it's too close to call and [that Gore] didn't need a recount. He covered it as Al Gore and the Democrats are sore losers and they are trying to steal the election."

More than any other TV network, Fox pushed the narrative of Bush as the presumptive winner with Gore trying to reverse that verdict. In some ways, that narrative sunk in with the broad public, even though other more neutral media outlets tried to portray the situation as a toss-up with the verdict not yet decided.

Right around this time I was communicating via email with my best friend I had known since grammar school. She still lived in New Jersey, and I was living in New York. She told me she hated Al Gore and that he was "a sore loser". Wanting to understand her POV, I asked her to please enumerate what she didn't like about him. I gave her a bulleted list about what I liked and didn't like about each candidate. She couldn't do that (she just found him "despicable!"), but that didn't stop her from calling me stupid and naive for preferring him over George Bush. I didn't understand her vehemence and change (she had been a Democrat and not political) until I learned that her new husband watched Fox religiously.

I had a similar exchange with another friend of mine. She read the Drudge Report. Both friends had changed dramatically. My determination to make this movie was strengthening.

Bush Is Handed the Presidency

The Bush/Gore race was finally resolved on December 12, 2000. The U.S. Supreme Court went against the Florida Supreme Court and made the decision to stop counting votes in Florida. Subsequently, the election was settled by a margin of 537 votes in Bush's favor, tilting the Electoral College his way and handing him the presidency. Al Gore had won the national popular vote by over five hundred thousand votes, and alarmingly, the exit polls in Florida showed a Gore win.

Greg Palast, an investigative journalist focusing mostly on election theft, wrote in his article "The Election Was Stolen— Here's How" that the "GOP Secretary of State Katherine Harris officially rejected 181,173 ballots as 'spoiled' because their chads were hung and other nonsense excuses. Those ballots overwhelmingly were marked for Al Gore."

There was hardly a peep regarding this and the other disturbing information. I wondered why the supposedly liberal mainstream media wasn't up in arms over this coup. The Right certainly would be if it happened to them. Didn't the press understand that this would be the first of many such coups if it weren't addressed? Where were the huge newspaper headlines? Where was the outrage? Were they that afraid of the Right? Maybe they just didn't want to admit what a huge blow had been struck to our democracy. It's human nature to try to rationalize the irrational, and at that point, it wasn't yet blatantly obvious that the Far Right had taken the reins of America with no intention of handing them back. The consequences of this election, of course, would echo for decades to come.

CHAPTER 9

9/11, Barack Obama, and Far-Right Extremism

For the ten days preceding September 11, 2001, I had been in Provence, France, on vacation with a friend. I arrived home to New York City on a Monday night and went to bed right away to try to sleep off the jet lag. The next morning, I was enjoying the exceptional French bread I had smuggled home. It was an absolutely stunning morning, sunny and warm. I felt peaceful and content. Then I heard a plane go right over my head, like it was just a few feet above the seven-story building I lived in. For some reason, I said to myself, almost as a joke, "Oh, Osama bin Laden and the terrorists must be bombing New York."

I gave the plane no further thought until the NPR radio show I was listening to announced that a plane had crashed into the World Trade Center. In the moment, it seemed like nothing more than an unfortunate accident. I didn't connect the news right away with the sound I had heard. By the time the second plane hit, however, we all realized our country was under attack.

An hour or two later, as I was lying on my bed, looking out the window and watching dazed people stream up Sixth Avenue away from the Trade Centers, I called my dad. Nobody knew where President Bush was, and Mayor Giuliani hadn't made a statement yet. I told Dad I felt abandoned, leaderless, like no one was in charge. I told him I missed Bill Clinton at that moment. I think he felt so bad for me, it was the only time in my memory that he didn't rail against Clinton. At that moment, in the midst of that trauma, he was in daddy mode.

Looking back on that morning, it seems pretty incredible that my first thought upon hearing a low-flying plane over New York City was that it must have been a terrorist attack organized by Osama bin Laden. Was I psychic? Of course not. But the media, both corporate mainstream and right-wing conservative, had been hyping up the threat of such an attack for months. That's the power of repeated media messages—they get burned into your subconscious, ready to influence you at the most unexpected of times.

Post-9/11 was an interesting time to be an American paying close attention to the media and how it presented different issues. President Bush and Vice President Cheney used the attacks and our collective fear to push a pro-war, pro-surveillance agenda that was (to me) obviously cloaked in fake patriotism. Bush made it seem like America's response to 9/11 was this grand struggle between good and evil and that "you are either with us or against us." News anchors across the board started wearing American flag pins, and everyone from politicians to pundits to the workers in the local supermarket became feverishly patriotic.

Gabriel Sherman described the Fox News coverage of 9/11:

How did Ailes cover that story? As a second Pearl Harbor—not that this is a terrorist attack, that there are other ways of dealing with terrorism; such as law enforcement and targeted strikes. Fox News more than any other media outlets sold the war as this grand struggle, and America was going to go there and kick ass, and George Bush was this John Wayne figure. I mean all of this symbolism in the response to 9/11 was driven by Fox News and the patriotism with the anchors wearing the flag pins. Roger Ailes knew that these stories...that these big stories can be boiled down to very simple plot lines.

Not wanting to be accused of being unpatriotic or, worse, liberal, many in the corporate media hopped on the bandwagon of selling the war too. Lucky for mainstream media, war sells.

One night around that time, I was at a party where people were talking about the possible war in Iraq. Most, I knew, were against it, but I remember my friend Irina, visibly upset, practically shaking, and leaning in to this guy she was challenging, saying, "I think we should bomb the shit out of them!" I didn't understand why she would feel so sure about it and have such strong feelings until I later learned that she watched Fox News with her father.

The result of this media-manufactured patriotism was basically a green light for the Bush administration to do anything they wanted as long as they connected it back to 9/11 and the idea of protecting our country from another attack. Fox News distributed lies every day, repeating that Iraq had weapons of mass destruction (WMDs), using scare tactics to garner support for the ill-advised Iraq War. The lies worked. Even in 2015, Fairleigh Dickinson University found that 51 percent of Republicans believed that we had found WMDs in Iraq when the United States invaded it in 2003. Of course, they couldn't find them because they weren't there. Eventually, even Bush finally had to admit that there was no active WMD program in Iraq. He made a joke about it at a black-tie event for journalists in 2004, pretending to look under a table for them. He joked as he lifted the tablecloth, "Those weapons of mass destruction have got to be here somewhere." It wasn't his best moment.

We eventually lost the sympathy of other countries when they saw how our government engaged in preemptive war and used 9/11 as an excuse for regime change in Iraq. Despite the uncertain public support for the war, however, the Bush administration and the media supporting it set him up for a solid reelection campaign against Democratic candidate John Kerry.

The Media Takes Down John Kerry

I braced myself for the 2004 election because I knew in my bones that the Republicans would do whatever they could to smear Kerry from the outset. And I knew my dad would believe whatever they came up with and would be sending me vitriolic emails against Kerry. I also dreaded how the Republicans might try to steal the election *this* time. Sure enough, in this election, the term *swift boating* (attacking one's opponent by questioning their credibility in a dishonest manner) was coined.

One of Kerry's strengths as a candidate was his Vietnam War heroism. He had been awarded the Silver Star, the Bronze Star, and three Purple Hearts for several incidents in which he showed incredible bravery and saved lives. So Republican strategist Karl Rove advised Bush's campaign to attack Kerry's military history. Rather than preying on the opponent's weaknesses like other political operatives did, Rove's plan was to attack the opponent's *strength*, to take out the one thing that could really tip the scales. Rove's goal, like other New Republicans, was a master thirty-year plan to build a permanent Republican majority. He was often referred to as "the architect."

Texas billionaire Bob Perry gave $4.4 million to a group of former POWs to make a video accusing John Kerry of exaggerating his heroism and distorting his conduct in the war. These POWs were called the Swift Boat Veterans for Truth. Plenty of people who saw the smear ads on TV and in books bought the false message. Because, well, who would lie that blatantly?

The mistake the Democrats made here was in ignoring the

lies rather than providing a swift and convincing rebuttal. The rationale was that the story would die out precisely because it wasn't true and as such didn't justify a response. As we have seen, however, "the big lie" is one of the Far Right's favorite tactics for spreading misinformation and winning people over to their side.

Kerry's campaign didn't anticipate how much these attacks would affect people's opinions. In an interview with Terry Gross in 2018, Kerry said his advisors told him they responded adequately to the swift boat veterans' story. Kerry's military record detailed his service and backed him, and major media did some reporting on it. But he acknowledged that right-wing funding got behind these "alternative facts." He said it was some of the same names still "doing major right-wing funding in the country today."

Additionally, Dick Cheney pumped fear into Americans by saying if they elected John Kerry, America would surely suffer another "devastating" terror attack because Kerry was "weak." Kerry was even falsely accused of having an affair. But the media's need to attract an audience caused them to focus on these kinds of sensational stories, no matter the cost to the candidate.

I watched this debacle in the media with despair. I thought, *Here we go again.* The Republicans would fall in line, and enough Democrats would be persuaded to either switch sides or not bother to vote that I felt defeated about the chances of getting Bush out of office.

Voter Suppression

The 2004 election was further marred by a rash of voter suppression supported across the Republican Party, intended to make it more difficult for Kerry to win. John Pappageorge, a Republican state legislature from Michigan, said, "If we do not suppress the Detroit vote, we're going to have a tough time in this election."

Then there was good old-fashioned intimidation. Uniformed officers with guns were sent out by Jeb Bush to question Black voters in Orlando who voted absentee in a mayoral election earlier that year as to why they had done so. Needless to say, given the bad (and sometimes fatal) experiences Black people have had with police, it was intimidating to many Black voters who had to vote absentee.

I was devastated. Kerry lost. The chance to right the ship slipped away again. The march to the right would continue with its stealthy one-party-rule plan, and worse yet, I believed the election was stolen again and there was no fight for it. What was to become of our country? I was emotionally exhausted.

Once again, the polls showed Kerry won but they were explained away by saying that people didn't want to admit they voted for Bush. Or the other lame excuse, that exit polls were no longer accurate.

There were major problems with Diebold voting machines in Ohio. For one thing, they were not the ones that had federal approval. They were also made by a company headed by Wally O'Dell, who had held massive fundraisers for Republicans.

One computer error gave "Bush 3,893 extra votes in suburban Columbus," and the Republican secretary of state, Kenneth Blackwell, in order to "clean up" voter lists, purged nearly one in four voters.

In New Mexico, machines malfunctioned and failed to properly register a vote on more than twenty thousand ballots. A federal commission on election reforms reported that at least one million ballots were spoiled by faulty voting equipment. Robert F. Kennedy Jr. also reported that "a consulting firm called Sproul & Associates, which was hired by the Republican National Committee to register voters in six battleground states, was discovered shredding Democratic registrations."

Despite the obvious issues, the Republicans and much of the media loudly accused people who questioned the validity of the election of wearing tin foil hats. Right-wing media beat their drums, so mainstream corporate media followed their lead and played the stories down, if they reported on any of them at all. As a result, the majority of Democratic voters didn't take it seriously either. If they didn't read about it in the *New York Times*, it was like it couldn't have happened. No one seemed to acknowledge the obvious: "Electronic totals can be changed without a trace." And without paper trails at that time there was no way to check the totals.

I felt like the Democrats just treated it as another conspiracy theory and acted as if they were afraid to address it. Were they shell-shocked from all the New Republican bullying? Were they afraid they'd get accused of hysteria or trying to steal the election themselves? Or was it just incomprehensible to think their fellow countrymen and women could be capable of stealing the vote? Was it just too monumental to deal with?

A study on media bias during the 2004 presidential election found that "the main effect of media coverage seems to be the media have become too cautious. Many cited the rise of Fox News as a force to moderate the other networks and conclude that media members are not asking hard enough questions. The media is also seen as afraid of being wrong and middle of the road."

I leave you with just one thought. What do you think the Republicans would do if *their* election was stolen? (Oh, wait! We know! And it wasn't even stolen. The attempted coup of January 6, 2021, was a result of the successful Big Lie that their election was stolen. Over sixty courts, even some with right-wing judges appointed by Trump, rejected the claim, as there was no evidence. This was the inevitable result—and perhaps the dream effect—of thirty some years of divisive, hateful media pushing the envelope.)

Hopelessness Sets In

To make matters worse, my dad was engaging in his own imaginary war with John Kerry. Rush Limbaugh bashed Kerry every day during the campaign, and my dad lapped it all up. One day when I happened to be standing in my parents' kitchen when Limbaugh had been on the radio railing against Kerry, I muttered under my breath about Limbaugh, "What a buffoon." My dad got an excited wild look in his eye, and he whispered to himself,

"Buffoon... Yeah!" The next day, I heard him call the stately John Kerry a buffoon. He was so happy to have a new term with which to disparage the image of his enemy.

My frustration was turning into hopelessness. When would Democrats get out of denial/apology mode and realize that an actual war was being waged against them, much of it mainlined straight into unwitting voters through right-wing media, compliant mainstream media, and with other tricks like disenfranchisement and gerrymandering? When would they fight back? *Would* they fight back at all?

The answer, in this case, was no. Despite major issues in the election, including voter disenfranchisement, Kerry conceded, saying there was not enough legal evidence to contest the votes. And the mainstream corporate media, too scared to be accused of liberal bias, remained too cautious to examine all the serious issues, many of which were repeats from the 2000 election. It seemed that we had learned nothing over the past four years.

What was to become of our country, I wondered. Republicans were full steam ahead with their stealthy one-party-rule plan that no one seemed to want to acknowledge. I was exhausted.

This right-wing extremism had affected the thinking of my father, some friends, and a lot of my relatives. It was no longer something just preying on my retired dad; it had become pervasive, and like a plague, it seemed to be spreading. It had in turn affected my relationships with these people, some of whom I loved very much. They would often repeat the same talking points during the same periods of time. I was no longer surprised when I heard my father say something like, "You know, Jennifer, there's no such thing as organic," and then a week later, my old college friend Elaine, who read the Drudge Report exclusively, made the same exact pronouncement, always starting with a confrontational, "Well, I bet you didn't know..." The consistency of the messaging was impressive...and frightening.

I shut down for a while. I couldn't reach my dad. It seemed our media was hijacked, and I was seeing the same behaviors my dad was displaying so fiercely in more and more loved ones and people I met. It was so frustrating and disheartening. I became despondent because my hope of Democrats or even mainstream media catching on to what was happening, striking back, and being able to reverse the direction we were going in seemed like it was becoming ever more out of reach.

I had to regroup and find my equilibrium again. I disengaged from politics and didn't email my dad about anything political, even when he emailed me political stuff. I might have even blocked him for a while.

Then, after some healing time, I finally made a plan to try to create some change. I would form my own little media watchdog group. I visited the café across the street from my apartment where all the people in my neighborhood went. I spoke to the owner, Claudia, about my frustration and how I wanted to start a local group. Did she know any people who might be interested? She did indeed, and she arranged a meeting.

I explained to the ten to fifteen people who showed up how I felt that the media, and particularly right-wing media, was at the root of the problems we were facing in our society. The next thing I knew, I had organized a small army of frustrated people, mostly from my New York City neighborhood. We met at my place once a week and formed an official group, People's Response to Inefficient Subservient Media (PRISM).

Our group was a diverse set of people focused on action and raising awareness about the rising (what is now called) whataboutism in mainstream media and the nefarious influence of right-wing media. We would watch, read, or listen to news or political talk, watching for bias, and then write letters to the station to tell them how a particular show had sponsored a guest or segment biased to the right. We wanted to counteract some of what we knew was a well-organized effort on the right and hopefully help some people working in media gain some understanding of how they were being manipulated and bullied by the right to cater to them.

We engaged in this activism for about two years, until the focus of the group shifted. Gradually, we turned into a documentary-watching group. For about three years, we watched documentaries every week and discussed them. And all the while, I was getting ideas for the documentary I hoped to make someday.

The Age of Social Media

In the meantime, new media forms were exploding on the scene. They started out as social interaction vehicles but soon also became instrumental in spreading misinformation, particularly in the political realm.

In February 2004, not long after we started our media watchdog group, Mark Zuckerberg launched Facebook. By 2012, it had over a billion users. Within a few years, millions of people were getting the majority of their news information from Facebook.

In 2005, YouTube, another means of spreading information via the internet, launched to early success. Twitter soon followed in 2006. And blogs were rising in popularity as well. It seemed there was suddenly no shortage of ways for everyday people to instantly share their opinions with the world, for better or worse.

The digital spread of information was initially challenging for networks like Fox News. Since their approach was to "win every news cycle, on every platform imaginable," they had to send out armies of staffers to counter anti-Fox content on popular political blogs. The effort was so massive that "one former staffer recalled using twenty different aliases to post pro-Fox rants. Another had one hundred."

All of a sudden, the lines between what was news and what was fake news became blurred, as the internet gave a platform to anyone with an agenda and a username to hide behind.

A Democrat Takes Back the Presidency

I remember when Senator Barack Obama first gave the keynote speech at the 2004 Democratic National Convention in Boston. My mom was so impressed by Obama's speech that she begged my father to watch it when it ran again on TV. She knew he wouldn't be able to help but be impressed with Obama's inclusive message. And he was! I think he liked that Obama said, "There

is not a liberal America and a conservative America. There is
the United States of America. There is not a Black America, a
White America, a Latino America, an Asian America. There's the
United States of America."

My dad was under the impression that all Democrats wanted
to fight for just those individual groups, that they were obsessed
with raising taxes, giving minorities special breaks over "regular"
(White male) Americans, and enacting full-fledged socialism.
But Obama gave him a different perspective on the Democratic
agenda. My dad nodded thoughtfully and said, "I like him!" My
mom said she thought she saw a glimpse of the old open-minded
Frank Senko when he watched Obama speak.

Unsurprisingly, as Obama's prominence and popularity grew,
he was relentlessly attacked by the Right in a way similar to what
had been done to Bill Clinton. As a result of the constant Obama
bashing by Limbaugh and Fox News and despite his initial positive impression, Dad became convinced that Obama was a far-left
socialist, born in Kenya, and a Muslim. Obama was a "radical" out
to make the country socialist and steal a third term and become
a dictator. Oh, and like all Democrats, he would take your guns
away (never mind the fact that my dad was never a gun person).

My dad and his friend Don were both hysterical about the
prospect of Barack Obama becoming president. I got all kinds of
emails from my dad, and even sometimes from Don, warning me
that Obama would dismantle our country "brick by brick"; he
would buy up all the ammo, start a civil war, and take a third term
if he became president.

Meanwhile, my mom was enamored with the charismatic senator. I would even say she was a bit smitten and had a little crush on the soon-to-be president.

Barack Obama won the race for president against John McCain in a landslide and became president in 2009. It was a hopeful sign to many of us who voted for him. Of course, the New Republicans were going to try to take him down by any means. Because Obama was Black and had a "funny" name and his father was from Kenya, they had extra toxic ammunition that would appeal to the White supremacists and closet racists who were fired up when faced with a Black president.

President Obama had his hands full when he took office. George W. Bush left the country with a huge deficit and the Great Recession. Additionally, Obama had to fight the far-right New Republicans working for one-party rule. In 2010, Senate minority leader Mitch McConnell said, "The single most important thing we want to achieve is for President Obama to be a one-term president." Rush Limbaugh said "he'd rather see the country fail than have President Obama succeed."

Fox News attacked Obama relentlessly and fanned any embers of racism until they became full flames. They talked about how much golfing he did, implying he was lazy (a racist dog whistle) or elite (a supposed liberal trait). Sean Hannity painted Obama as a terrorist because he had had a few dinners with Rashid Khalidi, a Palestinian-American history professor at Columbia. Glenn Beck was brought on to Fox and claimed Obama hated White people.

Fox often referred to Obama by his full name—Barack
Hussein Obama—emphasizing the "Hussein," clearly trying to
create an association between Obama and former Iraqi president
Saddam Hussein or at least claim he was not truly an American.
They even tried to fuse his name with Osama bin Laden occasionally, "accidentally" replacing *Obama* with *Osama*. Donald
Trump often phoned in to Fox to delegitimize Obama with his
birther conspiracy, claiming that Obama had not been born in
the United States but was born in Kenya and was therefore an
illegitimate president. These were vicious lies of course. Barack
Obama was born in Hawaii, though there are still Republicans
today who don't believe that.

Of course, we received emails from Dad spreading lies and
hysteria about President Obama. In one email, he wrote, "If
Obama gets elected again, it will be the last American election."

By Obama's presidency, my dad's views had done a complete
about-face from what they had been when I was growing up. He
had become a total devotee of the Far Right, and I could trace
every step of his evolution back to the media he was consuming
and the echo chamber created in his life.

The only view from Dad's former self that remained, surprisingly, was his thoughts on the right of a woman to have
an abortion. I found a Heritage Foundation questionnaire he
had filled out that was formatted with multiple-choice statements. Next to the statement "Abortion is morally wrong," he
checked "Disagree somewhat," indicating that he hadn't been
totally swayed to the far-right pro-life point of view. But all his

other answers mirrored exactly what I would have expected Rush Limbaugh himself to say in response to each statement. Watching my dad transform into someone I didn't recognize was chilling and infuriating. I could see what was happening to him but didn't have any power to stop it, and I couldn't find any way to make him see that he had stopped thinking for himself. And I know he was not alone in being bamboozled by the Right in some seriously scary ways.

The Documentary

I had been kicking around the idea of making a documentary about the damage right-wing media was inflicting on our country and families for years, and the time finally seemed right. I had a clear understanding of the role media played in everyday Americans' understanding of our political processes and how influential radio, TV, and the internet could be. I wanted to help save my country! I fervently believed that if the right-wing media train didn't slow down, it would surely have dire consequences that might disastrously divide our country and possibly damage or even destroy our democracy.

I did my first test interview with *both* my parents in May 2011. It was just a casual interview to get them used to me filming them and so I could see if it would work. They were naturals in front of the camera.

I had been scared to shoot my father talking about politics, but I got him alone and started questioning him. I tentatively held the camera, afraid to point it at him directly in case he reacted badly. As he got more carried away with the points he was making, I raised the camera. It worked. He didn't get angry with *me* because I stayed neutral and let him rant. He just expressed his anger toward Democrats and "government interference." Once I realized I could work on the film without damaging our relationship further, I knew I could it.

The first thing I needed to do was show who Dad had been before he changed, so I hunted around for the hours and hours of 16 mm footage my dad had shot while we were growing up. I found he had transferred the 16 mm footage to VHS tapes, which weren't quite ideal to work with but would have to do.

There were other logistical considerations to work out; putting together a documentary is time-consuming and complicated! I had saved $10,000 to get started on the film. With that I bought equipment and secured an editor and a small camera crew. We then interviewed a few media experts about some of the issues I wanted to cover so that I could get a trailer together for the purpose of fundraising.

Once the trailer was finished, my team and I were able to put together a Kickstarter campaign. It was during the ensuing Kickstarter campaign that I came to realize just how broadly shared my experience was. People across the country found out about the film, people whose experience mirrored mine. Almost overnight, I became the Ann Landers or Dear Abby of "What happened to my grandpa/mom/brother/uncle?" These people were really hurting. Like me when I started, they didn't understand why their relative or friend had become so unreasonable and angry and were relieved to know a documentary was being made on the subject. That's when I realized my experience was not unique. It was a national phenomenon at the crux of my project. I needed to include their voices. It hadn't just happened to my family or a handful of others, but hundreds, maybe thousands of others—eventually, now, in the millions.

Some of these people contributed money to the Kickstarter campaign, while others just wanted to tell their stories to someone who would understand. The stories I heard were so powerful that I reached out to some of the people who contacted me and asked them if they would want to be included in the film itself. We ended up taping many Skype interviews that made it into the documentary, hopefully giving viewers a window into other people's lives.

And as my team and I worked on the film over the course of more than two years (going through the Kickstarter funds, finding an investor, and receiving grant money to keep the project going), the world kept spinning, and the right-wing media kept doing their thing.

The Rise of Right-Wing Extremism

When we look back at the Black Lives Matter activism that sprung up after the murder of George Floyd in 2020, it's painful to think that back in 2009, we had some warning signs. Daryl Johnson, a former senior analyst for domestic terrorism at the U.S. Department of Homeland Security (DHS), tried to warn of the rise of right-wing violence. The DHS released his report that ideals of right-wing extremism and White supremacy were on the rise and were even spreading into military and law enforcement. But "the right-wing media machine went to DefCon1 and, eventually, got DHS to pull the report." John Boehner, then Speaker of the House, acted outraged that the DHS would call its own American people terrorists. It was just theater for the purpose of keeping the Dems, DHS, and whoever else in check.

I had not heard of the Southern Poverty Law Center (SPLC) until I started my film and a helpful friend turned me on to them. In 2011, the SPLC noted that the number of hate groups had reached more than one thousand for the first time. The SPLC defines a hate group as "an organization that—based on its official statements or principles, the statements of its leaders, or its activities—has beliefs or practices that attack or malign an entire class of people, typically for their immutable characteristics." They track them from "hate group publications, citizen reports, law enforcement agencies, field sources, web postings and news reports."

Paul Starr, a professor of sociology and public affairs, in his review of Andrew Marantz's book *Antisocial: Online Extremists, Techno-Utopians, and the Hijacking of the American Conversation,* gives the following reason for this growth in hate groups grounded in the Far Right:

In the United States, both the conservative media and the Republican Party helped keep a lid on right-wing extremism from the end of the McCarthy era in the 1950s to the early 2000s. Through his magazine *National Review,* the editor, columnist, and TV host William F. Buckley set limits on respectable conservatism, consigning kooks, anti-Semites, and outright racists to the outer darkness. The Republican leadership observed the same political norms, while the liberal press and the Democratic Party denied a platform to the fringe left.

Starr continues, "Those old norms and boundary-setting practices have now broken down on the right. No single source accounts for the surge in right-wing extremism in the United States or Europe." And of course, along with the rise and radicalization of conservative media, there was an opportunity for that ideology to expand into all the online outlets. But despite the growing popularity of these groups, the average American probably didn't know that hate groups were on the rise, unless of course they were Black or Latinx or transgender. One movement that we did hear a lot about, however, was the Tea Party. The story of how it started and how it grew is interesting. And disturbing.

In February 2009, Rick Santelli, a political commentator on CNBC, had an emotional response to President Obama's mortgage relief plan, which was designed to help lift the country out of the Great Recession. Alluding to the Boston Tea Party of 1773, Santelli took to the floor of the Chicago Mercantile Exchange, bellowing that the bailout would "subsidize the losers' mortgages." He announced, "We're thinking of having a Chicago Tea Party." The traders on the floor cheered. It was a dramatic TV moment, and right-wing media consumers who were already brainwashed to believe in free market ideology got hyped up. The group that rallied around this extremist conservative reaction to Obama's economic plans became known as the Tea Party. But the Tea Party had help—lots of it.

The Tea Party was popularized by right-wing pundits like Glenn Beck, Bill O'Reilly, Sean Hannity, and Rush Limbaugh. (I was thankful my dad never discovered Glenn Beck or Sean Hannity. They were probably on too late.) With ideological parallels to the John Birch Society, the Tea Party was funded by corporate billionaires like the Koch brothers and right-wing organizations like the Heritage Foundation, the Cato Institute, and Americans for Prosperity. These organizations had long been trying to sell their elite ideology to the non-elite, and finally huge numbers of everyday people were fighting for it, bringing their guns and babies to Tea Party rallies to rail against the "socialist" Affordable Care Act and other "entitlement programs." It was the height of irony, of course. The Boston Tea Party was staged as a reaction to being taxed without representation, while Obama, who *had* been elected to represent the American people, cut taxes and expanded health care, but that irony was lost on the Tea Partiers, who were woefully misinformed by the messages they had been fed.

The corporate media treated the Tea Party like a spontaneous, grassroots uprising rather than the heavily corporate-backed organization it truly was. As the unofficial mouthpiece of the organization, extremist conservative political commentator Glenn Beck was fed "embedded content" from the tax-exempt organization FreedomWorks that was intended to garner support for the Tea Party. Beck blended it right in with his own usual shtick, and Tea Party representatives gained influence quickly, with several of them being elected to Congress, bolstered by platforms focused on reducing debt, government spending (on social programs of course), and taxes.

With the Tea Party dominating headlines and Obama struggling to get anything done in office, thanks to the roadblocks the Republicans threw up at every turn, I was beyond frustrated with the political landscape. But then in 2010, my parents moved to a retirement community, and things with my dad slowly and miraculously began to change…for the better.

★ **CHAPTER 10** ★

The Return of Dad

My parents were getting older and started feeling like they could no longer take care of their house and huge yard. A retirement community seemed to be the perfect solution, so they packed up and moved once again. Somehow during the move, my dad's radio broke. He put it in the garage, where he planned to fix it one day, but he never got around to it. After the move, there were other things to take care of, and the radio fell down his to-do list. Without the radio, there were no Limbaugh lunches, and without Rush Limbaugh dominating the kitchen, my mom started eating in there with my dad again. My parents went back to chatting. And just as quickly as Limbaugh had taken over my father's life, the talk radio host disappeared from my parents' house.

Another miracle occurred shortly after the move when the old TV in the kitchen conked out and my parents got a new one.

My mom programmed the remotes for the new TV. She placed stickies all over them with little instructions on how to operate them. If my parents happened not to be eating together, my dad, not wanting to bother figuring out how to use the new remotes, ended up watching whatever news show Mom had left on. And she never watched Fox News.

Life moved forward. One day, my dad was in a lot of pain; it turned out he had kidney stones, so he went to the hospital for a week. While he was there, my mother became worried that his email was piling up and taking up space on his slow-running, ancient computer. I happened to be visiting that week to help out. She asked me if I could delete some of Dad's nonpersonal emails to save space. I found hundreds of right-wing political emails in his inbox.

As fast as I deleted them, the emails just continuously kept coming. Eventually, I told Mom it was pointless to try to keep up. So she decided that she would go into Dad's email herself and unsubscribe him from as many email lists as she could. As she went along unsubscribing and seeing more of these messages, she then got the idea of subscribing him to some of her more moderate and even liberal political emails. When my dad came back home, he just read whatever was in his inbox, seemingly not noticing or caring about the shift in messaging.

We finally began experiencing peace in the family. My dad was mellowing out; the anger he had been experiencing for years was eroding. We hadn't noticed when he stopped, but we certainly did notice that he was once again whistling or singing his

Polish and Ukrainian tunes, smiling, and enjoying afternoon tea with my mom. He stopped lashing out; he stopped sending those angry, fearful emails that said Obama was born in Kenya. Even from his home across the country in Oregon, my brother Greg could tell there had been a change in Dad.

One day, my mother called me and told me, "Guess what? Daddy said he liked Obama!"

I was shocked. A few weeks later, I was visiting for my dad's birthday. While we were having birthday cake, Mom asked him if he thought he would vote for Obama in the 2012 election. He said, "Yeah, he's doing all right. He's a pretty good guy."

That moment became burned into my mind. After everything Dad had previously said, sent, and felt about Obama, his response felt unreal. But that November, Dad voted for Barack Obama to serve a second term.

With all these changes, visits home were no longer a chore. Dad was beginning to have more health problems, and I went more often and doted on him. He began to just love it when I came to visit. We became good buddies. And my dad, who I had feared I would never be able to connect with again, became simply lovable. He was a cute and comedic old-timer who was happy to share a smile or a corny joke. He became the best of his old self, the dad I remembered and then some.

One sleepy summer day, he, my mom, and I had a remarkable conversation on my parents' back porch. By this time, I always had my camera ready to shoot as I continued work on the documentary.

I said to Dad, "Do you think your political views have changed?"

"Well, I'm halfway between a Republican and a Democrat," he said. "I'm not all Democrat, and I'm not all Republican"

"Do you believe in the minimum wage?" Mom asked.

"Minimum wage? Yes."

Mom pressed further. "Do you believe in personal freedom? Some people believe that gay people don't have the right to get married, and some people say, 'I couldn't care less. Let them get married if they want to.'"

Dad said, "Well, I guess if they want to do that, then go ahead and do it, yeah."

"Yeah, that's the way I figure it," Mom casually answered. But I could tell she had to stop herself from smiling.

It was an incredible thing to see my dad come full circle and watch how his thoughts evolved after being introduced to a variety of inputs. He was thinking independently again. I didn't care that he wasn't "all Democrat"; I wouldn't even have cared if he was still identifying as a Republican. I was just happy that he was content and no longer held prisoner to rage. The fear and anger from the agenda of the New Republicanism that had held him captive for so long had come to define him. The ebb of that rage gave me my father back.

On January 24, 2015, my dad forwarded me an email from Reader Supported News that had an article by Dennis Kucinich called "New Year's Resolution for America." It espoused some pretty liberal views for America, like getting rid of the Patriot Act and creating a Department of Peace to address police brutality, gun violence, and domestic abuse.

It was the last political email my dad ever sent.

When I asked my mother why she thought Dad fell for the right-wing ideology and she didn't, she said, "I think the reason for the differences in political opinion between me and Dad was partly the way we were raised. Dad was brought up where his parents spoke a different language, and he lived in poverty, as he thought everyone did that he knew.

"But when I was growing up, we always got at least a Sunday paper and would listen to the radio. I heard about Hoover being to blame for the Depression and heard how Franklin D. Roosevelt brought us out of the Depression. So in my teens, I learned how not to like Republicans and to admire Democrats."

I asked her to explain further.

"Well," she said, "he probably never heard of Republicans, so he never got a bad opinion of them, like blaming them for the Depression. Also, he never gave the Democrats praise for fixing the Depression, because he never knew there was a Depression. Everybody was a poor immigrant in his neighborhood growing up. So all this political stuff was new to him, and he got educated by the wrong people, like Rush Limbaugh, et cetera. And he would never think that they would lie—not educated people like politicians. Whereas I had opportunities to listen to radio, newspapers, et cetera and heard stuff as it was going on and formed my opinions this way."

Of course, I had been filming my father over the past couple of

years. He knew I had made two other films and that I often had a
camera with me, so he didn't question it too much. Sometimes he
even seemed to enjoy the attention. Finally, one day, he asked me
why I was shooting him. I told him I was making a movie about
him. That made perfect sense to him, because he thought he was
fascinating. When I explained that the film was about his personality change from being fanatical and kind of obnoxious about his
political views and then how he came back to being his jolly old
self, he laughed and jovially said, "I think I'd like to see that!"

Mom and Dad finally agree on gay marriage!

My Beloved Dad

In the last two months of 2015, my dad lost a lot of weight and
started getting headaches. I showed him my mostly completed
documentary, *The Brainwashing of My Dad*, one day when he was
feeling well. He loved it. He said, "Wow, Poody, I'm impressed

and so proud of you!" I took a picture of him holding the DVD and smiling proudly.

Shortly after Dad turned ninety-three and started suffering from headaches and some weight loss, we took him to see his doctor, and he indicated that my dad was in the natural process of dying. My father hated hospitals, so my mother and I got home-care hospice. I stayed with my parents, nursing my father until he died in his bed at home on January 21, 2016.

After Dad passed away, I helped my mom find an independent senior living apartment that would be manageable for her to live in alone. Once we found her a place, we had only a few months to go through some sixty years of stuff so she could downsize.

Dad kept *everything*, so he had years and years of papers and almost all his check ledgers from the past several decades. As I sat on the floor of the den, I flipped through some of these ledgers. I could not believe how much money he had given to causes like the Heritage Foundation, the National Right to Work, Citizens against Government Waste, Judicial Watch, Tea Party Patriots, Dittoheads of America—the list went on and on. All told, it must have added up to thousands of dollars. And to what end?

I am grateful that our family—mostly my mom, really—rescued my dad from the anger, paranoia, and hatred that imprisoned him for almost twenty years. Some may take issue with my mom's means, but I see in my mother a woman who stuck it out when her husband's personality changed, who was there with him through the arguing and anger, patiently nurturing and drawing out the man she had loved, a man who had almost disappeared.

Mostly through her simple act of distancing him from harmful messaging, he returned to his former self.

I am so glad that the last few years of Dad's life were filled with love and joy and happiness rather than right-wing rage and Limbaugh lunches. You could say that Dad was successfully "deprogrammed," something I honestly wouldn't have thought possible when he was at his worst. It didn't happen overnight. It took time and patience—lots of it. And love. Lots of love. But he eventually returned to us and to himself.

What this shift in my dad showed me was that when his media sources changed, his demeanor, thinking, and beliefs changed too. Media has a powerful, unseen effect on all of us; it's worth thinking carefully about our media diet and how we can manage it and help the people we care about think critically about their media choices. There's hope in Dad's journey, because understanding that he could change means others under similar "deprogramming" may be able to as well.

CHAPTER 11

After Dad

A lot has happened in the world since my dad passed away in early 2016. There have been times when I've wondered how he would react to different events and other times when I'm glad he isn't here to see what has happened to our country over the past few years. But from my perspective as someone who continues to be very interested in and critical of the media, it sure has been a wild ride!

With all the ups and downs, two things that have remained consistent are the Far Right's ability to flip the script to support their point of view and their unwillingness to play by the rules that used to govern politics in America. By the time the 2016 presidential election rolled around, the Far Right's plan to use media to influence America paid off in a bigger way than most people could have ever imagined.

Media Coverage of the 2016 Election

While our team hurried to get the documentary out before the election, we all watched the presidential race unfold. Quite stunningly, the contest came down to Donald J. Trump and Hillary Clinton. Clinton clearly had more experience—she was a successful politician, having been elected to the Senate in 2000 and serving as secretary of state in Obama's administration, and she had seen her husband, Bill, through eight years in the White House. Donald Trump had never held elected office and promoted himself as a billionaire real estate mogul and businessman, but he had gone bankrupt six times and was most well-known as the host of the reality TV show *The Apprentice*. Nearly everyone, including myself, thought Hillary was a shoo-in for the presidency.

But Donald Trump had some media advantages. Trump was obsessed with his image and TV ratings. He watched hours of TV every day and knew that if he said outrageous things, the corporate media couldn't help but report them. During the campaign, he was like a train wreck—you couldn't look away. His no-holds-barred demeanor, along with his racist "birther" theory about Obama's place of birth and supposed concern for the everyday American worker, won over many people who believed that politicians weren't looking out for their interests, who felt forgotten and left behind during America's march toward progress and equality for all. Many folks mistook his authenticity for sincerity; if he wasn't a "real" politician, that meant they could trust him. The more outrageous he was, the more folks assumed he was a regular person—just like them—but better because they believed he was a successful businessman who dared to 'tell it like it is" (except *it* wasn't). And the media played right into Trump's hands. Some analysts have reported that he earned himself nearly $5 billion worth of free promotion through the media that covered his every word in 2016.

The media was obsessed with Trump—there's no other way to describe it. And the more the media outlets covered him, the higher their ratings went and the more traction he gained. From there, his platform grew even larger, and he was able to more quickly spread lies and misinformation to the American people. Leslie Moonves, the former CEO of CBS, was quoted as saying, "It [the media's coverage of Trump] may not be good for America, but it's damn good for CBS." (Moonves later had to step down from CBS after six women accused him of sexual harassment and intimidation.)

One of Trump's outrageous and made-up accusations, which he returned to over and over again in the lead-up to the election, was that the election was rigged against him. Many have said he didn't believe he'd win, so this accusation provided a way for him to save face when he didn't. He was clearly sowing the seeds of division in a country that was about to become infinitely more divided over the next four years, and his voter base ate it all up.

I saw the repeating of Trump's lie in my own family. A cousin whispered to my mother during a family dinner, "The election is gonna be rigged!" My mother said yes, it will be, but she meant for Trump. He meant for Hillary.

Trump knew well how to exploit the polarization that already existed just under the surface of American society. He had been a fan of Fox News and Rush Limbaugh long before he ran for president. Far-right media had been his media diet for at least the last decade. Like many older American White men, he became addicted to it.

When he first took office, I at times wondered if it was possible that Trump, who is a former registered Democrat, was himself brainwashed by right-wing media during the 1990s and 2000s. It is apparent to most people now, however, that he doesn't really have any core values or beliefs other than whatever serves him personally in a given moment. In 1999 on *Meet the Press*, he said "I am very pro-choice." In the same interview, he said gays in the military would not disturb him. By the time he became the Republican presidential nominee, his views had shifted (at least publicly). Whether he became a Republican for expediency or because he was brainwashed, we can't be sure. Either way, he learned well how to work the crowd and rile the far-right media addicts up. He intuitively understood the power of the language of division.

Trump talked like a populist, allowing him to grow his base beyond the traditional Republican sympathizers and enroll independent voters and Democrats who were unhappy with their stagnant wages and inability to climb up the economic ladder. Rather than vote another perceived politician into office, they wanted someone different, and Trump was different all right. He promised that he alone could fix everything. He seemed like he could shake things up and said he would "drain the swamp" and change Washington for the good of the people.

Trump even appealed to some Obama voters because Obama promised them change they could believe in, but they didn't see that change in their lives. They felt unseen, unheard, and unrepresented and went with the guy who talked like he was a straight shooter. Except (spoiler), he wasn't.

But the most powerful factor was of course the right-wing media machine supporting him. Sean Hannity likened him to Ronald Reagan, and "Geraldo Rivera tweeted that Trump was 'more competent, creative, tough experienced and bold' than most of the other candidates." And of course, Limbaugh endorsed Trump daily on his show.

Mainstream media, unsurprisingly, did not do enough to counter Trump's boasts about himself and his abilities. They just let him speak, giving him a platform from which to spread lies. Jeff Jarvis of the Tow-Knight Center for Entrepreneurial Journalism put it well: "The mere fact of Donald Trump's candidacy is evidence of the failure of journalism."

Then there was the other right-wing outlets, like Breitbart and Alex Jones's InfoWars site, which generated conspiracy theories daily. "Pollsters would dismiss social media as a self-selecting group that doesn't reflect the whole voting population. But it does perhaps give a clue to the emotional impact of a candidate. Trump was giving people more to talk about," said David Sillito, a media correspondent. He continued, "The need for headlines that bring clicks and stories that get shared has changed everything."

Little did we know at the time that not only did we have Fox, the far-right talk radio guys, and Breitbart pushing Trump's agenda, the election media cycle would soon get even more complicated and darker. Russian interference through bots and trolls posting misinformation and spreading conspiracy theories infiltrated the social media networks that millions of Americans had come to rely on as important news sources, heavily influencing the public's opinion about what was true and what was false.

Journalist Luke Barnes wrote, "Part of the reason these conspiracy theories, and the death threats against survivors that accompany them, become so popular is because they manage to exploit the algorithms of major social media platforms that dictate what content is 'trending.'" Some of the Russian bots pushed hashtags they knew would resonate with the extreme Right and New Republicans. They also stirred up hatred not only between the Left and the Right but between those who had supported Bernie Sanders in the primary and were unhappy with Hillary Clinton as the Democratic candidate. About 4 percent of voters who had supported Obama were persuaded not to vote for Clinton by fake news stories. The fake news stories especially hurt Clinton in the three states that delivered the presidency: Michigan, Pennsylvania, and Wisconsin.

A study done at Ohio State University found that all the fake news that ran during the 2016 campaign "played a significant role in depressing Hillary Clinton's support on Election Day." This was not a surprise to me at all. After having studied the influence of media on politics for so long, I was incredibly worried about how Trump and his supporters were taking over the political messaging surrounding the election.

There was one other tactic that "rigged" the vote for Trump that got very little attention in the so-called liberal media. It was the use of the Interstate Voter Registration Crosscheck Program, Crosscheck for short, which took voters off the rolls (those thought to be Democrats) under the pretext of preventing voter fraud, even though voter fraud was a made-up issue.

If this had happened in reverse, the Cult Republicans would be out in the street—some heavily armed, as we saw in 2020 in Michigan when heavily armed protesters gathered at the state capital, just angry over having to wear masks to protect themselves and their fellow Michiganders from COVID-19. And as we saw on January 6, 2021, when thousands of Trump supporters like the Oath Keepers, the Proud Boys, and the One Percenters, etc., armed with bear spray, stun guns, baseball bats, and Trump flags stormed the U.S. Capitol to stop the Electoral College vote count in order to overturn the presidential election. Pipe bombs were also planted at the Democratic and Republican parties' headquarters because they believed the Big Lie that their election was stolen. The violence was predictable.

Issues arose from Kansas secretary of state Kris Kobach's use of Crosscheck. (Kobach was always for strong voter ID laws and had made ridiculously false claims about voter fraud.) With Crosscheck, if two voters had the same or a similar name and had the same birthday—it didn't matter if they were in two different states—one or both would be flagged as a "double voter" or as fraudulent voters and then thrown off the rolls. Most of the names it picked up were either Asian-, Hispanic- or Black-sounding names.

Crosscheck was a database developed in 2005 by then Kansas secretary of state Ron Thornburgh. In December 2019, a lawsuit filed by the American Civil Liberties Union of Kansas that challenged Kansas's management of the program resulted in the program being suspended indefinitely. Even before that, a dozen states had withdrawn from the program because of inaccurate data and the risk of violating the privacy rights of voters. Crosscheck was also accused of using racial discrimination to unlawfully purge voters. Before the 2016 election, Crosscheck had "tagged an astonishing 7.2 million suspects," yet no more than four perpetrators had been charged with double voting.

I asked Greg Palast about Crosscheck, and this is what he emailed back to me: "Crosscheck was a small, benign Kansas/Missouri program until Kris Kobach took over as Sec. of State of Kansas in 2013 and, with the Voting Rights Act gutted that year, began the national expansion to 30 states. With Kobach gone, Kansas shut the program in 2019. Its giant effect was felt in 2016—and still today as some states placed voters on their 'inactive' lists in past years—which could have caused a loss of votes in 2020."

Fox Carries on Ailes's Legacy

During the 2016 presidential campaign, Roger Ailes was ousted from his position as CEO of Fox News over sexual harassment charges. He then joined Trump's campaign as an advisor. Almost a year later, on May 18, 2017, he died after falling in his home and hitting his head.

During his long career in media, Ailes succeeded in creating a right-wing behemoth media machine. His genius was to tap into the wants and needs of television viewers, especially those of a vulnerable older audience looking for validation. He knew how to create compelling television programming perhaps better than anyone else in history, and he understood the human psyche: what people respond to and how you can use fear and anger to drive them to action.

It was the end of the Ailes era but not the end of Fox as we know it.

Murdoch himself took over at Fox News after Ailes's ousting. Later, he handed the reins over to his son Lachlan, whose political views leaned even farther right than his father's. When Trump became president, Fox News aligned itself with him and his administration in a way that had never been seen before in the history of American media.

Michael M. Grynbaum, media correspondent for the *New York Times*, wrote about the symbiotic relationship Trump and Fox News had: "The Trump-Fox connection, though, extends beyond friendship and flattery to outright advocacy. The president is the beneficiary of a sustained three-hour block of aggressive prime time punditry, which has amplified his unfounded claims and given ballast to his attacks on the news media as the 'enemy of the American people.'"

It was reported that Trump watched Fox News up to eight hours every day, then commented on the programming via Twitter, creating a feedback loop between himself and the network.

It had been surprising to me to see even mainstream corporate media and social media referring to Fox News as state-run TV. The connection was clearly observable because Trump got his talking points from Sean Hannity and sometimes from Murdoch. What did Trump know about governing and ideologies? Nothing. So he got his information and ideas mostly from Fox and sometimes Breitbart, Rush Limbaugh, Alex Jones, and other similar far-right kooks. It's not a surprise, then, that as mentioned before, Trump ordered the FDA to keep all the TVs in their break rooms, reception areas, or anywhere there is a TV tuned to Fox. This was explained to other staff members in an internal email but later denied by an FDA spokesperson.

The Supposed Liberal Bias That Has Social Media Companies Scared

In early 2016, the website Gizmodo accused Facebook of intentionally suppressing conservative articles. The Drudge Report hysterically reported Facebook was "leaning left," so even though Facebook's moderators found no evidence of bias, to avoid such charges, Facebook bent over backward to prove it was an unbiased platform. It fired almost all its editors "then reached out to conservative pundits for meetings" to insist it wasn't biased. It also shut down the Trending Topics section the conservatives had complained about. They became too soft on right-wing trolls. This accusation opened up a broader conversation about how the algorithms controlling what we see on our social media accounts function and what political and social biases might be baked into them.

In a 2018 article in the *Guardian*, Oscar Schwartz, an Australian journalist and researcher based in New York, discussed a claim made by Francesca Tripodi, a professor of sociology at James Madison University, that "anecdotal evidence of anti-conservative bias spreads as fact through the media in part because of a deep misunderstanding of how bias in search engines and content moderation practices work." Tripodi said, "These algorithms are very complex and not at all intuitive. They weigh things like how many people are linking to an article, what key words appear in the headline, and what specific phrases people are using in their search."

Schwartz wrote that "since technology companies ensure that their content moderation practices remain undisclosed, there is no way of definitively proving that algorithmic anti-conservative bias exists from the outside." In other words, it's nearly impossible to tell if the alleged bias really exists.

It is also quite inconvenient to be accused of anti-conservative bias when conservatives are in charge. In April 2018, Congress grilled Mark Zuckerberg, the founder and CEO of Facebook, about alleged anti-conservative bias on the platform. Extremist conservative groups put pressure on Facebook to address charges of censorship and bias. Under such scrutiny, Zuckerberg pledged to investigate the charges. "Facebook needs Republican support to ward off regulation threatened by Democratic lawmakers" reported *USA Today* senior technology writer Jessica Guynn.

Whether or not Facebook ever really had a bias against conservatism, the steady accusations and the threat of government regulation make it more likely that Facebook will be too fearful to exert discretion between fake news and real news and between hate speech and free speech in the future—even when Democrats are in charge, because they typically don't complain about anti-liberal bias.

Due to intense public pressure after 2016, ahead of the midterms in July 2018, Facebook took down thirty-two fake organization and event pages that were pushing disinformation and divisive messaging to American users. One of the pages had as many as eighteen thousand followers. These pages were involved in propaganda campaigns that looked similar to the ones run by Russia's Internet Research Agency. U.S. intelligence described the agency as a content farm "likely funded by a close Putin ally." Facebook was not sure where they originated, as the page owners' locations were difficult to detect. These pages featured divisive content about immigration, Trump, and especially targeted the Unite the Right rally. The various pages organized about thirty events during the first half of 2018. The pages looked legitimate, but looking closely, they were linked and seemed to be intentionally divisive, often organizing two opposing rallies or demonstrations on the same day. For example, one page would feature the Unite the Right march, while another event page called "No Unite the Right 2 DC" by a seemingly feminist-oriented group called "The Resisters" organized an opposing rally on the same day (the latter being fake).

The content contained the perfect ingredients for violence by using the online platform to instigate what would likely be the meeting of two opposing groups of people meeting in real life. When Facebook realized it was a fake ("coordinated inauthentic behavior"), they took the pages down. There were approximately twenty-six hundred users who had indicated their interest in the No Unite the Right 2 DC event.

The troubling aspect to this is that as Matt Taibbi explained in an article called "Beware the Slippery Slope of Facebook Censorship" in *Rolling Stone*, "Facebook was 'helped' in its efforts to wipe out these dangerous memes by the Atlantic Council, on whose board you'll find confidence-inspiring names like Henry Kissinger, former CIA chief Michael Hayden, former acting CIA head Michael Morell and former Bush-era Homeland Security chief Michael Chertoff."

So in other words, the council of those organized to monitor Facebook for bias would be considered to have a right-wing bias.

Because 62 percent of U.S. adults get their news from social media, we are vulnerable to bad actors, including foreign governments, who use social media networks—originally built to unite us—to divide us. But it can be tricky to know where the line between limiting false information and restricting speech falls. Although the First Amendment only applies to the *government's* limits on restricting speech (corporations like Facebook have the authority to limit content on their own platforms), Americans tend to get feisty when they encounter any form of suspected censorship. Since the growth of social media companies depends on an ever-expanding user base to advertise to, the last thing they want is to be perceived as having any kind of bias in their management of content, liberal or otherwise. Whether social media ends up contributing to the strengthening of our democracy or to its downfall remains to be seen.

CHAPTER 12

Brainwashing: The Amygdala and the Neuroscience

From the very beginning, I knew the title of my documentary would be *The Brainwashing of My Dad*. I am certainly not an expert in psychology or neuroscience and didn't even really know what brainwashing was, but it felt like the right language to describe what had happened to my father. Over time, I found that many people with similar experiences to mine felt the same way. While I was happy that the title of the documentary hit the nail on the head for its audience, it was deeply troubling that so many could relate to it.

My team and I did a lot of research about brainwashing and the neuroscience behind this personality-changing phenomenon. By the time work on the film was done, I realized that my father had indeed been brainwashed. What had started as my own anecdotal hypothesis and pure speculation on the topic turned out to have scientifically proven foundations.

A lot of my research on brainwashing was based on the work of Dr. Kathleen Taylor, a neuroscientist, author, and researcher in the areas of neuroimmunology and cognitive neuroscience at the University of Oxford. Dr. Taylor studies the phenomenon of brainwashing and has written numerous books about it.

My initial understanding of brainwashing was stereotypical and extreme: a harsh tactic that takes place in cults or in brainwashing camps where prisoners of war are locked away with no sleep and constantly inundated with propaganda designed to change their fundamental beliefs. The term *brainwashing*, in fact, has its origins in the Korean War, when POWs were subjected to this kind of intense indoctrination. Certain beliefs were instilled in them against their will through psychological torture.

CIA agent and author Edward Hunter was the first to use the term *brainwashing*. It comes from a kind of translation of a Chinese Communist term that means *wash brain*, referring to the process also known as political re-education. During the 1950s, brainwashing was used to describe the tactics used by totalitarian regimes. It later became a nonpolitical term often used in a more casual way to describe the effect of someone being indoctrinated by a cult or even how shoppers might be persuaded to buy something they don't need through incessant and convincing advertising.

According to Dr. Taylor, brainwashing is typically associated with beliefs that are damaging to the person being brainwashed. She says an extreme example of this is seen in cults like the one in Jonestown, Guyana, in which cult leader Jim Jones convinced almost all his followers to commit suicide by drinking Flavor Aid laced with poison.

Essentially, brainwashing is making someone adopt radically different beliefs by using systematic and often forcible pressure.

Two Different Methods of Brainwashing

Dr. Taylor cites two different means of brainwashing. The one most people are familiar with is brainwashing by coercive force, where the subject is actually browbeaten into believing something.

The more subtle means of brainwashing—which is what I feel many are subject to by media—is brainwashing by stealth. Dr. Taylor says the person:

is not so much forced to believe something but all of the information that is coming at them is pushing a line. There is no alternative in terms of information. So if you control the information that goes into the brain, to a great degree, you control what that brain is going to think and believe. That makes it difficult for the person to think anything else because the horizons are narrowed and everything is constricted down to what information is available to them.

Brainwashing by stealth occurs when someone either puts themselves in a bubble or they're put in a bubble (such as a nursing home) where they're hearing the same kind of stories and from the same voices over and over again. It's especially powerful when those stories are scary ones designed to appeal to and trigger a reaction from the primitive part of our brain that processes fear. The amygdala, or reptilian brain, isn't rational. No critical thinking happens there, only response to a perceived threat.

Advertising is an example of brainwashing by stealth. Not much attention may be being paid to the advertisement. It may be on in the background, but underneath that, you get a whole lot of new messages that come through that are saying it's really important to consume stuff. You are only worthwhile if you buy stuff or you're wearing makeup or you're driving a great car. All these messages are coming through even though they are on in the background. They create these thoughts via stealth.

Since brainwashing is all about belief change, I asked Dr. Taylor to describe the factors involved in creating it. She says there are five factors: isolation, control, uncertainty, repetition, and use of strong emotion.

1. **Isolation** is cutting the person off from other sources of information. Right-wing media, including Fox News, likes to do this all the time; they claim over and other that no other media tells the truth.

2. **Control** involves the brainwasher having control of the information that is going into the person's head, and nobody else is able to contribute other information to them.

3. **Uncertainty** involves the brainwasher attacking a person's

former beliefs so they are left feeling confused and unsure. That leaves the person in a state of not really knowing what is right and what is wrong about what they believe and, perhaps more importantly, what the truth really is.

4. **Repetition** involves repeating a message over and over again so the person can repeat it in their sleep, especially if other right-wing sources are in lockstep. It pushes the information into the brain, and competing information has no room to get in.

5. **Use of strong emotion**, particularly anger, with passion and emotive language is a very persuasive and powerful technique, especially when the anger is feeding off deeper fears.

George Lakoff said in an interview, "You can only understand what the neuro circuits of your brain allow you to understand. Any fact that doesn't fit that will be ignored or rejected as ridiculous, and so on. They don't know their brains are being changed. They don't know this mechanism. They're just there; they listen to it."

Dr. Taylor added, "We have very good psychological mechanisms for not even hearing and perceiving information that conflicts with what we believe. We have filters that shut down contrasting information."

Our strongest beliefs become a part of how we define ourselves. So when we challenge our loved ones' beliefs, we are in fact challenging *who* they are. Any belief that is threatened is going to be fiercely defended because people feel like they are literally defending themselves and their understanding of the world. It can be so uncomfortable to hear "facts" contrary to one's beliefs, there is even a term for it: *cognitive dissonance*. So once someone has settled on a certain belief, they are unlikely to seek information that will contradict that belief and will even bend evidence to match their understanding of the world and strengthen their convictions because it *feels* right.

The Key Role of the Amygdala

The amygdala is an almond-shaped grouping of neurons located in the temporal lobe of the brain. These two small areas, one in each hemisphere, are responsible for processing our emotions, particularly those of passion, such as fear, anger, and pleasure, along with our memory and survival instincts. When the amygdala is triggered, it disables the frontal lobes, where we have our impulse control mechanism and rational thought, and activates the fight-or-flight response. The amygdala, also known as our "reptilian brain," isn't rational—it's instinctual. No critical thinking happens there, only a response to a perceived threat.

These scary stories disguised as news—sometimes based in reality and sometimes not—have a function: they instill fear. They cause a feeling of loss of control first. As the fearmongering continues and the fear gets more deeply embedded, it becomes anger. When someone is overtaken with anger and anxiety, which then turns to rage, this is what is called *amygdala hijacking*.

Psychologist Daniel Goreman first coined the term *amygdala hijacking* in his book *Emotional Intelligence: Why It Can Matter*

More Than IQ to describe a circumstance when extreme negative emotion causes our critical thinking to become impaired or to shut down. People in this state can be easily manipulated because they need answers to be comforted out of their fear and because their rational thinking has been disabled by the amygdala's flight-or-fight response. They're essentially primed to be persuaded.

Addicted to Anger?

I sometimes felt that my dad lived for the anger on some level— that he was addicted to the rush of rage. He could not wait to shut himself in the kitchen, closing those big heavy doors he built, to listen to Rush Limbaugh for the full three hours and get all pissed off at Democrats and liberals. God have mercy on any who dared interrupt!

In order to see if anger addiction was possible, I found another neuroscientist, John Montgomery, who believed it was not only possible but had a compelling theory about it.

When I interviewed him for the documentary, he said that there is a lot of "evidence from neuroscience that stress hormones have the same effect in the brain as addictive drugs like meth and cocaine." He said when we experience a stressful situation, endorphins are released as a stress response to deal with the situation or pain. Endorphins are the main pleasure chemical of the brain. According to Montgomery, "Having them triggered can become like a chemical addiction." So, for example, he said, "in the case of your father, if he watches or listens to something that makes him very angry, he could get addicted to that because the stress response is releasing endorphins and dopamine. There is evidence that dopamine and endorphins are the two main chemicals that are involved in addiction to drugs and alcoholism." Anger creates a feeling of righteousness.

I believed anger was intoxicating to my dad. I felt it gave him purpose at a time in his life when he didn't have one, and it provided him with a frame from which to see and understand the world.

The release of endorphins in relation to anger is just a theory, but it does make sense if you consider similar behavior such as why some people like to watch horror movies for the rush of fear. Montgomery explained that "it sort of simulates being out in the wild—it's like feeling really alive. You know, having the high intensity of being alive and being surrounded by nature. Having an intense emotional connection."

So what exactly happened to make anger my dad's "fix"? And what happens when anger or fear rules our brains?

Groupthink

While we are all susceptible to brainwashing, those who are closely integrated into any kind of group are far more likely to be swept up and swayed by the group's beliefs than to keep their own beliefs if they conflict with those of the group. Most people adapt to the beliefs of the majority—or rather, of their tribe—because, as Dr. Taylor explains, they actually feel better if they believe what others around them do. This phenomenon is often referred to as *groupthink*.

As Dr. Taylor put it,

We evolved to live in a group, and our lives often depended on that group. So it was important to be in harmony with the people around us. That's why so often in workplaces or in politics, you have groupthink. Basically, people want to please their leader because their jobs and sometimes even their lives depend on it. They also want to maintain a status in the group. They don't want to step out of line, and so even if they disagree with the leader, they tend not to say so. The people who disagree then think that they better agree or at least pretend to. It's very hard to pretend to believe something, and so eventually they come to be a believer.

We also conducted an interview with Mike Lofgren, an author and former Republican staffer. He described groupthink in government this way:

It can happen in any group dynamic. It happens in governments and it happens in corporations, that you magically assimilate the views of your peers and your superiors, and as Upton Sinclair said, it's difficult to get a man to understand something if he is being paid not to understand it. In other words, this ostracism by the government of nonconformists within those institutions is because they all have a monetary or career interest in not understanding certain things. For instance, they didn't want to understand that getting us into wars in the Middle East is a dumb thing. Or understand that Wall

Street's business model of selling mortgages to people who couldn't pay them back was not the greatest business model in the world.

He added, "No one likes to be ostracized." These are other reasons people, especially in political parties, become susceptible to groupthink.

Cultlike Behavior

One of the behaviors I saw in my father that mirrored those seen in cults was his unquestioning devotion to a particular figure—in his case, Rush Limbaugh. Limbaugh set himself up, as many cult leaders do, as all-knowing. He would say things like "don't think about this until I get back on Monday." He would tell his listeners what the daily barrage of current events and politics meant, and his listeners would be relieved of the chore of figuring it out for themselves.

My dad often said Limbaugh was his hero. He said he always agreed with Rush. Rush was always right.

In a cult, no matter how harmful the leader's behavior is, those who follow him believe it is justified. The leader has exclusive access to the truth.

The Dittoheads, Fox followers, and Alex Jones devotees often exhibit another sign of cult behavior: a persecution complex. Criticism of the leader is characterized as persecution, and any outside group is billed as an enemy to be absolutely demonized, no matter what they say or do.

There is also the theme of exclusivity. Nonmembers are not welcome. Everyone else is in the wrong—there is no room for differences or dissent. It is an in-group/out-group kind of mentality. It makes the member feel important because they belong. And those who are not members, who don't belonging to the club, are looked down on. And that's an incentive to stay in the group.

Brain Differences between Conservatives and Liberals

In an article in *Psychology Today*, Dr. Bobby Azarian listed four ways in which he believes people who ascribe to conservative beliefs are different from those who are more liberal.

1. Conservatives tend to focus on the negative.

    Dr. Azarian cites a 2012 study where "liberal and conservative participants were shown" both negative and positive images "while their eye movements were recorded. While liberals were quicker to look at pleasant images," the conservatives tended to really inspect the threatening and disturbing pictures—which is what psychologists call a "negativity bias." So the world looks like a "much scarier place"—hence the irrational fears of equality for LBGTQ Americans, immigrants, vaccinations, etc.

2. Conservatives have a stronger physiological response to threat.

    He also cites "a 2008 study published in the journal *Science*" that "found that conservatives have a stronger physiological response to startling noises and graphic images," suggesting a "hypersensitivity to threat." The speculation for that kind of person supporting more conservative views would be that conservatism helps protect them because it provides a finite world. For example, Dr. Azarian said, "This could explain the two parties' different stances on gun control. It makes sense that those who startle more easily are also the ones that believe they need to own a gun."

3. Conservatives fear new experiences.

    The same 2008 study Dr. Azarian cites found that liberal college students owned more books and travel-related items and "conservatives had more things that kept order in their lives." The study suggests that conservatives seem to "prefer a more ordered, disciplined lifestyle" and may explain "why they can be resistant to change." This isn't too much different from George Lakoff's description of the conservative feeling more comfortable with authoritarianism.

4. Conservatives' brains are more reactive to fear.

    This one is familiar to us already: "Using MRIs, scientists from University College London found that students who identify themselves as conservatives have a larger amygdala than self-described liberals." So they are more "reactive to fearful stimuli" with a heightened sensitivity that may cause them to overreact. Azarian uses the example of how the Bush administration was able to gather wide public support among conservatives for invading Iraq.

We don't know definitively if conservatives' brains start out with larger amygdalae or if they become that way after being over-exposed to fear- and anger-inducing stimuli. In fact, Dr. Kathleen Taylor insists, "We are all vulnerable. We are pretty hopeless at realizing how much we are manipulatable." She said the people most shocked and shaken up by the "reeducation process that the Chinese Communists inflicted on their American POWs were the Americans, because the Americans have this idea of an individual self and being free."

Why Do They Believe Lies?

In my research for this book, I came across the work of John Ehrenreich. An author and professor of psychology at the State University of New York at Old Westbury, Ehrenreich's research is focused on why conservatives in particular willingly accept false-hoods as truth. Per an article he wrote in Slate, "as recently as 2016, 45 percent of Republicans still believed that the Affordable Care Act included 'death panels' (it doesn't!). A 2015 poll found that 54 percent of GOP primary voters believed then-President Obama to be a Muslim (he isn't!)."

What prompted me to look into his research was a post on Facebook, which was a response to my posting about something President Trump did that I didn't agree with. A commenter asked me if I'd rather have a Kenyan for president or a real American. I wasn't sure if this guy was just trolling me or not, but I also knew it was possible he really believed that. So why are some people so susceptible to believing ridiculous lies?

Ehrenreich had other examples: "Almost 1 in 6 Trump voters, while simultaneously viewing photographs of the crowds at the 2016 inauguration of Donald Trump and at the 2012 inauguration of Barack Obama, insisted that Trump's crowd size was larger." Estimates of Obama's inauguration suggest 1.8 million people attended while only 300,000 to 600,000 people attended Trump's inauguration. There were photographs showing the dramatic difference. But Cult Republicans still believed Trump had a bigger crowd. How could these particular Trump devotees not believe their own "lying eyes"? And most alarming to me was Ehrenreich's finding that 46 percent of Trump voters *still* believe Hillary Clinton was really connected to a child sex trafficking ring run from a pizza parlor in DC or weren't sure if it was true.

Many of my Democratic counterparts think people who believe lies and conspiracy theories are simply stupid or uneducated. Some are. Some aren't. But I know my dad wasn't stupid. He had a master's degree and was able to fix almost anything in our house. So chalking the gullibility up to *just* a lack of intelligence feels somewhat simplistic.

One thing my family noticed about my dad was that he had always been more gullible than my mother. I remember when we were kids how my younger brother could tell him a tall tale and he would believe it, eyes big as saucers, while my mom would roll her eyes. She heard Rush Limbaugh and read the stuff my dad sent her and lived through the same periods. *Why didn't she believe it while Dad got completely sucked in?* I entertained another possible explanation.

The other thing I remember about my dad was that he was not as introspective as my mother. So I wasn't surprised when I saw that in Ehrenreich's report, he also said "conservatives are less introspective, less attentive to their inner feelings, and less likely to override their 'gut'...and engage in further reflection to find a correct answer."

Ehrenreich, in the same Slate article, "Why Are Conservatives More Susceptible to Believing Lies?" wrote that "finding facts and pursuing evidence and trusting science is part of liberal ideology itself. For many conservatives, faith and intuition and trust in revealed truth appear as equally valid sources of truth." He poses Freud's theory that many of the Right's beliefs are "not merely alternate interpretations of facts but are instead illusions rooted in unconscious wishes."

Heuristics

Ehrenreich said we all use heuristics, or shortcuts in our thought processes, to make decisions quickly. These shortcuts are based on what we *think* we already know. It's a subconscious thing. Using heuristics is a strategy for making decisions quickly, so we use the information most readily available to us. How broad and accurate these shortcuts are dependent on the personality of the reasoner. We may have a confirmation bias, meaning we want to protect what we already know, so we will have *motivated* reasoning in our shortcuts.

After their immersion in right-wing media, so many people who used to be liberals are now conservatives—even extremist conservatives. Did they always have a conservative aspect to their personalities? Were they previously susceptible to group-think or a similar influence to perceive the world with a liberal slant? Perhaps we all have both liberal and conservative tendencies at work in our natures, and one aspect can be nurtured or suppressed depending on our groups, meaning either the media we consume or our tribes of friends and family members.

Exposing News as Fake Doesn't Always Help

Researchers Jonas De keersmaecker and Arne Roets at Ghent University wanted to study how "fake news" can distort people's beliefs even after the stories have been debunked. The example they gave was the fake news story that the pope had endorsed Donald Trump. Even when the story was proven false, people had a hard time rejecting that misinformation. They said there was still a "glow" created around Trump as a candidate. De keersmaecker and Roets's study, published in the journal *Intelligence,* suggested that those who continued to believe certain information after it was proven false had a low cognitive ability. They said this is exactly what is dangerous about fake news and viral misinformation—even when proven false, it still carries impact.

One of the tests they did that I found particularly interesting was they told two groups of people about a fictional woman. They said this woman, a nurse at a local hospital, "was arrested for stealing drugs from the hospital; she has been stealing drugs for two years and selling them on the street in order to buy designer clothes." The test subjects were then asked to rate the woman's traits—they were harsh, of course. Later, they were told that this information about the nurse was not true. Those who rated high in cognitive ability were able to adjust their opinions about her, and the subjects with lower cognitive ability "had more trouble shaking their negative first impression" of her. They were unjustifiably harsh when rating her traits again. This made me think of the false negative TV ads candidates sometimes run against each other or the harsh lies Sean Hannity or Laura Ingraham or Tucker Carlson say about someone who doesn't align with their beliefs. They know it sticks even after proven untrue. I had a friend who even after learning that Hillary Clinton did *not* run a child sex ring out of a pizza parlor could not shake a nefarious impression of her.

The fact that lies are repeated so often and across multiple platforms is even more of a reason someone with low cognitive ability may be resistant to the truth. It's really lodged in their brains!

Research indicates that as people get older, their cognitive ability declines, and they are therefore more vulnerable to fake news. The average age of Fox News viewers is sixty-eight. It has also been shown that with education, people develop "metacognitive skills." They become better able to monitor and reevaluate their own thinking. So more education is somewhat of an inoculation against fake news.

George Lakoff in his interview with us also noted one of the reasons conservatives may be more likely to believe lies:

personality differences. He explained in terms of how people respond to two specific parenting models. Those drawn to conservatism respond positively to the strict father model, while those who are more liberal tend to believe in the nurturant parent model. He said these are metaphors for how one believes the government should be run. The strict father model represents a parent who would raise their children to be more self-reliant, maybe letting a child cry themselves to sleep. The parent, particularly the father, would mete out rewards and punishment. In this model, father knows best, and spanking may be thought to be acceptable. The father is more of an authoritarian. This model, for instance, would never allow their kids to sleep with them as a habit, but the nurturant parent would.

Lakoff said the father "is in charge of the family. He's seen as the moral person. He knows right from wrong, and his job is to protect the family, to support the family, and to teach his kids right from wrong. And in order to do that, he has to maintain his authority, his word, his law. If they get moral discipline, they can go out in the world and become prosperous. If they are not disciplined or moral, they deserve the poverty."

The strict father type believes if you just work hard enough, you will be able to get by. Lakoff continued,

So you've heard the expression "let the market decide," right? What that says is the market is "the decider," as George Bush once said about himself—that the market is a kind of strict father who determines who gets rewarded and who gets punished in the market depending upon their financial discipline. But in addition to that, it says more. It says the market is fundamentally moral and natural. Natural, because people are naturally greedy—that's assumed. And moral because in the conservative interpretation of Adam Smith, if everybody pursues their own self-interest, the self-interest of all will be maximized. So that's seen as conservative morality.

A nurturant parent model assumes a respect for a child's intelligence, so they may be more likely to offer guidance rather than orders, or they may be more likely to pick the child up if they cry. They want the child to feel secure and comfortable talking about their feelings and thoughts, but at the same time, they want them to have self-discipline.

As Lakoff said, "Now, the nurturing parent families are different. If it has both a father and mother, both have equal responsibility. And their job is to empathize with their children. Empathy is the center of this. You have the idea that citizens are there to take care of each other and to empathize with each other and to be responsible both for themselves and for others."

Nurturant parent types believe the government should offer a safety net and a helping hand if needed.

So the way this works in a democracy from a progressive point of view is that the government is an instrument of people who care about other people and who provide what I call "public provisions." That is, they provide the roads and the bridges and the airports so you can move around. They provide public schools so that people can get educated, public health things like meat inspections, the Centers for Disease Control, so you take care of public health. They provide basic research in medicines and in other things. All of the internet was provided through government research, all of the major drugs we have came through government research, which then went into the private sector.

Lakoff feels we have a metaphor that the nation is a family and that in this theory, our moral frameworks shape our political views.

I feel for myself that I am a mix of both. So I asked, is it possible for anybody to have two contradictory views of morality in their brains? Lakoff said, "All over the brain, there are structures called mutual inhibition. That is, there are parts of the brain when the activation of one turns off the other. So when is it the case when people will have two different worldviews and it will shift without noticing it? The answer is Saturday night and Sunday morning. People who go to church on Sunday morning maybe have certain different moral views on Saturday night. And they don't even know that they're doing it. It is a perfectly normal, everyday experience." Some beliefs are just more dominant than others.

★ CHAPTER 13 ★

What We Can Do about Far-Right Media

After my dad passed away and the documentary was released, I traveled around the country to speak at screenings and met many other families who were experiencing strained relationships with their loved ones after their descent into the deviously addictive world of far-right media. Years later, I continue to get (even more) emails and social media messages from people who are distraught and confused about what has happened to their family members or friends. The problem grew worse as the divide between liberal and extremist conservative (which graduated to outright fascist) factions deepened over the COVID-19 pandemic and Donald Trump's refusal to admit to the danger the coronavirus posed to many Americans. The good news is that more people than ever before recognize how dangerous and destructive far-right media is. So what can we do about it?

What We Can Do

The first and most important thing to remember is to have hope. Whenever I feel discouraged about the monumental size of the task in front of us, I lean on my favorite quote from Margaret Mead: "Never doubt that a small group of thoughtful, committed citizens can change the world; indeed, it's the only thing that ever has."

I get a lot out of forming little groups of like-minded people: neighbors, friends, Twitter mates, or Facebook friends who understand how urgent it is to combat the influence of far-right media. You can discuss what you want to do every week and take action together, like an advocacy club. I find you can get more done, have moral support, and have more discipline if you form a group, but for those who don't do groups or can't for one reason or another, there are some actions you can do *either* as a group or as individuals:

1. Call and write to your congressional representatives to raise awareness about the dangers of the far-right media. Bring it up at town halls. The destructive nature of far-right media is rarely addressed as an issue by our representatives. They are often too intimated to bring it up. Make it clear that you need them to do so.

2. Support trustworthy independent media in all ways. Fairness and Accuracy in Reporting and Media Matters have easy-to-do, ready-made actions you can do almost every day that will preserve independent media voices. Join them.

3. Raise awareness of far-right media's effect on people whenever you can, however you can.

   a. If it seems safe to do so, speak up in a public place if someone is spouting hatred or false "facts." Don't let them be the loudest voice in the room.

   b. Ask business owners or public places like bars, doctor offices, gyms, and restaurants to turn off Fox. Explain it is divisive and will offend half their customers. Have zero tolerance. (If it's difficult for you to say something, you can buy and leave FoxOff cards from FoxIsToxic.org.)

   c. If you have older parents who spend a lot of time at home watching Fox or listening to fascist "conservative" talk radio, try to disrupt their media habits. Help them schedule activities to get them out of the house, consider blocking Fox from their TVs, or introduce them to more neutral entertainment channels or news feeds.

4. Contact your local radio stations and demand an end to hate speech and fake news if you live in an area with predominantly right-wing radio.

5. Contact the pundits at TV stations you watch and encourage them to call out far-right media or guests that either filibuster or lie or both.

6. Tell your TV provider to #UnFoxMyCableBox. Even if you never watch Fox News yourself, you are funding their programming through your cable subscription fees. Sixty percent of Fox's profits comes from subscription fees. The other 40 percent comes from advertisers. Visit https://unfoxmycablebox.com/ to learn more.

7. Boycott advertisers that engage with far-right media. Build your campaign on social media and educate them. Note that some media activists believe that corporate advertisers already have too much power over content and don't like empowering them further in letting them decide what or who gets on the air. The other problem is that some advertisers have then backed away from progressive hosts as well. So make it about truth and hate and not politics if you contact advertisers.

8. Fact-check news you see online, especially if it's information that seems to fit with everything else you already believe. Don't post or forward news articles without understanding where they come from and what their biases might be.

9. When you see a lie on social media, use fact-checking sites and politely enlighten and debunk, unless you can tell the poster is a bot or a troll. In that case, report the user and disengage.

10. Join a nationwide progressive advocacy group like Indivisible, Our Revolution, or RootsAction.org and aim to bring their attention to matters of right-wing media.

11. Watch your language. Do not call Fox News and the like "conservative media." Call it what it is: far-right, extreme-right media—even fascist media. Be judicious with how you use the term *the Far Left*. Do not use their language. Do not call Fox "News." Call it Fox Propaganda or Fox Noise or hate-for-profit media, and use the term *corporate media* instead of *liberal media*.

12. Educate yourself on how to talk to Cult Republicans through HearYourselfThink.org. They give workshops. Or read Steven Hassan's book *The Cult of Trump*. In order to evaluate if a group is a cult, Steven Hassan came up with what he calls the BITE model. (Different experts all give slight variations, but basically the characteristics are the same for a group using undue influence.) Hassan, who also wrote the book *Combating Cult Mind Control*, boils the characteristics down to four elements: Behavior Control, Information Control, Thought Control, and Emotional Control.

13. Do not call the *Cult* Republicans conservatives or Republicans. Call them Cult Republicans or the extreme Right. There are some old-school Republicans who no longer recognize their own party, and they deserve our respect.

14. Do not use Republican talking points, and don't fall for gotcha questions or whataboutism with right-wingers.

15. Report fake news on the radio and noncable TV, since they

are broadcast on public airwaves and are supposed to answer
to the FCC. You can write to them at:

Federal Communications Commission

Consumer and Governmental Affairs Bureau

Consumer Inquiries and Complaints Division

45 L Street NE

Washington, DC 20554

888-225-5322

Or file a complaint online: consumercomplaints.fcc.gov.

The Big Stuff

While the actions listed above are excellent steps for individual
people like you and me to take to raise awareness of far-right
media and weaken its power, we ultimately need to see change
in our institutions to make sure media serves its intended purpose—to inform and enlighten the public.

This list is by no means comprehensive. New ideas are being
discussed by media activists every day. You can find the latest
ideas posted on thebrainwashingofmydad.com.

Vermont senator Bernie Sanders is one elected official who
has tried to raise awareness about the importance of media. Some
of his ideas about policies that could improve the integrity of our
media landscape include the following:

- ▸ Stringently enforce antitrust laws.
- ▸ Support journalists' efforts to unionize.
- ▸ Reverse the Trump administration's moves gutting

media ownership rules. Trump allowed even more cross-ownership of media. A reversal would also better protect both local and national independent journalism.

► Before a major merger does occur, give the employees an opportunity, through employee stock-ownership plans, to purchase media outlets.

► Require major media corporations to disclose whether their transactions and mergers will involve significant journalism layoffs.

► Bar mergers or deregulatory actions that would dispro-portionately affect women and people of color as they are "woefully underrepresented" in the media landscape.

► Place a moratorium on mergers.

Additionally, the Center for American Progress suggests three ways to increase localism and diversify radio station own-ership to better meet local and community needs:

► Restore local and national caps on the ownership of commercial radio stations.

► Ensure greater local accountability over radio licensing.

► Require commercial owners who fail to abide by enforceable public interest obligations to pay a fee to support public broadcasting.

Another important step to creating an equitable media land-scape is to expand and restore net neutrality. Under net neutrality, internet providers must treat all internet content and communications equally and cannot charge more for "fast lanes" that prioritize certain content. But the FCC under Ajit Pai voted in 2017 to deregulate broadband/cable companies like Comcast and Verizon (which essentially kills consumer protection). On June 11, 2018, the repeal of the FCC's rules took effect, ending network neutrality regulation in the United States. Now cable companies can monitor what sites you go to and discriminate by slowing down sites that don't pay them. The DC circuit court upheld that FCC decision in 2019 but struck down a part of it, saying states could independently pass their own net neutrality rules. Some states have since enacted their own net neutrality bills.

As of this writing, the seats in the FCC are 2-2. If the Biden administration appoints "an aggressive consumer advocate" to the third seat, it is possible that net neutrality could be restored for the entire country. The new DOJ also dropped the lawsuit the Trump DOJ had against California for implementing net neutrality for their state.

Possible Legislative Actions

The biggest legislative impact would come from reversing the Trump administration's moves to gut media ownership regulation. Mega media mergers have allowed a handful of corporations to act as gatekeepers of information for most Americans over the past two decades. (Soon after the loss of FCC protections, the news became no longer just a public service but a money-making entity.) There are a myriad of problems with conglomerates owning news programming in particular: several major news sources could be owned by one holder; they have the ability to quash stories about other companies within the same holding company; coverage may lean toward political parties that are best for the company, not the viewer; and the temptation would be great to stay away from any story that would damage a major advertiser.

Cross-ownership and consolidated ownership with a handful of corporations owning most mainstream media have contributed to a decline in an informed citizenship and thus our democracy since 1996, when President Clinton "reformed" the Communications Act of 1934. The Telecommunications Act of 1996, which loosened the rules for cross-ownership, was a gift to media hogs, resulting in a narrowing of perspectives and information on which we form our political opinions. We must reinstate ownership caps and enforce antitrust laws.

There are arguments for and against reinstituting the Fairness Doctrine—which was only intended for the public airwaves, not cable, satellite, or the internet, etc. Some think a form of it should be reinstated and codified. Sue Wilson from the Media Action Center believes it should be framed as, and center around, The Right to Respond. She says the right-wing has trained its followers to attack anyone who even mentions the words "Fairness Doctrine," so it's time to use different language, and that we simply need to be able to respond not only to dangerous political speech, but also to personal attacks against which we are currently defenseless. Legislators need to invite various media experts to the table to discuss how it could best be done to emphasize the Fairness Doctrine's original purpose—to encourage news and public affairs programming in the public interest through balanced reporting—and the thought is to extend it beyond public broadcasting. Maybe we even need to rethink what constitutes "public airwaves." If you think about it, satellite TV broadcasts are not regulated, but could they exist without their use of the public airwaves?

There are a few on the left who argue against it as well as many on the right who are against it. Some people on the left who are against the reinstatement of the Fairness Doctrine rightly worry about who would be in charge of determining what fairness means. (The makeup of the FCC can change depending on who is in power, therefore the FCC should not have this power. It is beholden to the industry it oversees. Congress needs to make the rules.) The definition of fairness and the governing body responsible for moderating that balance should be fully transparent and accountable to the American people.

Many on the right say the purpose of reinstating the Fairness Doctrine is to silence voices that those on the left and in the middle don't like, when in reality the liberal voices are the ones that have been stifled by the death of the Fairness Doctrine. In fact, voices would not be silenced at all, because there would be no impact on opinion programming. The real reason right-wingers may be afraid of a reinstatement of the Fairness Doctrine is that it could affect their bottom line and/or ability to influence people in the way that has proven to be very effective—through the addictive nature of anger and fear, the telling of blatant lies, and being the only bully on the block.

As Steve Rendall said in our movie, "We want reform and restructuring, so where it could be done, we would like to see more progressive shows, more balance, more working people, the voices of working people, in our commercial and our public broadcasting."

Another issue: many of us concerned with the rampant and dangerous misinformation and disinformation in news media are especially concerned with those networks or programs that call themselves news. The word *news* itself connotes balance, sources, fairness, impartiality, and being in the public interest. Just as there are labels on food specifying the contents and whether it's natural, organic, or otherwise, we need to take this label more seriously to protect our democracy. So for instance, we all know by now that much of Fox News isn't really news. It's opinion and propaganda. In light of how Fox News deceived its audience during the COVID-19 pandemic, Kurt Eichenwald, *New York Times* bestselling author, tweeted, "Networks like Fox that knowingly spread disinformation about a health crisis should be taken off the air under a declaration of national emergency until the crisis passes. Or there should be a law allowing them to be held liable for broad public damage from their lies."

Another incident indicative of the problem is when a Florida court ruled some years ago that Fox's WTVT (a local Tampa Bay TV channel owned by Fox) did not have to report news accurately, as it was only an FCC rule to do so and not a law. Fox is cable TV (not public airwaves), so the FCC does not apply anyway. But should it really be allowed to call itself news and yet be registered as an entertainment channel (no different than the UFO Files channel)? A federal judge in September 2020 ruled in a defamation case against radical Fox host Tucker Carlson that he can't be sued because he is not a credible source of news. Then "news" should not be part of the name of the network. Again, this would be a challenge to figure out how much opinion is allowed in news and who the arbiter of that is. But it is important enough to try to solve.

Strengthening Nonprofit Media

Another way to combat right-wing bias would be to strengthen nonprofit media. One strategy, popularized by Jeff Cohen and Robert McChesney, relies on permitting tax deductions for contributions to nonprofit media. These tax deductions would enable ordinary Americans and not just those with significant disposable incomes to help create independent alternatives to corporate-run media outlets. We should also encourage wider ranges of media ownership, such as by universities, nonprofit organizations, and employee-owned cooperatives.

The United States spends far less public funds per person on public broadcasting than any other advanced country. As Jeff Cohen said, "Strengthening public broadcasting can be done by setting up a permanent, insulated, government-established trust fund that cannot be turned on or off by Congress. It's like most advanced countries."

Taxing Advertising Spending

Surprisingly, when corporations buy airtime from a broadcast company for advertising, they pay no sales tax on the transaction. Instead, giant corporations get to write off their ad expenses. Media activists Jimmy and India Burns advocate for a strategy for taxing these ad spends. Here is an example of how that might work. If a $5 million slot is taxed at 5 percent, that would result in $250,000 that could go toward a public media fund. This media sales tax could bring in upward of $3.5 billion a year. That would enable public media access stations to truly better serve the public.

Teaching Media Literacy in Our Schools

Children need to be taught to read and write in the new dominant medium of technology. They need to learn not only how to navigate various media sources but also how to construct and deconstruct media they encounter. As an example, they can be taught media tactics—they could learn to understand media manipulation and strategies to influence an audience. Simply by understanding how media is made, they are then taught not to passively consume it.

Best Practices for Journalists

Reporters can avoid reinforcing the effects of the lies by repeating them. A great formula George Lakoff suggests for journalists, reporters, and pundits is what he refers to as the "truth sandwich":

- ▸ Start with the truth. The first frame gets the advantage.
- ▸ Indicate the lie. Avoid amplifying the specific language if possible.
- ▸ Return to the truth. Always repeat the truth more than the lies.

For too long, the Far Right has persuaded journalists that journalism is about balance. But it shouldn't be, as that does a disservice to the public. Journalism is about the truth, objectivity and accuracy. If an argument is overwhelmingly truthful, and there is one lie refuting it, that lie does not merit the same weight in the argument. If that lie is mentioned, it should be framed as a fringe argument. Journalists and pundits must be courageous. When they see fascist tactics, they should name them fascist; when they see a coup attempt, they need to call it as such, etc. Journalists and pundits cannot be buddies with the politicians that they cover (and the political Sunday shows should not have on Republicans who supported the insurrection, as if it didn't happen!)

Good journalists are essential to a democracy and need to be able to freely report on issues. They need to be protected from attacks and from suffering negative consequences based on the angles of their reporting. Many journalists are American heroes who put their lives on the line to bring us the information we need to make informed decisions as a nation.

Using Technocognition

Another possible solution to the fake news phenomenon, proposed by Stephan Lewandowsky, Ullrich Ecker, and John Cook is called *technocognition*. It is about designing technology in a way that minimizes the impact of misinformation.

One of their ideas involves the establishment of an international nongovernmental organization that would create a rating system for disinformation. Some examples that already exist are Climate Feedback, Snopes, and PolitiFact. Of course, the challenge would be to convince right-wingers to accept a neutral arbiter of facts.

An article on Lewandowsky, Ecker, and Cook's study summarized their recommendations by saying, "These independent rulings could then be conveyed via technology. For example, Facebook could flag an article that's based on false information as an unreliable source, and Google could give more weight in returning factually accurate news and information at the top of its search results lists."

A related technique the study's authors have promoted is the inoculation technique. This strategy is focused on dislodging misinformation after it first takes hold and "involves explaining the logical fallacy underpinning a myth. People don't like being tricked, and research has shown that when they learn that an ideologically friendly article has misinformed them by using fake experts, for example, they're more likely to reject the misinformation."

Curbing the Abusive Use of Algorithms

One of the most insidious things that has happened at great speed in the past decade is that many of us are blindly being owned by algorithms.

As techno sociologist Zeynep Tufekci noted in a TED talk, the algorithms that "companies like Facebook, Google, and Amazon use to get you to click on ads are also used to organize your access to political and social information." Outrageously, private media regulators have already started using algorithms to deemphasize alternative news sites like AlterNet and Truthdig.

Algorithms are used to figure out what you like and what your friends like. They are used by advertisers to show you ads they think you are likely to respond to. However, political operatives use algorithms to profile users so they can come up with people who meet some designated demographic (single Black women raising two kids who are in charter schools and live in South Florida, for example). In 2016, Facebook embedded their employees in political campaigns to advise them on how to use algorithms for the 2020 election. After a backlash, Facebook said it would temporarily suspend political advertising after Election Day, "but researchers and political strategists say campaigns can still use Facebook to target the voters that they do—and don't—want to vote." Also in 2016, Trump's "campaign used data from Cambridge Analytica and other sources to identify Black voters who they thought could be dissuaded from voting. To do that, the campaign identified groups of users as Black, as voters, as living in swing states, and, finally, as persuadable. They flooded their Facebook feeds with negative ads."

Conversely, the practice of suggesting new videos with automated recommendations at the end of previously watched videos can radicalize and suck conspiracy theorists further down a rabbit hole. Author and technology columnist for the *New York Times* Kevin Roose also says that "software plays a huge role in what people watch," and it has been suggested that they stop this practice.

Moving Forward Together

The damage done by the forty-year rise of far-right, fascist media is so far-reaching and insidious (and multiplying daily), it sometimes feels like the damage done is insurmountable to overcome. But what choice do we have but to try?

Let's face it. War has been waged against the American people by Cult Republicans who gave up the principles of their party and became puppets for the plutocrats and megacorporations who used dark money and division to disenfranchise majority rule. It's past time to realize that the American dream has been insidiously attacked from the inside. We need to call it what it was and is: a vast, far-right conspiracy.

I hope we can all eventually find peace in our families and as a nation, but that will not happen if we do not address the problems within our media that have become blatantly obvious and destructive over the past few years. Humans are the frog in the pot with the flame under it—they don't realize they have to get out until they're being boiled.

Arguably, one of the United States' greatest strengths is our commitment to free speech, as enshrined in the First Amendment. To us Americans, freedom of speech represents our freedom and democracy. But the very thing we value as representing our democracy is being abused to destroy it. Unfortunately, lies and "alternative facts" have been allowed to creep into the American concept of free speech. This has left us all feeling captive in defending lies as a part of free speech. Allowing Murdoch and Fox News and other right-wing outlets to propagate lies and hatred over broadcast and cable has divided the country to such an extent that it led to an insurrection. We have to find a way to deal with this head-on before it's too late, if it's not too late already. (Not to be a downer.) Maybe we should look at other democracies that are still democracies and able to curb hate speech? It's something to think about.

But if we really open our eyes and seize this moment, we can work together as the people's voice and persist; we can get the change we need for a better country. Let's love one another instead of trying to take each other down. We are all on the same team ultimately. Let's also not depend so much on what any media tells us. Do our own research when we can.

My mother was able to repair our relationship with my father through love, patience, humor, and, I admit, a little trickery. (Not saying anyone else should do it.) Sometimes circumstances are such that you just can't save someone, and you must save yourself instead. You know what I'm talking about. But instead of blaming those you can't save, realize they've been bamboozled by a very sophisticated propaganda machine—which makes the conspiracy theorists blame the very people trying to save them.

The media is owned by just a handful of billionaires. We need this monopoly to be broken up and diversified. For the sake of our country, our families, and our survival, let's all of us (left, right, and center) act together to demand a more honest and equitable media landscape from our government and from our media companies. Let's make America great. It will never be perfect, but it can be better. Let's do it.

★ CHAPTER 14 ★

Your Stories

I have had so many people reach out to me over the years to share their own brainwashing stories that it has sometimes been a bit overwhelming. Today, the issues we outlined in our film have only been exacerbated by Donald Trump's time in office. The right-wing media's divisive tactics have been let off the leash, so the number of people witnessing changes in their loved ones and destructive divisions within their families expanded exponentially. Some of these stories are from a bit back ago, but they are still relatable today and show how it started. For the latest stories about family members lost to QAnon, go to thebrainwashingofmydad.com.

In an effort to show just how far the divide has come, I collected some of the many personal stories sent to me by people hoping to quell their heartache by sharing their despair at no longer being able to communicate with their loved ones. The stories are about their damaged relationships with fathers, mothers, sisters, brothers, cousins, husbands, wives, and friends.

Many people have found comfort in discovering that they are not alone. Right-wing media has strained relationships all over the country, in every community and demographic. I hope all those families can find peace and perhaps even get or do some deprogramming, as my own family did. As a final note of hope, I am also including a collection of testimonials from other families who successfully deprogrammed or found reconciliation with loved ones and were able to reclaim their relationships.

MARIA, FLORIDA

For me, it's my aunt and uncle. I was living nearer to them than I am now, and so we had Thanksgiving dinner together. My uncle was eighty at the time. We didn't usually talk politics because my views are liberal and my uncle was a hard-core Rush Limbaugh fan. But President Obama had just come into office, and the economy was in the toilet. I felt it was safe to discuss the economy because clearly President Obama couldn't have had anything to do with it—it was too soon. My uncle got very upset and started to rant about the president. I said this economy has nothing to do with him. He said, "You get out of my house. You can't stay here and talk to me about that guy!" So I said, "Don't be ridiculous. I'm not going anywhere."

He got up and came over to me as if to drag me [out]. My aunt stood up and got in the middle of us and said, "No, please don't do that!" He reached around her and smacked me in the face! I left the table. My aunt followed me, and we went into another room. She tried to comfort me, but he heard us and came down the stairs and said, "I told you to get out!" As he got to the bottom of the stairs, he raised his right hand, and I could see that he was holding a small pistol. He walked closer to me. I was shaken and said, "What are you doing? I'm going to call the police!" He dropped his hand and shot two rounds into the floor, and that was it. I never went back.

TOM (FORMER REPUBLICAN), NEW JERSEY

I first encountered [right-wing media] in the early '90s. My dad had retired in the late '80s. Finding time on his hands, he would use the radio to keep him company. This is where he, like so many others like him, discovered Rush Limbaugh.

Rush was catnip for an elderly Greatest Generation man. Spewing hate against those supposedly destroying our country that he had fought in World War II for.

Dad started visiting my house with books he had ordered from the Conservative Book Club that was advertised relentlessly on Rush's show. The books were all about the nefarious deeds of the Clintons. Including, yes, all the political opponents they had purportedly killed. He asked me to read them. I told him I would—after he had himself. He never did, of course. The message was all he cared about spreading. He was an Evangelical Christian. And prophesying was comfortable to him. And also made him easy prey for Rush.

I was a Republican at the time. Had voted for Bush Sr. in 1988 and 1992. Most of my fellow Republicans at that time still saw this stuff as fringe, if not outright lunacy. Those were the golden days that reasonable Republicans now look back on with despair today.

Ordering those books put him on a shared mailing list among conservative groups. After the onset of dementia, my sister and I had to take control and get a handle on his finances and mail. He would receive between ten and thirty mail solicitations a day. It turned out he was sending various groups between $200 and $350 a month—despite being a senior citizen on a fixed income with minimal investment assets.

His favorite "contributee" was Judicial Watch. An organization that today still thrives. They were relentless then and now in an endless attempt to investigate anything and everything "Clinton."

This was the right-wing hate machine that Hillary Clinton spoke of. I never believed it would morph into what it is today— what I commonly refer to as the right-wing hate machine version 2.0. The party of Breitbart and Trump. Which makes the original version 1.0 look like a diversity training seminar.

I have a family member who inevitably went 100 percent all in on the anti-Muslim sentiment and signed on to the resentment of the "ungrateful" Blacks and is all in on the White, Christian, ethnic nationalism messaging.

This is a person, mind you, of gentle heart and soul. However, they are emotionally needy. Needing something to grasp onto for anchoring. Driven greatly by fear.

Now they are a heart captured by hate.

My spirit weeps for the hearts they stole from me, within my own family, in my own home, while I was sleeping.

And that is why I am a former Republican. #MyPartyWas HijackedByWhackJobs

AMANDA, TEXAS

Five years ago, my father and my stepmother became involved with an RV camping group. They were retired, and that was their means of staying social. At that time, we noticed hateful and fearful conversations coming from them. Once we were able to track it back, we determined that it was from what they were watching on TV. It was Fox News. They spent hours watching it daily, and we noticed their language and their demeanor, their attitude all changed within a short span of five years.

My father and my stepmother used to be very loving and very caring, patient, very kindhearted individuals, and so we noticed when they became more hostile toward people not believing the way they did. Their conversation became very hateful.

I am mainly conservative. My husband and I have guns, but with my father and stepmother, it wasn't just a political view, it was a hostility toward the government and hatred toward different individuals that I had never seen before. They spent a lot of time on the gun range and had other weapons for protecting themselves. One Thanksgiving, they wanted my five- and ten-year-old girls to go with them to the gun range. I did not want them to go. My autistic child voted for Obama in her school election, and my dad said something like "Don't you dare." He unfriended me on Facebook. So they don't really have a need for us anymore because we don't believe what they believe. My ten-year-old is hurt and asks why they don't love her anymore.

DONNA, NASSAU COUNTY, LONG ISLAND

I grew up in a relatively conservative working-class White family on Long Island. Growing up, it was my mom, my four siblings, and I—all considerably older than me. My father had been a cop, and my eldest brother also became a cop. Eventually, my middle sister would as well. My mom was a lifelong Republican, and my siblings mostly all followed suit. But this wasn't some kind of hard-core ideological Republicanism. In fact, the way it played out was pretty varied: my mom was always pro-choice; we were Christian but not defensive about it; my eldest sister was pretty liberal and in the '90s was a big fan of the Clintons; my middle sister, always more conservative, would still criticize the televangelists of the day as hypocrites and defend the National Organization for Women to my mom, who called them "a bunch of crazy radicals."

We used to watch the Channel 7 news every night at dinner and read *Newsday* or the *Daily News*. We were a pretty raucous group, not shying away from arguments or giving each other shit over one thing or another—especially as I got older and began to develop my own, considerably more liberal political opinions. There were plenty of family arguments about various issues, but we all seemed to agree on the same basic set of facts. At various times in my life, I felt very close to both of my sisters. I always felt that even though we disagreed on certain issues—sometimes strongly, as in the case of the Gulf War—we were operating in the same reality, and we could relate to each other with kindness and humor in spite of our differences.

At some point in the early 2000s, my mom and sisters started watching Fox News, eventually to the exclusion of other news sources, although more recently, they have discovered some far-right websites like the Daily Caller and others. Over time, their views became harsher (drug addicts living in shelters were "losers," outspoken liberals were "pieces of shit"), and their views more extreme and often offered with little or no evidence to back them up (Hillary Clinton regularly has her political opponents assassinated, the Syrian refugee crisis is a secret Muslim plot to "infiltrate" the United States, and of course the "war on Christianity").

The degree of anger has been the most shocking thing. Both of my sisters are retired from good jobs and have good pensions and health insurance for the rest of their lives. They have made more money than I ever will and enjoy benefits I will never get. Yet one would think that their very lives are being threatened on a continual basis, so intense is the anger I've seen—at undocumented immigrants, at Black Lives Matter activists, at any liberal celebrity who speaks out against Donald Trump.

I think most painful to me has been seeing my middle sister, who stood by me and supported me when I was sexually assaulted as a child and who once considered becoming a sex-crimes police officer, defending men credibly accused of sexual assault. In her view, Bill O'Reilly and Donald Trump are victims of a liberal plot to drag them down—although, of course Harvey Weinstein and Eric Schneiderman are guilty as charged. A close second in terms of personal hurt is the strong sense that if my sisters didn't already know me, these days, they wouldn't want anything to do with me. Liberals are the enemy, the source of essentially everything wrong in America. And someone like me, who defends groups like Black Lives Matter and questions capitalism—forget it. Considering the anger I've experienced coming from someone I know who has genuinely loved me, I can only imagine what it would be like if I was just some random person expressing those opinions.

These days, we mostly just give each other space. We send birthday and Christmas greetings, but I often avoid family gatherings, except when my mother is up visiting from Florida. I've tried talking to each of them about various issues, carefully choosing my words, policing my tone, and lining up my evidence, and inevitably, they will drop the discussion. I try to keep myself open to connecting in what ways I can, but most often I find myself seeking the comfort and familiarity of those I can relate to without so much anxiety—my "chosen family" of friends and spiritual community.

MICHAEL (FORMER REPUBLICAN), TEXAS

I was positive that once Hillary Clinton won and became president in November 2016, the madness that I had seen descend on my fellow Republicans and fellow conservatives would finally be lifted. The 2016 election cycle had strained many relationships that my wife and I had built up over the years. I was shocked that we were in the minority of the people we went to church with and our neighbors. How could people be accepting this as the new normal?

When I ran for office, first for Congress and then for justice of the peace, I expected that the vast majority of my friends, neighbors, and church members would put away their politics to help a friend. I was thinking that people I would need to help me block walk, phone bank, and write postcards would come from friendships I had built over the years. None of them did. A few of them even campaigned for my opponent, even though they would have loved to vote for me if I were "still a Republican."

There were a few Republicans who had personally been sued by my opponent and had vowed to vote for and even campaign for me if he won the primary. When he won, they changed their mind because, and I quote, "voting red is more important than what happened to me personally." It was at this point that I realized there is a lot more than ideology at work with these people. It is like they have joined a cult.

Since the election of Donald Trump, this cultlike mindset has even gotten worse. We had a neighbor of ours who we have known for years ask us to leave their property and never come back because of our political and religious views. Just to give you some context of this shift, when this neighbor's wife went into labor early, it was my wife who delivered their baby.

Over the course of two years, my wife and I have lost many connections we thought were unbreakable. The good news is we have made so many newer ones and have been so blessed in my run for office as a Democrat, even when I had only been one for two days. The irrationality, the anger, and the tribalism that are so actively promoted by the right-wing media have done tremendous damage to this country. I am hopeful that we are able to reverse it.

MARIE, CALIFORNIA

Hi. My story is about one of my three brothers. I don't know if his demeanor can be completely blamed on Fox News, but I can definitely say he has the same anger, hatred, and uncaring attitude shown in your film.

It makes so much sense. I've been wondering, *Why do Repubs hate Hillary Clinton so much? How did we get Trump as pres? And what about the strong support for him?* No matter what he says, does, or has done, his supporters do not question or think anything other than "He's going to fix things."

I've had contentious, angry conversations with my brother about Obamacare, the Russia investigation, immigrants. He gets so angry that the only way I get through it is to laugh at him. He told me that if I can't afford health insurance (I'm single, support myself, and have Obamacare through Covered California), I have no right to have it. When I asked, "What if I get cancer? How would I pay for the treatment?" he said, "That's your problem. You would have to pay for it yourself." The meanness has been progressing over the last fifteen-plus years, and with Trump as pres, he is worse and more insulting to me—especially since I'm a Democrat and live in California, a combination not acceptable for any Trump/Fox News loyalist.

ANONYMOUS

I thought when our forty-fifth president (Trump) made fun of the disabled reporter (my daughter has special needs), my father would condemn him. When forty-five talked about grabbing women by the p*ssy, I thought surely my father, who is the father of a daughter and grandfather of two granddaughters, would condemn him.

But no, he makes excuses. We don't talk about it anymore, or much of anything else. It is heartbreaking, but I always knew him to be kind, compassionate, and loving. We had diverse family friends. We don't now. I just do not know what went wrong.

I defriended him on Facebook after he posted a photo of the plane hitting the Twin Towers that said, "Ask me if I give a shit about your Muslim ban." That photo was just pure propaganda. I replied, "Considering the ban is not in place due to any of the countries the 9/11 terrorists came from, I see this meme to be inaccurate." We parted ways after that.

I see what is happening as a moral stand, and if I lived in 1943 and my parents were Nazi sympathizers, I would have abandoned the relationship.

PAM, MISSOURI

My father voted Republican, and so did some of my friends. But it never became a hot topic; voting was just something citizens did. My friends didn't especially hate the military, and most of us identified with John Lennon's message much more than "Sweet Home Alabama."

Now, in the fifteen or so years since Fox took off the gloves and ceded the liberal cable position to MSNBC, the change in my friends is shocking. A high school reunion is marred by old friends who sneer and call me out because I vote Democrat. I point out that they have a pension thanks to their lifelong membership in a union, and they call me a commie. Men my age who dodged the draft religiously in the '60s and never volunteered for service now say any disagreement about American military strategy is an attack on the "fine men" in the military. There is no pleasant sharing a beer and conversation. Social events are minefields, as if the cheerful optimistic nature of our youth has been drained out of them.

A dear friend from the punk rock days now introduces me to new acquaintances as "my friend, the liberal," with a tone that implies she has to hold her nose to tolerate me. It is bizarre.

The common thread in this shift from laid-back tolerance is talk radio and Fox News. The seismic shift seems to have been the Iran-Contra hearings, when some of us saw Fawn Hall and Oliver North as sneaky, lying, seditious right-wing creeps. But others saw them as loyal to Reagan, Kissinger, and Haig. Cable news and Fox especially. The folks who listened to Rush Limbaugh for laughs, like me, turn out to have friends that bought his entertainment shtick. Now the divide is so wide, social events require warnings, quick whispers to watch out for the moment they get drunk enough to start in on the evil Clintons or whatever.

It's a lonely world for a Midwestern, older liberal.

ANONYMOUS

I think Fox is elder abuse. Ailes targeting those over fifty-five demonstrates that he knew exactly what he was after. That is no different than thieves marking a house that looks likely to be some senior's home.

LAURIE

My in-laws watch Faux Spews. I'm working on my bachelor's degree at age fifty-seven. My husband said something about the worst issue in this country now. Most of us might say "poverty" or "unemployment." My MIL replied "college." I told my husband a few days after that it was a very hurtful comment to me. He said, "Oh, she heard on Fox News that many Antifa members are college students." I replied, "Well, I don't watch that crap. How would I know?" Believe me, most college students are too busy working on assignments to be at every rally!

Testimonials of Successful Deprogramming

ZOSIA, CALIFORNIA

My husband was reasonably interested in politics, but around the time President Obama got elected, he started watching Fox News. Accidentally watching for a couple of minutes turned into tuning in to selected segments, and soon he was watching one to three hours a day. We both were working long hours; I thought TV was his way to chill out. Everybody needs a break. I didn't pay attention.

Within a couple of months, however, I found that he started

to change: from a nice, happy, friendly guy I always knew into an angry, resentful person, fearful of unspecified horrible restrictions prepared for guys like him by people like Obama or Hillary Clinton.

Once, he ordered a large batch of ammo for his hunting rifle, as he got convinced new rules would soon make ammo impossible to buy. Often I would hear from him the most surrealistic "news" he heard on Fox.

I realized he got psychotic after watching too much intense hate-filled shows on Fox News. I knew he needed to be cut off from the source of his psychosis; otherwise, anything could happen. So I canceled our cable, explaining that it's a waste of time and money, we could use this time much better, and all the info can be found on the internet anyway.

First weeks were rough. He was going through withdrawal: confused, angry, and easily triggered by anything. I tried not to notice his moods, offering activities we could do together: biking, going for a road trip, playing chess, doing home DIY projects, even hunting (I hate hunting!).

Slowly, he regained his old, nice personality. It took a couple of months until he got interested in his usual hobbies more than Fox shows.

He followed Trump's 2016 campaign. By that time, however, he was able to differentiate between made-up TV stories and the real world. Even if he rooted for Trump, he didn't vote, and after Trump fired Rex Tillerson, his comment was "Trump is crazy."

This is when I knew he was truly released from the Fox spell.

SARA, PANHANDLE, FLORIDA

I remarried two years after the death of my husband. The man I married had been an acquaintance of my husband and I assumed had similar ideas about things as they had participated in some political events together. We had two small houses. I sold mine and moved in with him. When I moved in with him, I quickly realized things were not at all as I had imagined. He was addicted to Fox News and was on numerous Facebook and email sites such as Oath Keepers, American News, Breitbart, Drudge, and Newsmax. The usual fare for this area of northwest Florida.

We would get into arguments when Fox was on, and I would try to explain what they were saying wasn't true. I also wouldn't be in the room if Fox was on. There wasn't a lot of space for me to retreat to, so I bought a big house on the other side of town.

I moved out.

I watched the documentary and then decided to try it. Your movie is one of the most important I've seen to highlight just how far down the rabbit hole we're falling. They're sowing the seeds of anger among an unstable, overly medicated, and undereducated population.

Each week, I deleted a "conservative" subscription from his email and added a progressive one in its place. Ring of Fire, Salon, the *Guardian*, Daily Kos, Join the Coffee Party. They weren't obvious by title. I also signed him up for Democracy Now and Truthdig. TYT [The Young Turks] is one of his favorites now. My husband now adores Bernie Sanders. He campaigned for him, phone banked, and went to the local DNC chapter to cast his ballot for a Bernie-friendly delegate to the convention in Philadelphia. It saved our marriage. We bought a house together and have lived in it now for three years.

So he's transitioned from a meat-eating, alt-right, if-you-don't-like-America-leave-it conservative to an almost-vegan, can't-we-just-leave-the-brown-people-in-peace, no-wall progressive who thinks Alexandria Ocasio-Cortez, Tulsi Gabbard, and Bernie Sanders are the only good politicians! He also wants to save the earth and whales and hates guns.

I'm still working on my father. It's that damned Fox News I cannot get him off. He's also a gun nut who receives tons of propaganda from the NRA. It's a little tougher project than the husband!

From the phony war for Panamanian independence to the current rhetoric involving Iran, the percentage of people who question anything is so small that it's terrifying. And it costs lives, both at home and abroad. It's killing the planet. If we can't figure out how to wake people up, the future looks pretty bleak.

STEVE DICUS (SELF-DEPROGRAMMED), TENNESSEE

So at first, I listened to thirty minutes of Rush Limbaugh, and I just didn't like him because he was critical to Clinton. But I had about an hour-and-fifteen-minutes commute to a factory two times over where I work. And I drove mid-day to the factory, and I would catch the last hour of his show on the radio. I ended up just immersing myself. I voted straight Republican. Clinton was more corrupt than Nixon. Clinton was part of this Global

Initiative to get to UN to control our country. Clinton is going to bring UN troops and take our guns and put dissidents in concentration camps.

Then one day I was playing around with the radio dial while I was driving in for work, and I found *Wait Wait...Don't Tell Me!* on NPR. Never really listened to this before. So I discovered they had great shows on the weekends and throughout the week. I stopped listening to Hannity and switched to *All Things Considered*. I'm not going to say that NPR has a left or liberal bias, but I think their journalism is solid. Basically, comparing the quality of how the information is presented and what I was being told, I could start seeing the right-wing talk radio as what it is: propaganda.

MELISSA (SELF-DEPROGRAMMED), MARYLAND

My "aha!" media moment was probably sometime in 2009, when Sarah Palin was a Fox consultant. I had the news on while chopping vegetables for dinner, and she was asked a simple question. I heard her reply and stopped what I was doing. I slowly turned around to face the television. With dread and fear, I used my remote to rewind so I could hear her answer again.

I remember saying out loud, "Noooo... Is it possible? The liberals were right all along?"

My question to myself was, How could someone fully engaged in politics and who watches four to five hours of news daily not know that Sarah Palin couldn't form a coherent thought? My conclusion: Fox had to be making a concerted effort to hide it from me. That's when I started switching to other news outlets. It was a long road, but that certainly was the beginning of the end of FNN for me.

LORETTA, BROOKLYN, NEW YORK

My mom was a homemaker who never concerned herself with politics at all: high school education, immigrant parents, growing up in an old-fashioned working-class Italian neighborhood.

She voted for "whomever Daddy says." She just adopted his views because he had to be right.

Daddy was a Republican. In fact, in 1960, he took me into the voting booth to pull down the brass tabs and pull the lever.

Turns out the first time I voted, it was for Nixon.

He had Fox on all the time. She hated that they just yelled at each other. She would put her hands over her ears and say, "Stop yelling." But she never turned the channel.

After my father died, I switched her over to MSNBC and CNN. She also wanted a radio talk show for what she called "nice conversation." I set her up with NPR. She started paying attention and started developing her own different opinions for the first time in her life.

She took a liking to President Obama. She said he was intelligent and he spoke quietly. She thought Bush was "a dum-dum."

One evening, we were watching TV and eating cookies, and there was that usual group of saggy old White Republicans, McConnell, Graham, the whole gang, talking about birth control and abortion. Not a female in sight.

Out of nowhere, she says, "What are these old men talking about? What do they know about what a woman needs?"

I believe I dropped my cookies.

This was the awakening of my mom.

DAVID WEISSMAN, FLORIDA

I was a Trump supporter and voter. When I got into politics after 9/11, I began to watch Fox News, because growing up as a conservative, that was the station being on at home. I, also being religious, thought the people at Fox News had very similar views as I did. So I never thought they would lie to me. I had branched out to other conservative news networks and really took in their indoctrination and hatred of Democrats, immigrants, Muslims, and even the group Black Lives Matter.

After knowing I could have a respectful dialogue about Trump with progressive comedian Sarah Silverman, I began asking questions about liberal values, wondering why they believed in the things they did, like why do they care more about illegal aliens than the military, or why do they want to take our guns away. Through the dialogue with her and a lot of others, I've learned that conservative media was wrong. I've also learned they were wrong about Democratic politicians like President Obama and Hillary Clinton. Everything I believed turned out to be false because I learned it was fear-based that turned to hate. Dems weren't taking away our rights; they were fighting for the rights of others.

This led me to question, were they wrong about Trump?

And they were. He was not the patriotic businessman I thought I voted for; he was a corrupt draft dodger who aligned himself with a corrupt Republican Party.

Acknowledgments

Thanks above all to my dad for being supportive of my unconventional path in life and my filmmaking and for allowing me to capture in film the return to his wonderful self, all of which made this book possible. Huge and loving thanks to my mom for rescuing my dad and making the film and the book not only possible but with a happy ending. Thanks also to her for answering all kinds of questions about my dad and their life for when I wasn't around. Thanks, Mom, for reading an early draft of my book and your helpful notes. Thanks also to my brother, Greg Moores (lost to COVID Jan. 6 2021. I will miss him.), historian and writer, for an early read, accuracy check of history, and for writing tips. I very much appreciated the patience of my cousin Patricia on my father's side for answering so many questions about the Senko past.

I owe a lot to author and friend Joselin Linder for practically holding my hand during the process early on in getting a book proposal together. Then I threw questions at her like one of those softball throwing machines at a batting range, and she took the time to answer each one with careful thought.

For his steadfast support, patience with me, and fact-checking whenever I needed it, I could not have done the film or the book without the help of the incredible Jeff Cohen. He is my mentor and hero. I thank his friend Crystal Zevon for introducing us. And I thank Jeff for introducing me to his friend, professor, author, and media activist Robert W. McChesney, who I also bugged with questions. Jeff played a big role in the film as consulting producer and almost instantly answering my questions having to do with this book. Another person I interviewed for the film who helped answer my incessant questions for whom I am grateful is Thom Hartmann. Though his interview did not make it into the film, Mike Lofgren, former Republican staffer and author, allowed me to pepper him with questions as well.

I also thank Sue Wilson, "badass activist journalist," media watchdog at SueWilsonReports.com, who has always answered questions when I wasn't clear about something. Her film *Broadcast Blues* is what made me aware of the importance of the Telecommunications Act. By the same token, thanks to director and producer Frances Causey. Her film *Heist: Who Stole the American Dream* educated me and made me aware of the Lewis Powell memo.

For allowing me to pepper her with questions about the

Religious Right, many thanks to Anne Nelson, author of *Shadow Network*.

Thank you to all the experts who appear in the film and book who allowed me to interview them and pick their brains. Thank you also to Bobby Kirk, a Facebook friend who gave advice and sacrificed his weekend and a couple of days to read an early version of the entire manuscript. His comments encouraged me, and his notes were just what I needed at that time.

I also am truly moved by the patriotic military captain who took the time to educate me further about psychological tactics, specifically psyops.

Thank you to media consultant and documentarian Jillian Hurley, who jumped in last minute to read the section on possible legislative actions and reminded me of some very important points to make.

For all the years, from the time I started the film and since then, of voluntary research and unending support, I warmly thank David Dudine. I also thank my dear friend Melodie Bryant for early- and late-stage editing help. Thank you to my film editor and friend Käla Mandrake for her valuable input and for really getting me!

For various contributions here and there, I warmly thank my Facebook friend Thomas C. Kahn and all the other people who generously allowed me to use their stories.

Thank you to my editor, Anna Michels, for believing in my vision.

For some initial editing: Miracle Jones, a.k.a. Justin Humphries.

Thanks especially to John Oaks of Or Books for recommending Justin Humphries to me, but especially for an introduction to my wonderful agent, Tina Pohlman. And thank you to Medea Benjamin for introducing me to John Oaks. Thank you to Jodie Evans for introducing me to Medea! Thanks to my good friend, Patrick McDermott for exploring and arguing some issues with me. It was helpful.

Thank you to Gretchen Crary for help with the proposal early on. I met Gretchen on Facebook through Tobin Smith. Thanks to Tobin Smith and Steven Hassan for reaching out to me and then being able to learn even more from you both and allowing me to quote from your books.

Special thanks to Joshua Stern for always believing in me and always encouraging me.

Thanks to my friends and relatives who are friends for being patient with me for telling them I can't talk while working on this book: Amy, Patrick, Robin, Charlie, Arley, Merle, Steve, Tommy, Elaine, Patricia, and Anna-Mária Vág.

Notes

The Great Depression, the New Deal, and the Nazi Propaganda That Paved the Way for Extreme Right-Wing Media

"During the 1920s": Kimberly Amadeo, "1920s Economy: What Made the Twenties Roar," The Balance, updated April 13, 2020, https://www.the balance.com/roaring-twenties-4060511.

"In a market": "Comparing Economies: Traditional, Command, Market, and Mixed," Cheney268, accessed November 4, 2020, http://www.cheney 268.com/chs/HSSS/Hibbs/assessment/comparing_economies.htm.

"The Republican party": Encyclopaedia Britannica Online, s.v. "Presidents of the United States," updated July 17, 2019, https://www.britannica.com/topic /Presidents-of-the-United-States-1846696.

"Though there were": Encyclopaedia Britannica Online, s.v. "Great Depression," by Richard H. Pells and Christina D. Romer, updated September 10, 2020, https://www.britannica.com/event/Great-Depression.

"Billions of dollars": Harold Bierman Jr., "The 1929 Stock Market Crash," EH.net, updated March 26, 2008, https://eh.net/encyclopedia/the-1929 -stock-market-crash/.

"Many folks rushed": Britannica, "Great Depression."

"Unemployment levels rose": Kimberly Amadeo, "Unemployment Rate by Year Since 1929 Compared to Inflation and GDP," The Balance, updated September 17, 2020, https://www.thebalance.com/unemployment-rate-by-year-3305506.

"President Hoover believed": Bierman, "1929 Stock Market Crash."

"The jobless and homeless": Britannica, "Great Depression."

"FDR's first move": Stephen Greene, "Emergency Banking Act of 1933," Federal Reserve History, updated November 22, 2013, https://www.federalreservehistory.org/essays/emergency_banking_act_of_1933.

"Within his first": D. D. Guttenplan, *The Next Republic: The Rise of a New Radical Majority* (New York: Seven Stories, 2018), 193.

"Many of the laws": Encyclopaedia Britannica Online, s.v. "New Deal," updated September 10, 2020, https://www.britannica.com/event/New-Deal.

"The Communications Act": Encyclopaedia Britannica Online, s.v. "Communications Act of 1934," by Robert Gobetz, updated June 12, 2020, https://www.britannica.com/event/Communications-Act-of-1934.

"Day by day": Britannica, "Great Depression."

"economic royalists": Franklin D. Roosevelt, "Acceptance Speech for the Renomination for the Presidency, Philadelphia, Pa.," June 27, 1936, The American Presidency Project, transcript, https://www.presidency.ucsb.edu/documents/acceptance-speech-for-the-renomination-for-the-presidency-philadelphia-pa.

"Adolf Hitler was born": Encyclopaedia Britannica Online, s.v. "Adolf Hitler," by John Lukacs, Alan Bullock, and Wilfrid F. Knapp, updated April 26, 2020, https://www.britannica.com/biography/Adolf-Hitler.

"unrelenting propaganda": Britannica, "Adolf Hitler."

"the Jews" and *"like a disease"*: Timothy Snyder, "How Hitler Pioneered 'Fake News,'" New York Times, October 16, 2019, https://www.nytimes.com/2019/10/16/opinion/hitler-speech-1919.html.

"propaganda organs": Snyder, "How Hitler Pioneered 'Fake News.'"

"task is not": "Nazi Propaganda," United States Holocaust Memorial Museum, accessed November 20, 2018, https://encyclopedia.ushmm.org/content /en/article/nazi-propaganda.

"must confine itself": Snyder, "How Hitler Pioneered 'Fake News.'"

"the broad masses": Adolf Hitler, *Mein Kampf,* trans. James Murphy (London: Hurst and Blackett, 1939), http://gutenberg.net.au/ebooks02/0200601 .txt.

"Hitler met the writer": *Encyclopaedia Britannica Online,* s.v. "Joseph Goebbels," by Helmut Heiber, updated October 25, 2020, https://www.britannica .com/biography/Joseph-Goebbels.

"What the press": C. N. Trueman, "Radio in Nazi Germany," History Learning Site, March 9, 2015, https://www.historylearningsite.co.uk/nazi-germany /radio-in-nazi-germany/.

"the still-new": Trueman, "Radio in Nazi Germany."

"designed to mobilize": "Nazi Propaganda."

"a treasonable offense": Trueman, "Radio in Nazi Germany."

"If you tell": "Big lie," Wikipedia, updated November 5, 2020, https:// en.wikipedia.org/wiki/Big_lie.

"Avoid abstract ideas": Garth S. Jowett and Victoria J. O'Donnell, *Propaganda and Persuasion,* 4th ed. (Thousand Oaks, CA: Sage, 2006), 230.

"In the 1920s": Jennie Rothenberg Gritz, "Early Warnings: How American Journalists Reported the Rise of Hitler," *The Atlantic,* March 13, 2012, https://www.theatlantic.com/national/archive/2012/03/early-warnings -how-american-journalists-reported-the-rise-of-hitler/254146/.

"most German Jews": Leon Botstein, "Why Jews Didn't Leave Europe," *Orchestra of Exiles,* PBS, April 14, 2013, https://www.pbs.org/wnet/orchestra-of -exiles/why-jews-didnt-leave-europe/.

"In 1934": *Britannica,* "Adolf Hitler."

"By 1944": "75th Anniversary of the End of WWII," National WWII Museum, accessed September 29, 2020, https://www.nationalww2museum.org /war/topics/75th-anniversary-end-world-war-ii.

"The GI Bill": "The G.I. Bill," History.com, updated June 7, 2019, https://www
.history.com/topics/world-war-ii/gi-bill.

The Right Is Declared Dead

"Then, on November": "November 22, 1963: Death of the President," John F.
Kennedy Presidential Library and Museum, accessed December 3, 2019,
https://www.jfklibrary.org/learn/about-jfk/jfk-in-history/november-22
–1963-death-of-the-president.

"President Kennedy died": *All Things Considered*, "Walter Cronkite on the
Assassination of John F. Kennedy," hosted by Melissa Block and
Robert Siegel, aired November 22, 2013, on NPR, https://www.npr.org
/transcripts/246628793.

"Those whose jobs": "Cronkite on the Assassination."

"Buchanan has been called": Sam Tanenhaus, "The Architect of the Radical
Right," The Atlantic, July/August 2017, https://www.theatlantic.com/
magazine/archive/2017/07/the-architect-of-the-radical-right/528672.

"In 1963, the country": "Congress Profiles: 88th Congress (1963–1965),"
History, Art & Archives, United States House of Representatives, accessed
November 4, 2019, https://history.house.gov/Congressional-Overview
/Profiles/88th/.

"Former Arizona senator": Larry J. Sabato, "How Goldwater Changed Campaigns
Forever," *Politico Magazine*, October 27, 2014, https://www.politico.com
/magazine/story/2014/10/barry-goldwater-lasting-legacy-112210.

"Operation Dixie": Sue Sturgis, "Paul Manafort's Role in the Republicans'
Notorious 'Southern Strategy,'" *Facing South*, November 3, 2017, https://
www.facingsouth.org/2017/11/paul-manaforts-role-republicans-notorious
-southern-strategy.

"The South had been": Noam Chomsky, in discussion with the author, March 13,
2013, Cambridge, MA.

"Robert W. Welch Jr.": "Our History," John Birch Society, updated February 25,
2020, https://jbs.org/about/history/.

"Claire Conner": Claire Conner, in discussion with the author, May 14, 2014, Dunedin, FL.

"declared dead": Bart Barnes, "Barry Goldwater, GOP Hero, Dies," *Washington Post*, May 30, 1998, https://www.washingtonpost.com/archive/politics /1998/05/30/barry-goldwater-gop-hero-dies/22107068-2842-4505-bb1d-ec9e4783d206/.

News in the Age of Walter Cronkite and Nixon on the Rise

"most trusted man in America": David Folkenflik, "Walter Cronkite, America's 'Most Trusted Man,' Dead," NPR, July 18, 2019, https://www.npr.org /templates/story/story.php?storyId=106770499.

"liberal bias": Nicole Hemmer, "The Conservative War on Liberal Media Has a Long History," *The Atlantic*, January 17, 2014, https://www.theatlantic .com/politics/archive/2014/01/the-conservative-war-on-liberal-media -has-a-long-history/283149/.

"In 1969, Reed Irvine": "History of AIM," Accuracy in Media, accessed October 19, 2020, https://www.aim.org/about/history-of-aim/.

"Basically, the idea": David Brock, in discussion with the author, April 18, 2014, New York, NY.

"There was a universal": Brock, discussion.

"These rebels also wanted": *Encyclopaedia Britannica Online*, s.v. "Hippie," updated May 22, 2020, https://www.britannica.com/topic/hippie.

"Along with the social": Britannica, "Hippie."

"strong sense of ambition": "Richard M. Nixon," History.com, updated May 16, 2019, https://www.history.com/topics/us-presidents/richard-m-nixon.

"zealous McCarthyite": Lance Selfa, "1968: The Nixon Backlash and the 'Silent Majority,'" *Socialist Worker*, November 8, 2018, https://socialistworker. org/2018/11/08/1968-the-nixon-backlash-and-the-silent-majority.

"In 1952": "Richard M. Nixon."

"When Nixon was": George Lakoff, interview by Nico de Miranda, August 13, 2014, Berkeley, CA.

"The first of those": Lakoff, interview.

"traditional family values": Michael P. Riccards, "Richard Nixon and the American Political Tradition," *Presidential Studies Quarterly* 23, no. 4 (Fall 1993): 739–45, http://www.jstor.org/stable/27551150.

"Nixon was not": Tom Wicker, "Richard Nixon," Character Above All, PBS, updated October 18, 2017, https://www.pbs.org/newshour/spc/character /essays/nixon.html.

"Roger Ailes": Joe Flint, "Roger Ailes, Former Fox News Chief, Dies at 77," *Wall Street Journal*, updated May 18, 2017, https://www.wsj.com/articles /former-fox-news-chief-roger-ailes-dies-1495112318.

"Nixon appeared sweaty": "Richard M. Nixon."

"personally infatuated": Tim Dickinson, "How Roger Ailes Built the Fox News Fear Factory," *Rolling Stone*, May 25, 2011, https://www.rollingstone .com/politics/politics-news/how-roger-ailes-built-the-fox-news-fear-factor -244652/.

"he blamed the media": "Richard M. Nixon."

"Roger Ailes understood": Gabriel Sherman, in discussion with the author, June 2014, New York, NY.

"Roger Ailes coached": Sherman, discussion.

"The staged town halls": Gabriel Sherman, *The Loudest Voice in the Room: How the Brilliant, Bombastic Roger Ailes Built Fox News—and Divided a Country* (New York: Random House, 2014).

"over a droopy sock": Olivia B. Waxman, "Before Fox News, Roger Ailes Helped Get Richard Nixon Elected," *Time*, May 18, 2017, https://time.com /4784104/roger-ailes-richard-nixon/.

"silent majority": Selfa, "Nixon Backlash."

"blue-collar strategy": Arlie Hochschild, "Why Blue Collar Populism Works for the Republicans," History News Network, October 2003, http://hnn.us /articles/1715.html.

"he created conservative": Lakoff, interview.

"The brilliance of Nixon": Rick Perlstein, in discussion with the author, April 2014, New York, NY.

"handwritten notes": Michael Golden, "How Nixon's Legacy Is Protecting Trump," *Washington Post*, May 1, 2019, https://www.washingtonpost.com /outlook/2019/05/01/how-nixons-legacy-is-protecting-trump/.

"people are lazy": John Cook, "Roger Ailes' Secret Nixon-Era Blueprint for Fox News," Gawker (blog), June 30, 2011, https://gawker.com/5814150/roger -ailes-secret-nixon-era-blueprint-for-fox-news.

"Ailes was eventually": Cook, "Secret Nixon-Era Blueprint."

"The Coors family": Jack Shafer, "Fox News 1.0: Revisiting TVN, Roger Ailes' First Stab at Running a TV News Operation," Slate, June 5, 2008, https:// slate.com/news-and-politics/2008/06/revisiting-tvn-roger-ailes-first -stab-at-running-a-tv-news-operation.html.

"Their goal was": Reese Schonfeld, in discussion with the author, February 2014, New York, NY.

"Ailes was the perfect": Simon Houpt, "How Fox News's Roger Ailes Divided Journalism and Conquered," *Globe and Mail*, December 4, 2018, https:// www.theglobeandmail.com/arts/article-how-fox-newss-roger-ailes-divided -journalism-and-conquered/.

"No thoughtful person": Lewis F. Powell Jr., "Attack on American Free Enterprise System," August 23, 1971, Lewis F. Powell Jr. Papers, Washington and Lee University School of Law, https://scholarlycommons.law.wlu.edu /powellmemo/.

"Ralph Nader": "The Essential Nader," accessed August 14, 2020, https://nader .org/biography/essential-nader/.

"We have to get": Lakoff, interview.

"It hardly need be": Powell, "Attack on American Free Enterprise System."

"vast right-wing conspiracy": David Maraniss, "First Lady Launches Counterattack," *Washington Post*, January 28, 1998, https://www.washingtonpost.com/wp -srv/politics/special/clinton/stories/hillary012898.htm.

"The Powell memo": Powell, "Attack on American Free Enterprise System."

"You had a series": Jeff Cohen, in discussion with the author, April 2, 2013, Saugerties, NY.

"Think tanks": Eric Lipton and Brooke Williams, "How Think Tanks Amplify Corporate America's Influence," *New York Times*, August 7, 2016, https://www.nytimes.com/2016/08/08/us/politics/think-tanks-research-and-corporate-lobbying.html.

"The vast majority": Jack Anderson, "Powell's Lesson to Business Aired," *Washington Post*, September 28, 1972, http://jfk.hood.edu/Collection/Weisberg%20Subject%20Index%20Files/P%20Disk/Powell%20Lewis%20F/Item%2028.pdf.

"So they set up": Cohen, discussion.

From Nixon to Reagan and the Rise of the New Republicans

"were worried about": Encyclopaedia Britannica Online, s.v. "United States Presidential Election of 1972," updated October 31, 2020, https://www.britannica.com/event/United-States-presidential-election-of-1972.

"the widest margin": "Winning Margins in the Electoral and Popular Votes in United States Presidential Elections from 1789 to 2020," Statista, accessed December 22, 2020, https://www.statista.com/statistics/1035992/winning-margins-us-presidential-elections-since-1789/.

"broadcast evangelism": Jeffrey K. Hadden, "The Rise and Fall of American Televangelism," *Annals of the American Academy of Political and Social Science* 527, no. 1 (May 1993): 113–30, https://doi.org/10.1177/0002716293527001009.

"Mr. Graham took": Laurie Goodstein, "Billy Graham, 99, Dies; Pastor Filled Stadiums and Counseled Presidents," *New York Times*, February 21, 2018, https://www.nytimes.com/2018/02/21/obituaries/billy-graham-dead.html.

"the Federal Communications Commission": Anne Nelson, *Shadow Network: Media, Money, and the Secret Hub of the Radical Right*, (New York: Bloomsbury, 2019), 43.

"Paul Weyrich": Encyclopaedia Britannica Online, s.v. "Moral Majority," updated February 12, 2018, https://www.britannica.com/topic/Moral-Majority.

"an ever-widening sewer": Nelson, Shadow Network, xvii.

"characterized by racism": Janice Peck, The Gods of Televangelism: The Crisis of Meaning and the Appeal of Religious Television (New York: Hampton, 1993), 81.

"The televangelist broadcasters": William F. Fore, "The Unknown History of Televangelism," Religion Online, January 2007, https://www.religion-online.org/article/the-unknown-history-of-televangelism/.

"Someone needs to say": John MacArthur, "A Colossal Fraud," Grace to You, December 7, 2009, https://www.gty.org/library/articles/a391.

"pardoned all the draft evaders": Lee Lescaze, "President Pardons Viet Draft Evaders," Washington Post, January 22, 1977, https://www.washingtonpost.com/archive/politics/1977/01/22/president-pardons-viet-draft-evaders/dfa064a5-83fc-4efb-a904-d72b390a909e/.

"put solar panels up": Jimmy Carter, "Solar Energy Remarks Announcing Administration Proposals," June 20, 1979, American Presidency Project, transcript, https://www.presidency.ucsb.edu/documents/solar-energy-remarks-announcing-administration-proposals.

"an advocate": Merriam-Webster, s.v. "libertarian (n.)," accessed September 20, 2020, https://www.merriam-webster.com/dictionary/libertarian.

"strong rights": Bas van der Vossen, "Libertarianism," Stanford Encyclopedia of Philosophy, updated January 28, 2019, https://plato.stanford.edu/archives/spr2019/entries/libertarianism/.

"We urge the repeal": Thom Hartmann, "Alexander Hamilton Was Preoccupied with the Threat That a Presidency Like Trump's Posed for America," Common Dreams, September 20, 2018, https://www.commondreams.org/views/2018/09/20/alexander-hamilton-was-preoccupied-threat-presidency-trumps-posed-america.

"Let's Make America Great Again"

"*Ronald Reagan*": Encyclopaedia Britannica Online, s.v. "Ronald Reagan," updated June 10, 2020, https://www.britannica.com/biography/Ronald-Reagan.

"*The economic ills*": Ronald Reagan, "Inaugural Address," January 20, 1981, Ronald Reagan Presidential Foundation & Institute, transcript, https://www.reaganfoundation.org/media/128614/inaguration.pdf.

"*One of the brilliant*": Perlstein, discussion.

"*Reagan claimed*": "Reaganomics," U.S. History, accessed July 19, 2020, https://www.ushistory.org/us/59b.asp.

"*trickle-down economics*": Mehrun Etebari, "Trickle-Down Economics: Four Reasons Why It Just Doesn't Work," United for a Fair Economy, July 17, 2003, http://www.faireconomy.org/trickle_down_economics_four_reasons.

"*hurting the very*": Michael Ettlinger and Michael Linden, "The Failure of Supply-Side Economics," Center for American Progress, August 1, 2012, https://www.americanprogress.org/issues/economy/news/2012/08/01/11998/the-failure-of-supply-side-economics/.

"*There are two*": Perlstein, discussion.

"*Let's Make America*": Britannica, "Ronald Reagan."

"*They [the Birch Society]*": Conner, discussion.

"*One of the first*": Bryan Craig, "Reagan vs. Air Traffic Controllers," Miller Center, accessed October 28, 2020, https://millercenter.org/reagan-vs-air-traffic-controllers.

"*the 70 percent rate*": Monica Prasad, "Actually, It Was Democrats Who Killed the 70 Percent Tax," Politico, February 5, 2019, https://www.politico.com/agenda/story/2019/02/05/democrats-70-percent-tax-rate-000879/.

"*Grover Norquist*": "About Grover Norquist," Americans for Tax Reform, accessed September 28, 2020, https://www.atr.org/about-grover.

"*We have now*": Thom Hartmann, in discussion with the author, February 2014, Washington, DC.

"*previously unimaginable rise*": Michael I. Niman, "Five Forces Driving the

Rise of Fascism in 2019," Truthout, January 13, 2019, https://truthout.org
/articles/five-forces-driving-the-rise-of-fascism-in-2019/.

"figured the country": William Greider, "Reagan's Reelection: How the Media
Became All the President's Men," *Rolling Stone*, December 20, 1984,
https://www.rollingstone.com/politics/politics-news/reagans-reelection
-how-the-media-became-all-the-presidents-men-73809/.

"the oil industry": Greider, "Reagan's Reelection."

"reacting to the battering": Greider, "Reagan's Reelection."

"In 1985, Reagan made": "Murdoch Becomes U.S. Citizen, Can Buy TV
Network," *Los Angeles Times*, September 4, 1985, https://www.latimes
.com/archives/la-xpm-1985-09-04-mn-23112-story.html.

"Keith Rupert Murdoch": Encyclopaedia Britannica Online, s.v. "Rupert Murdoch,"
updated March 26, 2020, https://www.britannica.com/biography
/Rupert-Murdoch.

"He even successfully": Julia Baird, "Why Australia Killed Its Carbon Tax," *Seattle
Times*, updated July 30, 2014, https://www.seattletimes.com/opinion/why
-australia-killed-its-carbon-tax/.

"He purchased a British": Britannica, "Rupert Murdoch."

"He became": "Murdoch Becomes U.S. Citizen."

"Reagan's first step": Richard E. Wiley et al., "Broadcast Deregulation: The
Reagan Years and Beyond," *Administrative Law Review* 40, no. 3 (Summer
1988): 345–76, http://www.jstor.org/stable/40709586.

"staffed the FCC": Steve Kangas, "ABC and the Rise of Rush Limbaugh," updated
March 19, 1999, http://www.huppi.com/kangaroo/L-libmedia.htm.

"a toaster with pictures": Milton Mueller, "Interview with Mark S. Fowler,"
Reason, November 1981, https://reason.com/1981/11/01/interview-with
-mark-fowler/.

"They also lifted": Wiley et al., "Broadcast Deregulation."

"was block Congress": Penny Pagano, "Reagan's Veto Kills Fairness Doctrine
Bill," *Los Angeles Times*, June 21, 1987, https://www.latimes.com/archives
/la-xpm-1987-06-21-mn-8908-story.html.

"Broadcasters were required": Steve Rendall, in discussion with the author, January 2013, New York, NY.

"Reagan had repealed": Marjorie Hunter, "Concern on Aid for Mental Health is Raised in Light of Law's Repeal," *New York Times*, October 15, 1981, https://www.nytimes.com/1981/10/15/us/concern-on-aid-for-mental-health-is-raised-in-light-of-law-s-repeal.html.

How Talk Radio Hijacked My Dad

"Reagan was reelected": Britannica, "Ronald Reagan."

"Often called": Paul Vitello, "Bob Grant, a Combative Personality on New York Talk Radio, Dies at 84," *New York Times*, January 2, 2014, https://www.nytimes.com/2014/01/03/nyregion/bob-grant-a-pioneer-of-right-wing-talk-radio-dies-at-84.html.

"savages": Jim Naureckas, "50,000 Watts of Hate: Bigotry Is Broadcast on ABC Radio's Flagship," Fairness and Accuracy in Reporting, January 1, 1995, https://fair.org/extra/50000-watts-of-hate/.

"slimeball": Peter Hart, "How Racist Do You Have to Be Before the New York Times Calls You a Racist?" Fairness and Accuracy in Reporting, January 3, 2014, https://fair.org/home/how-racist-do-you-have-to-be-before-the-new-york-times-calls-you-a-racist/.

"music had moved": Joseph Turow, Joseph N. Cappella, and Kathleen Hall Jamieson, "Call-In Political Talk Radio: Background, Content, Audiences, Portrayal in Mainstream Media," Annenberg Public Policy Center of the University of Pennsylvania. In Report Series, no. 5 (August 7, 1996), https://repository.upenn.edu/cgi/viewcontent.cgi?article=1410&context=asc_papers.

"new accessibility of satellite": Turow, Cappella, and Jamieson, "Call-In Political Talk Radio."

"1–800 numbers": Turow, Cappella, and Jamieson, "Call-In Political Talk Radio."

"Father Charles Coughlin": "Charles E. Coughlin," United States Holocaust

Memorial Museum, updated October 9, 2020, https://encyclopedia
.ushmm.org/content/en/article/charles-e-coughlin.

"Joe Pyne": Donna Halper, "Joe Pyne—Talk Radio Pioneer," Broadcaster's
Desktop Resource, June 2017, https://www.thebdr.net/joe-pyne-talk
-radio-pioneer/.

"simply failed": Abram Brown, "Why All the Talk-Radio Stars Are
Conservative," *Forbes*, July 13, 2015, https://www.forbes.com/sites/abram
brown/2015/07/13/why-all-the-talk-radio-stars-are-conservative/.

"it's not the same": Brown, "Talk-Radio Stars."

"Tell your audience": Brown, "Talk-Radio Stars."

"Killers often": Samantha Power, "Bystanders to Genocide," *The Atlantic*,
September 2001, https://www.theatlantic.com/magazine/archive/2001/09
/bystanders-to-genocide/304571/.

"Rush Limbaugh": *Encyclopaedia Britannica Online*, s.v. "Rush Limbaugh,"
updated April 9, 2020, https://www.britannica.com/biography/Rush
-Limbaugh.

"The allure": Rendall, discussion.

"Rush Limbaugh started": miggsb [Miggs Burroughs], "Rush Limbaugh's First
TV Interview from 1988," *Miggs B on TV*, July 6, 2008, YouTube video,
9:08, https://www.youtube.com/watch?v=z15uiwHfhbI.

"People who see you": miggsb, "Rush Limbaugh's First TV Interview."

"the most listened": Britannica, "Rush Limbaugh."

"Limbaugh provided plenty": Brian Rosenwald, "The Divisive Case for Giving
Rush Limbaugh the Medal of Freedom," *Washington Post*, February 6,
2020,   https://www.washingtonpost.com/outlook/2020/02/06/divisive
-case-giving-rush-limbaugh-medal-freedom/.

"In terms of people": Cohen, discussion.

"He wasn't just": Cohen, discussion.

"Cohen and Rendall": Steven Rendall, Jim Naureckas, and Jeff Cohen, *The Way
Things Aren't* (New York: New Press, 1995).

"more Native Americans": Rush Limbaugh, *See, I Told You So* (New York: Atria, 1993), 68.

"ice caps melting": Brandon Moseley, "Rush Limbaugh: Mo Brooks' Rebuttal of Manmade Climate Change Was 'Brilliant,'" *Alabama Political Reporter*, July 17, 2020, https://www.alreporter.com/2019/07/17/rush-limbaugh-mo -brooks-rebuttal-of-manmade-climate-change-was-brilliant/.

"no conclusive proof": The Rush Limbaugh Show, aired April 29, 1994, on WABC.

"or that cigarettes cause": The Rush Limbaugh Show, aired April 17, 2015, on WOR.

"into a Muslim outreach": The Rush Limbaugh Show, aired March 6, 2014, on WOR.

"Most people don't think": Rendall, discussion.

The Vast Right-Wing Conspiracy Takes Off

"brat": Hanna Rosin, "Among the Hillary Haters," *The Atlantic*, March 2015, https://www.theatlantic.com/magazine/archive/2015/03/among-the-hillary -haters/384976/.

"There is this backlash": Cohen, discussion.

"He was found": Ronald J. Ostrow and Ron Broder, "Bitter Lament by Foster Revealed Depth of Despair," *Los Angeles Times*, August 11, 1993, https:// www.latimes.com/archives/la-xpm-1993-08-11-mn-22695-story.html.

"no other president": Cohen, discussion.

"It stated that": David Brock, "His Cheatin' Heart: Living with the Clintons: Bill's Arkansas Bodyguards Tell the Story the Press Missed," *American Spectator*, July 1994, 18–30.

"Paula Jones": Peter Baker, "Clinton Settles Paula Jones Lawsuit for $850,000," *Washington Post*, November 14, 1998, https://www.washingtonpost.com /wp-srv/politics/special/clinton/stories/jones111498.htm.

"Brock, along with Ann": "David Brock," Live Online, *Washington Post*, February 26, 2002, https://www.washingtonpost.com/wp-srv/liveonline/02/politics /brock022602.htm.

"The conspiracy came": "David Brock."

"In early 1998": Brock, discussion.

"number one voice": David Remnick, "Day of the Dittohead," *Washington Post*, February 20, 1994, https://www.washingtonpost.com/archive /opinions/1994/02/20/day-of-the-dittohead/e5723f05-04d8-4ccb-98c9 -8b1ba6c358d2/.

"Democratic Party should": Sheryl Gay Stolberg, "A Scorched Earth Style of Politics; Gingrich Has Long Treated His Opponents More as Enemies Than Adversaries," *International Herald Tribune*, January 28, 2012.

"This war has": Stolberg, "Scorched Earth Style."

"encouraged the Republican": Evan Philipson, "Bringing Down the House: The Causes and Effects of the Decline of Personal Relationships in the U.S. House of Representatives," *College Undergraduate Research Electronic Journal*, University of Pennsylvania, April 8, 2011, https://repository .upenn.edu/curej/141/.

"weekly strategy meetings": Bob Dreyfuss, "Grover Norquist: 'Field Marshal' of the Bush Plan," *The Nation*, April 26, 2001, https://www.thenation.com /article/archive/grover-norquist-field-marshal-bush-plan/.

"The Wednesday meetings": Thomas Medvetz, interview by Melodie Bryant, March 2014, Berkeley, CA.

"If the conservative": Medvetz, interview.

"So when Hillary": Medvetz, interview.

"drown it in a bathtub": "Conservative Advocate," *Morning Edition*, NPR, May 25, 2001, https://www.npr.org/templates/story/story.php?storyId=1123439.

"they have people": Lakoff, interview.

"They try to empathize": Julie Hotard, "What Most People Never Noticed about the Presidential Debate: About the Guiding Light of Truth," Medium, October 2, 2020, https://upine.medium.com/what-most-people-never -noticed-about-the-presidential-debate-about-the-guiding-light-of-truth -7b06ce21d178.

"socialistic": Ian Millhiser, "A Brief, 90-Year History of Republicans Calling Democrats 'Socialists,'" ThinkProgress, March 6, 2019, https://archive

.thinkprogress.org/a-history-of-republicans-calling-democrats-socialists
-777bcd2b7a6d/.

"My dad also believed": Russell Watson, "Vince Foster's Suicide: The Rumor
Mill Churns," *Newsweek,* March 20, 1994, https://www.newsweek.com
/vince-fosters-suicide-rumor-mill-churns-185900.

"Foster was deeply": Ostrow and Broder, "Bitter Lament by Foster."

"alternative facts": Aaron Blake, "Kellyanne Conway Says Donald Trump's
Team Has 'Alternative Facts.' Which Pretty Much Says It All," *Washington
Post,* January 22, 2017, https://www.washingtonpost.com/news/the-fix
/wp/2017/01/22/kellyanne-conway-says-donald-trumps-team-has-alternate
-facts-which-pretty-much-says-it-all/.

"Brainwashing is the concept": *Merriam-Webster,* s.v. "brainwashing (n.)," accessed
December 23, 2020, https://www.merriam-webster.com/dictionary/brain
washing.

"in February 1996": "Telecommunications Act of 1996," Federal Communications
Commission, updated June 20, 2013, https://www.fcc.gov/general/tele
communications-act-1996.

"One of the biggest": Cohen, discussion.

"in 1983, there were": *Democracy on Deadline: The Global Struggle for an
Independent Press,* directed by Calvin Skaggs (New York: Independent
Lens and Thirteen WNET, 2006), film, 120 min.

"by 2015, Rupert Murdoch": "Our Leadership," News Corp, accessed October
28, 2020, https://newscorp.com/leader/rupert-murdoch/.

"Murdoch launched": "Rupert Murdoch Fast Facts," CNN, updated April 13,
2020, https://www.cnn.com/2013/06/10/world/rupert-murdoch-fast-facts
/index.html.

"long wanted in": Mark Sweeney, "Roger Ailes Career Timeline: From Trusted
Nixon Ally to Fox News Kingpin," *Guardian,* May 18, 2017, https://www
.theguardian.com/media/2017/may/18/roger-ailes-career-history-nixon
-fox-news.

"Sometime in the fall": Sherman, Loudest Voice in the Room, 170.

"fair and balanced": Sherman, Loudest Voice in the Room, 170.

"Ailes wanted to be": Eric Alterman, "Fox News Has Always Been Propaganda," The Nation, March 14, 2019, https://www.thenation.com/article/archive /fox-news-propaganda-eric-alterman/.

"I know certain": Dickinson, "How Roger Ailes Built."

"He [Ailes] says": Perlstein, discussion.

"Roger Ailes feels": Sherman, discussion.

"Ailes believed displaying": Dickinson, "How Roger Ailes Built."

"riling up the crazies": Maureen Dowd, "Riling Up the Crazies," New York Times, October 27, 2018, https://www.nytimes.com/2018/10/27/opinion /sunday/donald-trump-fear.html.

"Fox was another opportunity": Jim Hayes, "Rupert Furthers Strategy to Crash into Social Media," The Pen, July 3, 2018, http://the-pen.co/aim-is-to -extend-control-and-political-influence/.

"He would support": John Gapper, "The Two Sides of Rupert Murdoch," Financial Times, October 6, 2006, https://www.ft.com/content/73de2d8c -555d-11db-acba-0000779e2340.

"authoritarian countries can work": Ken Auletta, "The Pirate," New Yorker, November 5, 1995, https://www.newyorker.com/magazine/1995/11/13 /the-pirate.

"Fox News is a real": Edward S. Herman, in discussion with the author, January 2013, Philadelphia, PA.

"The most dangerous": Brock, discussion.

"Emory University study": Dylan Matthews, "A Stunning New Study Shows That Fox News Is More Powerful Than We Ever Imagined," Vox, September 8, 2017, https://www.vox.com/policy-and-politics/2017/9/8/16263710/fox -news-presidential-vote-study.

"a glitch": Emily Dreyfuss, "Want to Make a Lie Seem True? Say It Again. And Again. And Again," Wired, February 11, 2017, https://www.wired .com/2017/02/dont-believe-lies-just-people-repeat/.

"What these news": Jonathan Schroeder, in discussion with the author, June 20, 2014, Rochester, NY.

"The noise machine": Eric Boehlert, in discussion with the author, 2014.

"One of the worst things": Chomsky, discussion.

"Doubt is our product": "Tobacco: 'Doubt Is Their Product,'" Collaborative on Health and the Environment, accessed October 5, 2020, https://www .healthandenvironment.org/environmental-health/social-context/history /tobacco-doubt-is-their-product.

"Instead of presenting": Heather Hogan, "How Fox News Brainwashes Its Viewers: Our In-Depth Investigation of the Propaganda Cycle," Autostraddle, September 2, 2015, https://www.autostraddle.com/this-is -how-fox-news-brainwashes-its-viewers-our-in-depth-investigation-of-the -propaganda-cycle-297107/.

"gaslighting, a manipulation": Sarah DiGiulio, "What Is Gaslighting? And How Do You Know if It's Happening to You?" Better by *Today*, July 13, 2018, https://www.nbcnews.com/better/health/what-gaslighting-how-do-you -know-if-it-s-happening-ncna890866.

"once two groups": Anonymous psyops captain, email message to author, February 29, 2020.

"It's just so clear": Anonymous captain, email.

"Branding works by": Elizabeth Smithson, "What Is Branding and Why Is It Important for Your Business?" *Brandingmag*, October 14, 2015, https://www .brandingmag.com/2015/10/14/what-is-branding-and-why-is-it-important -for-your-business/.

"all major news": *The Myth of the Liberal Media : The Propaganda Model of News*, directed by Sut Jhally (San Francisco: Kanopy Streaming, 2014), film, 60 min.

"Well, part of it": Schroeder, discussion.

"The idea is": Cynthia Boaz, "14 Propaganda Techniques Fox 'News' Uses to Brainwash Americans," *Georgia Straight*, July 2, 2011, https://www.straight

.com/news/dr-cynthia-boaz-14-propaganda-techniques-fox-news-uses
-brainwash-americans.

"When the story": Jessica Bennett, "The Shaming of Monica: Why We Owe
Her an Apology," Time, May 9, 2014, https://time.com/92989/monica
-lewinsky-slut-shaming-feminists-media-apology/.

"Today Lewinsky runs": Catherine Thorbecke and Nicole Pelletiere, "Monica
Lewinsky Launches Anti-Bullying Campaign, Calls Kavanaugh Accuser 'A
Role Model in Bravery,'" ABC News, October 5, 2018, https://abcnews
.go.com/GMA/News/monica-lewinsky-launches-anti-bullying-campaign
-calls-kavanaugh/story?id=58239336.

"subordinate to her husband": Ken Auletta, "The Hillary Show," New Yorker,
May 26, 2014, https://www.newyorker.com/magazine/2014/06/02/the
-hillary-show.

"The cleverest trick": Joseph Goebbels, "Goebbels at Nuremberg: 1934," German
Propaganda Archive at Calvin University, accessed November 1, 2020,
https://research.calvin.edu/german-propaganda-archive/goeb59.htm.

"Donald Trump": Peter Beinart, "The Projection President," The Atlantic, July 14,
2017, https://www.theatlantic.com/politics/archive/2017/07/the-success
-of-smoke-and-mirrors/533706/.

"There is more of a chance": "Debunking the Voter Fraud Myth," Brennan Center
for Justice, January 31, 2017, https://www.brennancenter.org/sites/default
/files/analysis/Briefing_Memo_Debunking_Voter_Fraud_Myth.pdf

"Lindsey Graham lying": Kenny Stancil, "Lindsey Graham Admits that Making
Voting More Accessible Renders GOP Victories Impossible," Salon, Nov.
11, 2020, https://www.salon.com/2020/11/11/lindsey-graham-admits
-that-making-voting-more-accessible-renders-gop-victories-impossible
_partner/.

"only 3.9 percent": "Armed Forces Radio gets a 'Rush' from Limbaugh," UPI,
December 7, 1993, https://www.upi.com/Archives/1993/12/07/Armed
-Forces-Radio-gets-a-Rush-from-Limbaugh/3879755240400/.

"Republican representative Robert Dornan": Carol Wallin, in discussion with the author, March 2014, New York, NY.

"In 2018, the FDA": Laura Strickler, "At FDA, TVs Now Turned to Fox News, and Can't Be Switched," *CBS News*, updated May 8, 2017, https://www.cbsnews.com/news/at-fda-tvs-now-turned-to-fox-news-and-cant-be-switched/.

"when he would try": Aaron, email message to author, February 29, 2020.

"Pew Research found": Amy Mitchell et al., "Political Polarization & Media Habits," Pew Research Center, October 21, 2014, https://www.journalism.org/2014/10/21/political-polarization-media-habits/.

"roughly 91 percent": "Talk Radio by the Numbers," Center for American Progress, July 10, 2007, https://www.americanprogress.org/issues/economy/news/2007/07/10/3297/talk-radio-by-the-numbers/.

"is due to structural": "Talk Radio by the Numbers."

"first blatantly right-leaning": Herman, discussion.

"first to use": Bryant Welch, *State of Confusion: Political Manipulation and the Assault on the American Mind.* (New York: Thomas Dunne, 2008), 150.

"The sound and visual": Welch, *State of Confusion*, 150.

"After Roger Ailes": Gabriel Sherman, "Women Can Wear Pants on Fox News Now, But Not Much Else Has Changed," *New York Intelligencer*, May 14, 2017, https://nymag.com/intelligencer/2017/05/rupert-murdoch-disaster-at-fox-news.html.

"It's a visual medium": Sherman, discussion.

"It's not just language": Frank Luntz, in discussion with the author, November 2014, New York, NY.

"trickle-down economics": Kimberley Amadeo, "Why Trickle-Down Economics Works in Theory but Not in Fact," The Balance, updated September 24, 2020, https://www.thebalance.com/trickle-down-economics-theory-effect-does-it-work-3305572.

"the state is one": James C. McKinley Jr., "Texas Conservatives Win Curriculum Change," *New York Times*, March 12, 2010, https://www.nytimes.com/2010/03/13/education/13texas.html?hpw.

"Darwin's theory": McKinley, "Texas Conservatives Win Curriculum Change."

"All the Republicans": Richard Adams, "Texas Conservatives Rewrite History," *Guardian*, March 13, 2010, https://www.theguardian.com/world/richard-adams-blog/2010/mar/13/texas-textbooks-republicans-education.

"In articles and speeches": Steven Thomma, "Not Satisfied with U.S. History, Some Conservatives Are Rewriting It," McClatchy, updated April 3, 2010, https://www.mcclatchydc.com/news/politics-government/article24578641.html.

"Newt Gingrich recognized": GOPAC, *Language: A Key Mechanism of Control*, 1990, https://connectionslab.org/wp-content/uploads/2017/05/information clearinghouse-info-a-key-mechanism-of-control.pdf.

"Newt's political action committee": Clarence Page, "Talk Like a Newt with the Gingrich Diatribe Dictionary," *Chicago Tribune*, September 19, 1990, https://www.chicagotribune.com/news/ct-xpm-1990-09-19-9003180664-story.html.

"The pamphlet provided": Peter Stone, "How Newt Gingrich's Language Guru Helped Rebrand the Kochs' Message," *Mother Jones*, December 8, 2014, https://www.motherjones.com/politics/2014/12/frank-luntz-helped-the-koch-brothers/.

"He also provided": GOPAC, *Language*.

"Language is not neutral": Lakoff, interview.

"Clear Skies Initiative": James R. Lyons et al., "Red, White, Blue, and Green: Politics and the Environment in the 2004 Environment," *Yale School of the Environment Publications Series*, 6 (2004), https://elischolar.library.yale.edu/fes-pubs/6/.

"Healthy Forests Initiative": P. C. Pezzullo, "Teaching Environmental Communication through Rhetorical Controversy," in *Teaching Environmental Literacy: Across Campus and Across the Curriculum*, ed. Heather L. Reynolds, Eduardo S. Brondizio, and Jennifer Meta Robinson (Bloomington: Indiana University Press, 2010), 98–108, https://www.researchgate.net/publication/290928403_Teaching_environmental_communication_through_rhetorical_controversy.

"so-called death tax": Mark Abadi, "Republicans Say 'Death Tax' while Democrats Say 'Estate Tax'—and There's a Fascinating Reason Why," *Business Insider*, October 19, 2017, https://www.businessinsider.com/death-tax-or-estate-tax-2017-10.

"this law is only": Ashlea Ebeling, "IRS Announces Higher Estate and Gift Tax Limits for 2020," *Forbes*, November 6, 2019, https://www.forbes.com/sites/ashleaebeling/2019/11/06/irs-announces-higher-estate-and-gift-tax-limits-for-2020/.

"I have fought": Luntz, discussion.

"80 percent": Frank Luntz, interview, *Frontline*, PBS, December 15, 2003, https://www.pbs.org/wgbh/pages/frontline/shows/persuaders/interviews/luntz.html.

"Framing is about": George Lakoff, "The Power of Positive Persistence," *George Lakoff* (blog), January 17, 2018, https://georgelakoff.com/2018/01/17/the-power-of-positive-persistence/.

"The right-wing movement's": Dave Johnson, "Who's Behind the Attack on Liberal Professors?," History News Network, updated May 14, 2006, http://www.hnn.us/articles/1244.html.

"are somehow the anointed": Roy H. Copperud, *American Usage and Style: The Consensus* (New York: Van Nostrand Reinhold, 1980), 101–102.

"Cognitive psychologist": Paul Farhi, "'The Democrat Party': Trump Needles Opposition by Truncating Its Name," *Washington Post*, March 7, 2019, https://www.washingtonpost.com/lifestyle/style/the-democrat-party-trump-needles-the-opposition-by-truncating-its-name/2019/03/06/a1a3e3dc-3f6b-11e9-922c-64d6b7840b82_story.html.

"Many called themselves": Linda Shrieves, "Dittoheads: Limbaugh's Faithful," *Orlando Sentinel*, August 28, 1993, https://www.orlandosentinel.com/news/os-xpm-1993-08-28-9308270768-story.html.

Is Dad Brainwashed?

"*nearly 10 percent*": Farhad Manjoo, "Jurassic Web," History News Network, February 24, 2009, https://historynewsnetwork.org/article/63799.

"*the emails most often*": David Brock, *The Republican Noise Machine: Right-Wing Media and How It Corrupts Democracy* (New York: Crown, 2004), 155–56.

"*a woman sued McDonald's*": *Hot Coffee*, directed by Susan Saladoff (New York: The Group Entertainment, 2011), film, 88 min.

"*George W. Bush*": *Encyclopaedia Britannica Online*, s.v. "United States Presidential Election of 2000," by Michael Levy, updated October 31, 2020, https://www.britannica.com/event/United-States-presidential-election-of-2000.

"*I took the initiative*": Glenn Kessler, "A Cautionary Tale for Politicians: Al Gore and the 'Invention' of the Internet," *Washington Post*, November 4, 2013, https://www.washingtonpost.com/news/fact-checker/wp/2013/11/04/a-cautionary-tale-for-politicians-al-gore-and-the-invention-of-the-internet/.

"*Al Gore was criticized*": "Bush, Gore Go Deep on Issues in First Debate," ABC News, October 4, 2000, https://web.stanford.edu/class/polisci179/ABCNEWS_com%20%20Bush,%20Gore%20Go%20Deep%20on%20Issues%20in%20First%20Debate.htm.

"*at 9:55, CNN*": David Bauder, "Networks Try to Explain Blown Call," *Washington Post*, November 8, 2000, https://www.washingtonpost.com/wp-srv/aponline/20001108/aponline183922_000.htm.

"*hanging or dimpled chads*": Jessica Reaves, "The Dimpled Chad Dilemma," CNN, November 22, 2000, https://www.cnn.com/2000/ALLPOLITICS/stories/11/22/ballot.tm/index.html.

"*being purged*": Katie Sanders, "Florida Voters Mistakenly Purged in 2000," *Tampa Bay Times*, June 14, 2012, https://www.tampabay.com/news/politics/stateroundup/florida-voters-mistakenly-purged-in-2000/1235456/.

"*lost votes*": Jessica Reaves, "Counting the Lost Votes of Election 2000," *Time*, July 17, 2001, http://content.time.com/time/nation/article/0,8599,167906,00.html.

"one computer even showed": Bob Fitrakis and Harvey Wasserman, "Diebold's Political Machine," *Mother Jones*, March 5, 2004, https://www.motherjones.com/politics/2004/03/diebolds-political-machine/.

"What happens in 2000": Sherman, discussion.

"The Bush/Gore race": Britannica, "United States Presidential Election of 2000."

"Al Gore had won": Greg Palast, "The Election Was Stolen—Here's How...," Greg Palast, November 11, 2016, https://www.gregpalast.com/election-stolen.

"GOP Secretary of State": Palast, "Election Was Stolen."

9/11, Barack Obama, and Far-Right Extremism

"How did Ailes": Sherman, discussion.

"Fairleigh Dickinson University": Dan Cassino, "Ignorance, Partisanship Drive False Beliefs About Obama, Iraq," Fairleigh Dickinson University's Public Mind Poll, January 7, 2015, http://publicmind.fdu.edu/2015/false/.

"He made a joke": David Teather, "Bush Jokes about Search for WMD but It's No Laughing Matter for Critics," *Guardian*, March 26, 2004, https://www.theguardian.com/world/2004/mar/26/usa.iraq.

"swift boating": Lexico, s.v. "swift-boat," accessed October 31, 2020, https://www.lexico.com/en/definition/swift-boat.

"He had been": Mark Hemingway, "Setting the Record Straight on the Swift Boat Veterans," *Washington Examiner*, October 7, 2016, https://www.washingtonexaminer.com/weekly-standard/setting-the-record-straight-on-the-swift-boat-veterans.

"the architect": Wayne Slater, interview, *Frontline*, PBS, March 2, 2005, https://www.pbs.org/wgbh/pages/frontline/shows/architect/interviews/slater.html.

"Texas billionaire Bob Perry": William Yardley, "Bob Perry, Big Backer of 'Swift Boat' Ads, Dies at 80," *New York Times*, April 15, 2003, https://www.nytimes.com/2013/04/16/us/politics/bob-perry-swift-boat-ad-backer-dies-at-80.html.

"In an interview": Terry Gross, "John Kerry Reflects on Smear Campaigns and

Not Taking Anything for Granted," *Fresh Air*, NPR, September 5, 2018, https://www.npr.org/2018/09/05/644830886/john-kerry-reflects-on -smear-campaigns-and-not-taking-anything-for-granted.

"Dick Cheney pumped fear": Julie Hirschfeld Davis, "Cheney Hails Bush's Policies, Scorns Kerry," *Baltimore Sun*, September 2, 2004, https://www .baltimoresun.com/news/bs-xpm-2004-09-02-0409020339-story.html.

"Kerry was even": Suzanne Goldenberg, "Take One Part Kerry, One Part Fonda...," *Guardian*, February 18, 2004, https://www.theguardian.com /media/2004/feb/18/newmedia.uselections2004.

"If we do not suppress": Bob Herbert, "Protect the Vote," *New York Times*, September 13, 2004, https://www.nytimes.com/2004/09/13/opinion /protect-the-vote.html.

"Uniformed officers with guns": Bob Herbert, "Suppress the Vote?" *New York Times*, August 16, 2004, https://www.nytimes.com/2004/08/16/opinion /suppress-the-vote.html.

"They were also made": Fitrakis and Wasserman, "Diebold's Political Machine."

"One computer error": John McCarthy, "Voting Machine Error Gives Bush 3,893 Extra Votes in Ohio," WFMY News, November 5, 2004, https://www .wfmynews2.com/article/news/politics/voting-machine-error-gives -bush-3893-extra-votes-in-ohio/83–402226666.

"The federal commission": Robert F. Kennedy Jr., "Was the 2004 Election Stolen?," *Rolling Stone*, June 15, 2006, https://www.rollingstone.com/news /story/10432334/was_the_2004_election_stolen.

"a consulting firm": Kennedy, "Was the 2004 Election Stolen?"

"Republicans and much": Kennedy, "Was the 2004 Election Stolen?"

"electronic totals can be": Mark Crispin Miller, "Let's Get Real," *In These Times*, November 16, 2004, https://inthesetimes.com/article/let-get-real.

"the main effect": Adam Lasecki, "Leaning Left: A Case Study of Media Bias in the 2004 Presidential Election" (master's thesis, Rowan University, 2005), 33, https://rdw.rowan.edu/etd/1025.

"Kerry conceded, saying": Kennedy, "Was the 2004 Election Stolen?"

"millions of people": Irfan Ahmad, "The History of Social Media," Social Media Today, April 27, 2018, https://www.socialmediatoday.com/news/the -history-of-social-media-infographic-1/522285/.

"win every news cycle": David Folkenflik, *Murdoch's World: The Last of the Old Media Empires* (New York: Public Affairs, 2013), 67.

"one former staffer": Folkenflik, *Murdoch's World*, 67.

"There is not a liberal": Barack Obama, "Barack Obama's Remarks to the Democratic National Convention," *New York Times*, July 27, 2004, https://www.nytimes.com/2004/07/27/politics/campaign/barack-obamas-remarks -to-the-democratic-national.html.

"Barack Obama won": Encyclopaedia Britannica Online, s.v. "United States Presidential Election of 2008," updated October 28, 2020, https://www .britannica.com/event/United-States-presidential-election-of-2008.

"left the country": Kimberley Amadeo, "US Budget Deficit by President," The Balance, updated November 2, 2020, https://www.thebalance.com/deficit -by-president-what-budget-deficits-hide-3306151.

"The single most important": Glenn Kessler, "When Did Mitch McConnell Say He Wanted to Make Obama a One-Term President?," *Washington Post*, January 11, 2017, https://www.washingtonpost.com/news/fact-checker /wp/2017/01/11/when-did-mitch-mcconnell-say-he-wanted-to-make -obama-a-one-term-president/.

"he'd rather see": W. Gardner Selby, "Mark Strama Says Rush Limbaugh Made It Clear He'd Rather See the Country Fail than President Barack Obama Succeed," PolitiFact, September 13, 2012, https://www.politifact.com /factchecks/2012/sep/13/mark-strama/mark-strama-says-rush-limbaugh -made-it-clear-hed-r/.

"implying he was": Allison Graves, John Kruzel, and Manuela Tobias, "Who Plays More Golf: Donald Trump or Barack Obama," PolitiFact, updated May 18, 2018, https://www.politifact.com/article/2017/oct/10/who-plays -more-golf-donald-trump-or-barack-obama/.

"Sean Hannity painted": Sean Hannity, "Khalidi Praises Palestinian Terrorist,"

Fox News, November 3, 2008, https://www.foxnews.com/printer _friendly_story/0,3566,446187,00.html.

"Glenn Beck was": David Bauder, "Fox's Beck: Obama Hates White People, Culture," NBC News, July 28, 2009, https://www.nbcdfw.com/news /national-international/natlfoxs-beck-obama-hates-white-people-culture /1855065/.

"Fox often referred": Sabrina Siddiqui, "Fox News: How an Anti-Obama Fringe Set the Stage for Trump," *Guardian*, March 19, 2019, https://www .theguardian.com/media/2019/mar/18/fox-news-donald-trump-barack -obama-election.

"Donald Trump often phoned": Siddiqui, "Anti-Obama Fringe."

"The DHS released": Daryl Johnson, "I Warned of Right-Wing Violence in 2009. Republicans Objected. I Was Right," *Washington Post*, August 21, 2017, https://www.washingtonpost.com/news/posteverything/wp/2017 /08/21/i-warned-of-right-wing-violence-in-2009-it-caused-an-uproar-i -was-right/.

"the right-wing media": Charles Pierce, "'We' Did Not Miss the Rise of Right-Wing Extremism. You Did," *Esquire*, December 13, 2018, https:// www.esquire.com/news-politics/politics/a25574930/new-york-times -rightwing-extremism-white-supremacist/.

"John Boehner, then Speaker": "GOP's Overdone Outrage about a Homeland Security Memo," *Los Angeles Times*, April 17, 2009, https://www.latimes .com/opinion/editorials/la-ed-extremism17–2009apr17-story.html.

"the SPLC noted": "U.S. Hate Groups Top 1,000," Southern Poverty Law Center, February 23, 2011, https://www.splcenter.org/news/2011/02/23/us-hate -groups-top-1000.

"an organization that": "Frequently Asked Questions about Hate Groups," Southern Poverty Law Center, March 18, 2020, https://www.splcenter .org/20200318/frequently-asked-questions-about-hate-groups.

"hate group publications": "Methodology: How Hate Groups Are Identified and Categorized," Southern Poverty Law Center, March 18, 2020, https://

www.splcenter.org/news/2020/03/18/methodology-how-hate-groups
-are-identified-and-categorized.

"In the United States": Paul Starr, "How the Right Went Far-Right," *American Prospect*, March 31, 2020, https://prospect.org/culture/books/how-the
-right-went-far-right/.

"Those old norms": Starr, "How the Right Went Far-Right."

"Rick Santelli": "Santelli's Tea Party Rant, February 19, 2009," CNBC, updated February 6, 2015, https://www.cnbc.com/video/2015/02/06/santellis
-tea-party-rant-february-19–2009.html.

"subsidize the losers' mortgages": Michael Ray, *Encyclopaedia Britannica Online*, s.v. "Tea Party Movement," updated November 11, 2019, https://www
.britannica.com/topic/Tea-Party-movement.

"we're thinking of having": Steven Perlberg, "Rick Santelli Started the Tea Party with a Rant Exactly 5 Years Ago Today—Here's How He Feels about It Now," *Business Insider*, February 19, 2014, https://www.businessinsider
.com/rick-santelli-tea-party-rant-2014–2.

"popularized by right-wing pundits": Britannica, "Tea Party Movement."

"corporate billionaires": Jeff Nesbit, "The Secret Origins of the Tea Party," *Time*, accessed August 7, 2020, https://time.com/secret-origins-of-the-tea
-party/.

"bringing their guns": Alex Seitz-Wald, "Gun Rights and Tea Party Activists Encourage People to Bring Guns to New Mexico Protest," ThinkProgress, January 3, 2010, https://archive.thinkprogress.org/gun-rights-and-tea
-party-activists-encourage-people-to-bring-guns-to-new-mexico-protest
-ee22ebff3af/; Angela Brandt, "Tea Party Bear Arms at Rally," *Independent Record*, March 5, 2011, https://helenair.com/news/tea-party-bears-arms
-at-rally/article_cfd1e6b6-46f7-11e0-997e-001cc4c002e0.html.

"entitlement programs": Vanessa Williamson, Theda Skocpol, and John Coggin, "The Tea Party and the Remaking of Republican Conservatism," *Perspectives on Politics* 9, no. 1 (March 2011): 25–43, https://doi.org/10.1017/S1537
59271000407X.

"embedded content": "Tea Party," Center for Media and Democracy, updated July 21, 2018, https://www.sourcewatch.org/index.php?title=Tea_Party.

The Return of Dad

"It espoused": Dennis J. Kucinich, "New Year's Resolution for America," *Huffington Post*, December 31, 2014, https://www.huffpost.com/entry /new-years-resolution-for-_2_b_6400848.

After Dad

"the contest came down": David C. Beckwith, *Encyclopaedia Britannica Online*, s.v. "United States Presidential Election of 2016," updated November 11, 2019, https://www.britannica.com/topic/United-States-presidential-election -of-2016.

"racist 'birther' theory": Ashley Parker and Steve Eder, "Inside the Six Weeks Donald Trump Was a Nonstop 'Birther,'" *New York Times*, July 2, 2016, https://www.nytimes.com/2016/07/03/us/politics/donald-trump-birther -obama.html.

"Some analysts": Emily Stewart, "Donald Trump Rode $5 Billion in Free Media to the White House," The Street, November 20, 2016, https://www .thestreet.com/politics/donald-trump-rode-5-billion-in-free-media-to -the-white-house-13896916.

"Leslie Moonves said": Paul Bond, "Leslie Moonves on Donald Trump: 'It May Not Be Good for America, but It's Damn Good for CBS,'" *Hollywood Reporter*, February 29, 2016, https://www.hollywoodreporter.com/news /leslie-moonves-donald-trump-may-871464.

"Moonves later had": Ronan Farrow, "As Leslie Moonves Negotiates His Exit from CBS, Six Women Raise New Assault and Harassment Claims," *New Yorker*, September 9, 2018, https://www.newyorker.com/news/news -desk/as-leslie-moonves-negotiates-his-exit-from-cbs-women-raise-new -assault-and-harassment-claims.

"the election was rigged": Stephen Collinson, "Why Trump's Talk of a Rigged

Vote Is So Dangerous," CNN, October 18, 2016, https://www.cnn
.com/2016/10/18/politics/donald-trump-rigged-election/index.html.

"Far-right media": James Poniewozik, "Trump Isn't Watching Too Much TV. He's
Watching the Wrong Kind," *New York Times*, December 12, 2017, https://
www.nytimes.com/2017/12/12/arts/television/trump-isnt-watching-too
-much-tv-hes-watching-the-wrong-kind.html.

"I am very pro-choice": Donald Trump, interview by Tim Russert, *Meet the
Press*, NBC, October 24, 1999, https://www.nbcnews.com/meet-the-press
/video/trump-in-1999-i-am-very-pro-choice-480297539914.

"grow his base": Perry Bacon Jr., "How the 2016 Election Exposed America's
Racial and Cultural Divides," NBC News, November 11, 2016, https://
www.nbcnews.com/politics/white-house/how-2016-election-exposed
-america-s-racial-cultural-divides-n682306.

"drain the swamp": Peter Overby, "Trump's Efforts to 'Drain the Swamp' Lagging
Behind His Campaign Rhetoric," NPR, April 26, 2017, https://www.npr
.org/2017/04/26/525551816/trumps-efforts-to-drain-the-swamp-lagging
-behind-his-campaign-rhetoric.

"Trump even appealed": Nate Cohn and Toni Monkovic, "How Did Donald
Trump Win Over So Many Obama Voters?" *New York Times*, November
14, 2016, https://www.nytimes.com/2016/11/15/upshot/how-did-trump
-win-over-so-many-obama-voters.html.

"Geraldo Rivera tweeted": Conor Gaffey, "A Short History of Donald's Trump
Relationship with Fox News," *Newsweek*, March 29, 2017, https://www
.newsweek.com/donald-trump-fox-news-576064.

"Limbaugh endorsed Trump": Travis Hale, "Rush Limbaugh Is a Hypocrite
When It Comes to Trump," *The Hill*, November 25, 2015, https://thehill
.com/blogs/pundits-blog/presidential-campaign/261258-when-it-comes
-to-trump-rush-limbaugh-is-a-hypocrite.

"The mere fact": David Sillito, "Donald Trump: How the Media Created the
President," BBC News, November 14, 2016, https://www.bbc.com/news
/entertainment-arts-37952249.

"Pollsters would dismiss": Sillito, "Donald Trump."

"Russian interference": Gabe O'Conner and Avie Schneider, "How Russian Twitter Bots Pumped Out Fake News During the 2016 Election Cycle," *All Things Considered*, NPR, April 3, 2017, https://www.npr.org/sections /alltechconsidered/2017/04/03/522503844/how-russian-twitter-bots -pumped-out-fake-news-during-the-2016-election.

"Part of the reason": Luke Barnes, "Death Threats Force Parkland Shooting Survivor to Leave Facebook," ThinkProgress, February 23, 2018, https://archive .thinkprogress.org/parkland-shooting-survivor-forced-off-facebook-6fc3 97ab2b9f/.

"Some of the Russian": O'Conner and Schneider, "Russian Twitter Bots."

"About 4 percent": Aaron Blake, "A New Study Suggests Fake News Might Have Won Donald Trump the 2016 Election," *Washington Post*, April 3, 2018, https://www.washingtonpost.com/news/the-fix/wp/2018/04/03/a-new -study-suggests-fake-news-might-have-won-donald-trump-the-2016 -election/.

"played a significant role": Blake, "Study Suggests Fake News."

"Kobach was always": David A. Graham, "The Last Time Trump Alleged Massive Fraud," *The Atlantic*, November 12, 2020, https://www.theatlantic .com/ideas/archive/2020/11/kris-kobach-and-search-mythical-voter -fraud/617069/.

"tagged an astonishing": Greg Palast, "The GOP's Stealth War Against Voters," *Rolling Stone*, August 24, 2016, https://www.rollingstone.com/politics /politics-features/the-gops-stealth-war-against-voters-247905/.

"Crosscheck was a small": Greg Palast, email message to author, November 18, 2020.

"Roger Ailes was ousted": John Koblin, Emily Steel, and Jim Rutenberg, "Roger Ailes Leaves Fox News, and Rupert Murdoch Steps In," *New York Times*, July 21, 2016, https://www.nytimes.com/2016/07/22/business/media /roger-ailes-fox-news.html.

"He then joined": Maggie Haberman and Ashley Parker, "Roger Ailes Is Advising

Donald Trump Ahead of Presidential Debates," *New York Times*, August 16, 2016, https://www.nytimes.com/2016/08/17/us/politics/donald-trump -roger-ailes.html.

"on May 18, 2017": Clyde Haberman, "Roger Ailes, Who Built Fox News into an Empire, Dies at 77," *New York Times*, May 18, 2017, https://www.nytimes .com/2017/05/18/business/media/roger-ailes-dead.html.

"During his long": Haberman, "Roger Ailes."

"Murdoch himself": Jonathan Mahler and Jim Rutenberg, "How Rupert Murdoch's Empire of Influence Remade the World," *New York Times Magazine*, April 3, 2019, https://www.nytimes.com/interactive/2019/04/03/magazine /rupert-murdoch-fox-news-trump.html.

"Later, he handed": Peter Maass, "Power Transfer: How Lachlan Murdoch Went from Studying Philosophy at Princeton to Exploiting White Nationalism at Fox News," The Intercept, March 30, 2019, https://theintercept .com/2019/03/30/lachlan-murdoch-fox-news/.

"The Trump-Fox connection": Michael M. Grynbaum, "Fox News Once Gave Trump a Perch. Now It's His Bullhorn," *New York Times*, July 1, 2018, https://www.nytimes.com/2018/07/01/business/media/fox-news-trump -bill-shine.html.

"up to eight hours": Poniewozik, "Trump Isn't Watching."

"anchors will speak": Jane Mayer, "The Making of the Fox News White House," *New Yorker*, March 4, 2019, https://www.newyorker.com/magazine /2019/03/11/the-making-of-the-fox-news-white-house.

"even mainstream media": Mayer, "Fox News White House."

"Trump get his talking": Grynbaum, "Fox News Once Gave Trump."

"Trump ordered the FDA": Strickler, "At FDA, TVs Now Turned."

"Gizmodo accused Facebook": Michael Nunez, "Former Facebook Workers: We Routinely Suppressed Conservative News," Gizmodo, May 9, 2016, https:// gizmodo.com/former-facebook-workers-we-routinely-suppressed-conser -1775461006.

"leaning left": John Herrman and Mike Isaac, "Conservatives Accuse Facebook

of Political Bias," *New York Times*, May 9, 2016, https://www.nytimes
.com/2016/05/10/technology/conservatives-accuse-facebook-of-political
-bias.html.

"bent over backward": Phil McCausland, "GOP Accuses Facebook of Censorship,
but Conservative Media Flourishes Online," NBC News, April 15, 2018,
https://www.nbcnews.com/tech/social-media/gop-accuses-facebook
-censorship-conservative-media-flourishes-online-n865276.

"then reached out": Mathew Ingram, "Facebook and Twitter Still Trying to
Convince Conservatives They Aren't Biased," *Columbia Journalism Review*,
June 27, 2018, https://www.cjr.org/the_new_gatekeepers/facebook
-twitter-bias.php.

"anecdotal evidence": Oscar Schwartz, "Are Google and Facebook Really
Suppressing Conservative Politics?," *Guardian*, December 4, 2018, https://
www.theguardian.com/technology/2018/dec/04/google-facebook-anti
-conservative-bias-claims.

"Since technology companies": Schwartz, "Are Google and Facebook."

"Extremist conservative groups": Jessica Guynn, "Is Facebook Too Liberal? It
Pledges to Investigate Charges It's Biased Against Conservatives," *USA
Today*, May 3, 2018, https://www.usatoday.com/story/tech/news/2018
/05/03/facebook-pledges-investigate-charges-bias-against-conservatives
/574505002/.

"Facebook needs Republican": Guynn, "Is Facebook Too Liberal?"

"ahead of the midterms": Elizabeth Dwoskin and Tony Romm, "Facebook
Says It Has Uncovered a Coordinated Disinformation Operation ahead
of the 2018 Midterm Elections," *Washington Post*, July 31, 2018, https://
www.washingtonpost.com/technology/2018/07/31/facebook-says-it-has
-uncovered-coordinated-disinformation-operation-ahead-midterm-elections/.

"likely funded by": Dwoskin and Romm, "Facebook Says It Has Uncovered."

"coordinated inauthentic behavior": Taylor Hatmaker, "Activists Push Back on
Facebook's Decision to Remove a DC Protest Event," TechCrunch, August

1, 2018, https://techcrunch.com/2018/08/01/facebook-organizers-protest-no-unite-the-right-2/.

"Facebook was 'helped'": Matt Taibbi, "Beware the Slippery Slope of Facebook Censorship," *Rolling Stone*, August 2, 2018, https://www.rollingstone.com/politics/politics-features/facebook-censor-alex-jones-705766/.

"62 percent": Jordan Crook, "62 Percent of U.S. Adults Get Their News from Social Media, Says Report," TechCrunch, May 26, 2016, https://techcrunch.com/2016/05/26/most-people-get-their-news-from-social-media-says-report/.

"Since the growth": Taibbi, "Beware the Slippery Slope."

Brainwashing: The Amygdala and the Neuroscience

"The term brainwashing": John D. Marks, *The Search for the Manchurian Candidate: The CIA and Mind Control* (New York: Times Books, 1979), 125.

"CIA Agent and author": Marks, *Search for the Manchurian Candidate*, 125.

"It comes from": "'Brainwashing': A History," *Merriam-Webster*, accessed October 8, 2020, https://www.merriam-webster.com/words-at-play/brainwashing-word-history.

"brainwashing is typically": Kathleen Taylor, in discussion with the author, March 2014, London, England.

"is not so much": Taylor, discussion.

"five factors are": Ibid.

"You can only understand": Lakoff, interview.

"We have very good": Taylor, discussion.

"cognitive dissonance": "Cognitive Dissonance," *Psychology Today*, accessed July 21, 2020, https://www.psychologytoday.com/us/basics/cognitive-dissonance.

"amygdala hijacking": Nancy Moyer, "Amygdala Hijack: When Emotion Takes Over," Healthline, April 22, 2019, https://www.healthline.com/health/stress/amygdala-hijack.

"evidence from neuroscience": John Montgomery, in discussion with the author, 2014.

"it sort of simulates": Montgomery, discussion.

"We evolved to live": Taylor, discussion.

"It can happen": Mike Lofgren, in discussion with the author, August 12, 2014, Alexandria, VA.

"No one likes": Lofgren, discussion.

"the event held": Aamer Madhani and Mary-Claire Jalonick, "Amy Coney Barrett Swearing-In Differs Markedly from 'Superspreader' Rose Garden Event," Chicago Tribune, October 26, 2020, https://www.chicagotribune .com/nation-world/ct-nw-amy-coney-barrett-celebration-superspreader -rose-garden-20201027-riunvoij5vgjllzjbzq73cbjza-story.html.

"Trump's rallies have been": Berkeley Lovelace Jr., "Trump Campaign Rallies Led to More Than 30,000 Coronavirus Cases, Stanford Researchers Say," CNBC, October 31, 2020. https://www.cnbc.com/2020/10/31/coronavirus -trump-campaign-rallies-led-to-30000-cases-stanford-researchers-say .html.

"Criticism of the leader": Father Dwight Longenecker, "4 Danger Signs of Cult-Like Behavior, and 4 Antidotes" Catholic Education Resource Center, April 23, 2017, https://www.catholiceducation.org/en/religion-and-philosophy /other-topics/4-danger-signs-of-cult-like-behavior-and-4-antidotes.html.

"no room for differences": Longenecker, "4 Danger Signs."

"four ways he believes": Bobby Azarian, "Fear and Anxiety Drive Conservatives' Political Attitudes," Psychology Today, December 31, 2016, https://www .psychologytoday.com/us/blog/mind-in-the-machine/201612/fear-and -anxiety-drive-conservatives-political-attitudes.

"We are all vulnerable": Taylor, discussion.

"reeducation process": Taylor, discussion.

"as recently as 2016": John Ehrenreich, "Why Are Conservatives More Susceptible to Believing Lies?," Slate, November 9, 2017, https://slate .com/technology/2017/11/why-conservatives-are-more-susceptible-to -believing-in-lies.html.

"Estimates of Obama's": Sarah Frostenson, "A Crowd Scientist Says Trump's Inauguration Attendance Was Pretty Average," Vox, January 24, 2017,

https://www.vox.com/policy-and-politics/2017/1/24/14354036/crowds
-presidential-inaugurations-trump-average.

"46 percent of Trump": Amanda Robb, "Anatomy of a Fake News Scandal,"
Rolling Stone, November 16, 2017, https://www.rollingstone.com/feature
/anatomy-of-a-fake-news-scandal-125877/.

"conservatives are less introspective": Ehrenreich, "Why Are Conservatives More
Susceptible."

"finding facts": Ehrenreich, "Why Are Conservatives More Susceptible."

"Ehrenreich said we all": Ehrenreich, "Why Are Conservatives More Susceptible."

"Researchers Jonas De keersmaecker": David Z. Hambrick and Madeline
Marquardt, "Cognitive Ability and Vulnerability to Fake News," *Scientific
American,* February 6, 2018, https://www.scientificamerican.com/article
/cognitive-ability-and-vulnerability-to-fake-news/.

"those who continued": Jonas De keersmaecker and Arne Roets, "'Fake News':
Incorrect, but Hard to Correct. The Role of Cognitive Ability on the Impact
of False Information on Social Impressions," *Intelligence* 65, (November
2017): 107–110, https://doi.org/10.1016/j.intell.2017.10.005.

"was arrested for": De keersmaecker and Roets, "'Fake News.'"

"as people get older": Daniel L. Murman, "The Impact of Age on Cognition,"
Seminars in Hearing 36, no. 3 (August 2015): 111–21, 10.1055/s-0035-1555115

"average age": Bill Carter, "Fox Viewers May be Graying, but Their Passion
Still Pays," *New York Times,* July 22, 2013, https://www.nytimes.com
/2013/07/23/business/its-viewers-are-graying-but-their-passion-pays
-for-fox-news.html.

"meta-cognitive skills": Hambrick and Marquardt, "Cognitive Ability and
Vulnerability."

"Those drawn to conservatism": Lakoff, interview.

"is in charge": Lakoff, interview.

"So, you've heard": Lakoff, interview.

"Now the nurturing": Lakoff, interview.

"So the way this": Lakoff, interview.

"All over the brain": Lakoff, interview.

What We Can Do about Far-Right Media

"Never doubt that a small": Donald Keys, *Earth at Omega: Passage to Planetization* (Boston: Branden, 1982), 79.

"Stringently enforce antitrust": "Sanders Releases Media Reform Plan to Protect Journalism from Billionaires, Monopolies & Trump," Democracy in Action, August 27, 2019, https://www.democracyinaction.us/2020 /sanders/sanderspolicy082719mediareform.html.

"Restore local and national": "Talk Radio by the Numbers."

"Some states have": Heather Morton, "Net Neutrality Legislation in States," National Conference of State Legislatures, January 23, 2019, https://www .ncsl.org/research/telecommunications-and-information-technology/net -neutrality-legislation-in-states.aspx.

"seats in the FCC": Karl Bode, "New Interim FCC Boss Jessica Rosenworcel Will Likely Restore Net Neutrality, Just Not Yet," Tech Dirt, January 25, 2021, https://www.techdirt.com/articles/20210125/07374446112/new-interim-fcc-boss-jessica-rosenworcel-will-likely-restore-net-neutrality-just-not-yet.sht

"Many on the right": Tom Rosentiel and Dante Chinni, "Is the Fairness Doctrine Fair Game?" Pew Research Center, July 19, 2007, https://www .pewresearch.org/2007/07/19/is-the-fairness-doctrine-fair-game/.

"Networks like Fox": Kurt Eichenwald (@kurteichenwald), "Networks like Fox that knowingly spread disinformation about a health crisis should be taken off the air under a declaration of national emergency until the crisis passes," Twitter, September 9, 2020, 10:32 p.m., https://twitter.com /kurteichenwald/status/1303883927489314817.

"A federal judge": David Folkenflik, "You Literally Can't Believe the Facts Tucker Carlson Tells You. So Say Fox's Lawyers," NPR, September 29, 2020, https://www.npr.org/2020/09/29/917747123/you-literally-cant-believe -the-facts-tucker-carlson-tells-you-so-say-fox-s-lawye.

"One strategy": Robert W. McChesney, "Making Media Democratic," *Boston Review*, June 1, 1998, http://bostonreview.net/forum/robert-w-mcchesney-making-media-democratic.

"The United States spends": Michael J. Coren, "Americans Could Barely Buy a Coffee with What They Spend per Year on Public Media," Quartz, September 9, 2018, https://qz.com/1383503/americans-could-barely-buy-a-coffee-with-what-they-spend-per-year-on-public-media/.

"Strengthening public broadcasting": Cohen, discussion.

"historians say there": Daniel Dale, "The First 5,276 False Things Donald Trump Said as U.S. President," *Toronto Star*, June 2, 2019, https://projects.thestar.com/donald-trump-fact-check/.

"truth sandwich": George Lakoff (@GeorgeLakoff), "Truth Sandwich," Twitter, December 1, 2018, 10:37 a.m., https://twitter.com/GeorgeLakoff/status/1068891959882846208.

"These independent rulings": Dana Nuccitelli, "Fake News Is a Threat to Humanity, but Scientists May Have a Solution," *Guardian*, December 27, 2017, https://www.theguardian.com/environment/climate-consensus-97-per-cent/2017/dec/27/fake-news-is-a-threat-to-humanity-but-scientists-may-have-a-solution.

"involves explaining": Nuccitelli, "Fake News."

"companies like Facebook": Zeynep Tufekci, "We're Building a Dystopia Just to Make People Click on Ads," September 2017, TED video, 22:46 https://www.ted.com/talks/zeynep_tufekci_we_re_building_a_dystopia_just_to_make_people_click_on_ads.

"private media regulators": Taibbi, "Beware the Slippery Slope."

"but researchers and political": Sidney Fussell, "Facebook Tweaked Its Rules, but You Can Still Target Voters," *Wired*, October 12, 2020, https://www.wired.com/story/facebook-tweaked-rules-still-target-voters/.

"software plays a huge role": Shira Ovide, "Take YouTube's Dangers Seriously," *New York Times*, April 20, 2020, https://www.nytimes.com/2020/04/20/technology/youtube-conspiracy-theories.html.

Index

Note: Page numbers in italic refer to illustrations.

About the Author

Jen Senko is an award-winning documentary filmmaker based in New York City. Her documentaries focus on sociopolitical themes with the intent of inspiring discussion and fomenting change. Senko's most recent documentary, *The Brainwashing of My Dad*, tracks the disturbing rise of right-wing media. The film is told through the lens of her father, whose politics and personality were radically transformed after he discovered talk radio. This widely acclaimed project has won numerous awards and has been screened in festivals and theaters across the United States, Canada, England, Ireland, and Sweden.

Senko's previous documentary, *The Vanishing City*, codirected with Fiore DeRosa, exposes gentrification's dire consequences in New York City and illustrates how it is typical of major cities around the world. Kathryn Erbe of *Law & Order* narrates the film.

Senko's first documentary, *Road Map Warrior Women*, is a road trip documentary about extraordinarily independent women in the West and has also won numerous awards.

In addition to filmmaking, Senko is frequently invited to speak at screenings of her films. She defines herself as a social justice activist and documentarian with a focus on media.

Senko graduated on the dean's list from Pratt Institute, New York City, where she studied communications design and painting.